# AN OCEAN APART

## Explaining Three Decades of U.S.-Japanese Trade Frictions

Stephen D. Cohen

PRAEGER

Westport, Connecticut
London

**Library of Congress Cataloging-in-Publication Data**

Cohen, Stephen D.
    An ocean apart : explaining three decades of U.S.-Japanese trade frictions / by Stephen D. Cohen.
      p.   cm.
    Includes bibliographical references and index.
    ISBN 0–275–95686–5 (alk. paper)
    1. United States—Foreign economic relations—Japan. 2. Japan—Foreign economic relations—United States. 3. Balance of trade—United States. 4. Balance of trade—Japan. 5. United States—Commercial policy. 6. Japan—Commercial policy. I. Title.
HF1456.5.J3C64    1998
337.73052—dc21    97–22802

British Library Cataloguing in Publication Data is available.

Library of Congress Catalog Card Number: 97–22802
ISBN: 0–275–95686–5

First published in 1998

Praeger Publishers, 88 Post Road West, Westport, CT 06881
An imprint of Greenwood Publishing Group, Inc.

Printed in the United States of America

The paper used in this book complies with the Permanent Paper Standard issued by the National Information Standards Organization (Z39.48–1984).

10 9 8 7 6 5 4 3 2 1

To my mother and

the memory of my father

# Contents

III: CONCLUSIONS

# Introduction

In 1969, the United States was annoyed with Japan's import barriers, export aggressiveness, and $1 billion bilateral trade surplus with the United States. In 1997, the United States was annoyed with Japan's import barriers, export aggressiveness, and annual bilateral trade surpluses in the range of $50 billion. The intervening years witnessed the world's biggest and longest contemporary trade fight. What is going on here? Although an enormous body of literature has emerged discussing these bilateral disagreements, no international consensus exists on exactly what caused and perpetuates them.

My purpose in writing this book is to offer an improved analytical framework for explaining the long-running strains in U.S.-Japanese trade relations. If successful, the book will bring an enhanced sense of order — and perhaps a better set of policy responses — to the controversy surrounding the high-stakes dispute between the world's two largest, strongest national economies. More heat than light has been generated in seeking answers to why these two economic superpowers have experienced three consecutive decades of trade frictions and trade balance disequilibria — with no end in sight — despite continuous efforts by both countries to correct them. The serious knowledge gap needs to be narrowed.

The means to these ends is a comprehensive, dispassionate examination of the multifaceted encounters among governmental policymakers, corporations, and consumers within as well as between the United States and Japan. The complexity of the subject requires a broader inquiry than a study of a single aspect of bilateral relations (the lack of U.S. saving and capital investment, Japanese industrial policy, and so on). The myriad nuances of bilateral economic relations preclude definitive answers emerging from an effort limited to analyzing only one economy or to praising one country while deriding the strategies and values of the other. This study is designed to transcend the relatively concentrated focus of existing academic studies and governmental reports on this subject by developing a broad, integrating thesis explaining the longevity of U.S.-Japanese trade frictions and disequilibria. The validity of this thesis can be evaluated in part by observing the accuracy of its straightforward forecast of a continuing stream of new trade problems and persistent Japanese bilateral trade surpluses in the future — barring an unprecedented commitment by at least one country to effectively address causes rather than symptoms.

As an agnostic scholar who has been struggling since the late 1960s to understand how the many complex strands of bilateral trade dynamics ultimately fit together, I am highly sensitive to the inherent limitations of anyone trying to get this story just right. I certainly do not claim to have divined all the right answers because, like others writing on U.S.-Japanese trade relations, I cannot claim expertise in all of the social sciences — economics, politics, history, social psychology, and even theology — necessary to put bilateral trade problems in full context. Nor can I claim any breakthrough in creating controlled scientific experiments that precisely measure either who is doing what to whom or irrefutable cause and effect relationships.

The idea that books one day might be transformed from ink and paper to electronic blips on a computer screen normally makes me recoil in horror. However, once I started writing this book, I quickly came to the belief that it would be an excellent candidate for on-line dissemination. The internet would allow a significant portion of the text to be presented on a split-screen basis, thereby allowing arguments complimentary to the United States literally to share the same page with counter-arguments giving the pro-Japan viewpoint. No matter how well reasoned, no study can alter the fact that logical rejoinders exist for every major argument advanced in assessing a tempestuous bilateral trade relationship incorporating precious few universally accepted truths and dozens of differing interpretations of "reality."

Despite these limitations, I still believe that my many years of observing non-stop trade frictions and my determination not to take sides have allowed me to produce a unique synthesis of the underlying forces of U.S.-Japanese trade relations. The synthesis provides a verifiable hypothesis explaining past economic behavior on both sides of the Pacific with relatively few inconsistencies and gaps. My approach seeks the proper trade-off between the need to be reasonably specific and the need to operate in the large gray area that separates the tiny slivers of black and white absolutes. Despite the rush of new events and trends in bilateral economic relations, certain core themes remain unaffected. Nothing has occurred yet to discredit my basic argument that a systemic problem exists in the form of a series of deeply-rooted, mostly uncorrected mismatches between the United States and Japan.

On a stylistic note, I have Westernized the sequence of Japanese proper names, that is, family names come last.

# Acknowledgements

A number of people provided invaluable assistance in the preparation of this book. First, I thank my four graduate assistants for their exceptionally able research and editing assistance: Mary Catherine Fish, Hilary A. Smith, T. J. Grubisha, and David F. Helvey. I am also grateful for the very useful suggestions by Ed Lincoln and Warren Farb concerning selected chapters. As author, I accept full responsibility for errors of fact and the many subjective judgments rendered about the United States and Japan.

# Acronyms

| | |
|---|---|
| GATT | General Agreement on Tariffs and Trade |
| ITC | International Trade Commission |
| JFTC | Japan Fair Trade Commission |
| MITI | Ministry of International Trade and Industry |
| NEP | New Economic Policy |
| NIC | Newly Industrialized Country |
| OECD | Organization for Economic Cooperation and Development |
| OMA | Orderly Market Agreement |
| OPEC | Organization of Petroleum Exporting Countries |
| SII | Structural Impediments Initiative |
| USTR | United States Trade Representative |
| WTO | World Trade Organization |

# I

## WHAT HAPPENED

# 1

# Defining the Nature and Causes of Structural Problems in U.S.-Japanese Trade Relations

The Hare, one day, laughed at the Tortoise for his short feet, slowness and awkwardness.

"Though you may be swift as the wind," replied the Tortoise good naturedly, "I can beat you in a race. . . ."

The rivals started, and the Hare, of course, soon left the Tortoise far behind. Having reached midway to the goal, she began to play about, nibble the young herbage, and amuse herself in many ways. The day being warm, she even thought she would take a little nap in a shady spot, for she thought that if the Tortoise should pass her while she slept, she could easily overtake him again before he reached the end.

The Tortoise meanwhile plodded on, unwavering and unresting, straight towards the goal.

The Hare, having overslept herself, started up from her nap, and was surprised to find that the Tortoise was nowhere in sight. Off she went at full speed, but on reaching the winning-post, found that the Tortoise was already there, waiting for her arrival.

*— Aesop's Fables*

We live in a unique period in modern history. On a global basis, the question of how governmental policies can best nurture the private sector in the pursuit of economic prosperity has eclipsed great power rivalries over territory and ideology. Capital and technology are displacing weapons stockpiles as the measure of a country's international influence. Executives of the handful of companies that rate the safety and financial attractiveness of bonds issued by governments and corporations around the world can command more fear than any general. As economic issues assume increasingly dominant roles in both domestic and international politics, Japan and the United States, the world's two largest, most dynamic national economies, arguably represent the world's most important bilateral relationship.

The two countries are closely linked through a security treaty that provides Japan with U.S. military protection and makes Japan the most important U.S. ally in the western Pacific. The two countries are also closely linked through a vast web of economic interdependence. Two-way trade exceeds $200 billion annually. The United States is Japan's largest export market (it buys 30 percent of all Japanese exports) and is the largest host country for Japanese foreign direct investment, accounting for about 40 percent of the total. Japan is the second largest U.S. export market (after Canada) and is the largest single source of capital inflows to finance the U.S. current account (goods and services) deficit and to bolster the relatively low U.S. saving rate. The struggle for global leadership in most of the important new technologies is dominated by U.S. and Japanese corporations. Uncommonly intense competition in the high-tech sector seems to instill corporations in both countries with a relentless commitment to minimizing costs and accelerating new product innovation.

No matter how great the mutual benefits of cooperative interdependence, the friendship between the United States and Japan is far from secure. For the past three decades, their economic relationship has resembled a stormy marriage in which the partners find that their distinctive neuroses threaten to overwhelm mutual attraction. The United States is still trying to make up for time lost while it mistakenly believed that size and momentum would be sufficient to sustain the extraordinary level of economic power it enjoyed following World War II. The U.S. industrial sector should have looked over its shoulder in the late 1960s. It was about to pay a stiff price for being unable to keep pace with its enormously capable, more determined Japanese competition.

Many U.S. government officials, politicians, and business leaders have accused the Japanese of playing the international trade game unfairly. Their specific charges include excessive import barriers, restrictive business practices in their home market that discriminate against outsiders, and aggressive targeting of foreign markets for export drives. The Japanese respond by accusing the United States of making unjustified criticisms and ill-conceived economic demands, and of using Japan as a scapegoat for its own industrial shortcomings. The accumulating stresses from ongoing trade disagreements and imbalances are of major consequence because so much is at stake. The international economic order cannot avoid being sensitive to serious problems between two countries who account for approximately 40 percent of world gross domestic product

(GDP) and more than 20 percent of world trade. Differences in their values, priorities, and style caused the United States and Japan to experience pronounced differences in economic performances that determine the growth of well-paying, high-skilled jobs and real national incomes.

Developing from different cultures and historical circumstances, the U.S. and Japanese economies have been out of sync. Domestically, the United States has embodied the cowboy spirit: an emphasis on consumption and recreation, the spirit of individual freedom and new frontiers to conquer, distrust of government, and the glory of the free market. Meanwhile, Japan has embodied the samurai spirit: an emphasis on production and the rewards of hard work, loyalty and subordination of self-gratification to group interests, respect for governmental authority, and the need for limiting the free rein of the invisible hand of the marketplace.

Internationally, the United States has been relentless in its pursuit of international political security. Its size and talents have enabled it to sustain the roles of global military superpower and defender of democratic values. Internationally, Japan has been relentless in its pursuit of economic strength and industrial competitiveness. Both countries have been remarkably successful in attaining dissimilar international priorities.

Although the likelihood of a total breakdown in U.S.-Japanese economic relations in the foreseeable future remains remote, the probable continuation of unabated discord could be mutually costly. Unchecked intensification of the respective stereotypes of Japan as an aggressive adversarial trader with a double standard for imports and exports and of the United States as a sour-grapes–spouting bully in denial over its declining economic strength poses the risk of trade hostilities in the form of a spiral of retaliation and counter-retaliation against the goods of the other country. A serious escalation of bilateral trade tensions eventually would put at risk the willingness of the two countries to cooperate on national security issues. To reduce the risk of mutually damaging economic and political divisiveness, a better understanding of the causes of trade frictions is urgently needed. This is easier said than done. Despite the tens of millions of words written and spoken on this subject, the communications and perceptions gaps between the two countries are still as wide as the Pacific Ocean.

## MULTIPLE VERSIONS OF REALITY

A critical element is missing in the English language literature on contemporary U.S.-Japanese trade frictions and disequilibria. The best efforts of government officials, business executives, and academics notwithstanding, no one has yet produced a universally accepted explanation of the causes and significance of bilateral trade problems. Lack of consensus on the causes of these problems has contributed to their perpetuation.

Seeking explanations as to why observers passionately disagree is an important, but long overdue, exercise. Most commentators on the subject simply take it as a given that they have divined the indisputable cause of bilateral trade frictions.

For good reasons, conflicting perceptions and value judgments together with an abundance of economic data have created multiple versions of reality in bilateral relations. Some interpretations are more complete or plausible than others, and all have attracted supporters as well as critics. Some interpretations represent an objective search for the truth, some seek merely to amplify the author's preexisting notions, and some are paid public relations exercises in image-building.

*Rashomon*, a widely acclaimed 1950s movie by the noted Japanese director Akira Kurosawa, provides a striking metaphor for multiple versions of reality in U.S.-Japanese trade relations. The film's plot revolves around three characters retelling the events surrounding a thief's rape of a woman and the murder of her husband in an isolated forest. All three eyewitness accounts are inconsistent in their portrayal of critical details, yet all are equally plausible. Viewers are left on their own to calculate the self-serving content of each account and then to decide whether to believe one version, reject them all, construct a composite, or to seek expert opinion.

Depictions of three decades of bilateral trade frictions and imbalances can be likened to observations made when looking through a "*Rashomon* lens."[1] Conflicting beliefs and subjective interpretations of events influence what people see in bilateral trade relations, thereby creating a number of credible, but mutually exclusive, images of who is doing what to whom and why.

At the heart of the trade frictions controversy is the difficulty of identifying which country has been the victim and which has been the aggressor. Although Japan has initiated more unilateral trade liberalization measures over the past three decades than any country in history it remains on the receiving end of more foreign complaints about barriers to imports than any country in recent times. Has Japan been practicing "techno-nationalism," or has the United States been practicing "economic under-achievement?" A harsh answer comes from an American teaching at a Japanese university: evidence is mounting "that what we had been taking as a rough but friendly competition has been all along for the Japanese a deliberate, humorless economic war — a retaliation, even, for their . . . military defeat at our hands."[2] Most Japanese would argue that this statement — and the root cause of bilateral problems — reflects the Americans' inability to accept gracefully Japanese economic superiority and their desire to ward off economic defeat by seeking to modify the rules of economic engagement. An unusually blunt articulation of this version of reality is the assertion of a retired Japanese Finance Ministry official that the United States "believes that by rights it ought to be stronger than Japan; since it cannot be, it tries to hold Japan back." Even if Japan gives in to U.S. demands on all fronts, the "U.S. economy will not improve."[3]

Some observers saw as intolerably aggressive the Clinton administration's demands that the United States receive a greater share of the Japanese automobile and auto parts markets, and they considered it a mistaken embrace of managed trade. They cheered at Japan's refusal to acquiesce to these allegedly misguided demands. Hard-liners offered a radically different assessment of what happened. They saw the last minute withdrawal of U.S. threats to impose 100 percent tariffs on imports of Japanese luxury cars — despite Japan's refusal to provide meaningful new concessions — as an ill-advised show of weakness and indecisiveness that will encourage Japan to be inflexible in future trade disputes.

The Japanese and U.S. versions of a market access dispute consist of so many contradictory "facts" that neutral observers of the debate in effect become viewers of a real-life version of *Rashomon*. For example, during Motorola's bitterly contested ten-year fight beginning in the mid-1980s to gain additional access to the Japanese cellular telephone market, an impartial observer could choose between mutually exclusive versions of who was aggressor and who was victim. The U.S. version alleged a classic example of discriminatory regulations and delaying tactics being employed by Japan's Ministry of Posts and Telecommunications for the express purpose of helping Japanese cellular telephone makers and the Nippon Telegraph and Telephone Corporation neutralize the superior design and quality standards of Motorola's system. The other version of reality accused the U.S. government of flagrantly intruding into Japan's internal affairs by demanding that the latter add a second cellular phone operating system to accommodate Motorola, whose technical standards were incompatible with the system initially established in Japan.[4]

Another example of massively conflicting facts is the melange of charges, rebuttals, and counterarguments associated with Eastman Kodak's complaint that illegal market access barriers in Japan were hurting sales of its photographic film. To be fully informed, one would need to study 2,000 pages (and still growing) of public argumentation released by the law firms representing Kodak and Fuji Photo Film Company. The former's case pictures government-encouraged domination by Fuji over the four leading national wholesalers of film that severely restricts access of competing companies to camera shops — the major retail outlets for film. Fuji's denial of all anti-competitive charges includes the allegation that Kodak's retailing problems mainly stem from its ill-advised delays in establishing marketing facilities in Japan and the suggestion that, because the case fails to meet the criteria of U.S. trade law, Kodak should have filed an antitrust complaint with the Japanese Fair Trade Commission.

Distinctive visions of reality among Americans closely correlate with their degree of first-hand knowledge of Japan, academic training, and professional experience. In public forums, Japanese people tend to speak with one voice, all defending their country's economic practices. Typically, U.S. economists view the problem through a lens that hones in on traditional free trade theory. The latter emphasizes the mutual advantages of foreign trade whose primary logic lies in importing goods produced more efficiently overseas and the self-defeating nature of import barriers, which only serve to subsidize inefficient domestic production. Political economists, who utilize a multidisciplinary approach, often view bilateral problems as a function of differentials in each country's competitiveness as caused by divergent macroeconomic trends, government policies, managerial capability, and cultural factors.

U.S. foreign policy specialists tend to observe relations with Japan through a lens that magnifies three things: the strategic and political importance of good relations with Japan, the need to prevent an alliance between friends from being endangered by relatively less important commercial squabbles, and the need to appreciate Japanese good faith in responding to U.S. demands. Finally, most U.S. business people and trade policymakers (as well as a few academic specialists on Japan) look through a lens that is configured to illuminate the dark side of Japan's mercantilist streak. They see Japan rejecting market forces and friendly commercial competition in favor of a selfish promotion of national economic power based on maximization of exports and discouragement of both imports and inward foreign direct investment. In sum, some Americans look at Japan and see the image of a political friend and a noble economic success story; others look at Japan and see the reflection of avoidable U.S. economic decline.

Another factor contributing to the multiple realities syndrome is the difficulty in keeping pace with a moving object: an economic relationship in which key events and trends are constantly changing. An accurate assessment of the Japanese government's impact on the industrial sector will differ depending on the specific time period being examined. Conventional wisdom sometimes is quickly and unceremoniously discredited. For example, during the 1980s a number of U.S. officials and industry representatives believed that only billions of dollars of government subsidies would enable the United States to catch up with Japan's development of high-definition television technology, potentially a multibillion-dollar consumer electronics product. Their argument vanished in the wake of a privately-financed, U.S.-based breakthrough to a digital-based technology that leap-frogged Japan's high-definition television system.

Projections of where bilateral trade relations are headed have produced incompatible forecasts because of very different views of domestic economic realities appearing in the "*Rashomon* lens." Both the U.S. and Japanese economies have gone through distinct phases over the past two decades. The rapid pace of change in the U.S. economy spawned two contradictory perceptions of end-of-century reality. The U.S. industrial sector was all but written off in the 1980s as being unable to compete against Japan because of its apparent loss of direction, obsolete factories, unattractive products, and high costs. By the mid-1990s, conventional wisdom was heaping lavish praise on an apparently revived, technologically innovative, and low-cost U.S. industrial sector.

Predictions of runaway Japanese industrial dominance were inspired by the unprecedented increases in competitiveness and stock market prices recorded during the latter half of the 1980s, referred to as the "bubble years," when Japan seemed to have perfected the role of unstoppable industrial juggernaut. Conversely, the so-called bursting of the bubble in 1990 inspired an entirely new vision of reality depicting a potentially unraveling Japanese economy amid its most prolonged period of slow growth, asset deflation, and a banking crisis.[5] The implication of this negative view of Japan's economic future is that its trading partners should stifle their criticism; temper their demands; and not try to take advantage of a weakened, unstable Japanese economy.

Americans taking a hard-line approach do not see an image of Japanese weakness; instead, they still see a dangerous threat to U.S. prosperity and leadership. Typically, they foresee Japan cleansing itself of the wretched excesses of the bubble years and moving to a new phase of enhanced international economic strength. Their version of reality inspires fear that Japan's unsuspecting trading partners eventually will be blindsided by the carefully orchestrated enhancement of Japan's global economic leverage. Typical of this school of thought is the belief that Japan is moving to consolidate its long-sought goal of "comprehensive economic security" through a planned transition to a powerful headquarters economy. The latter would be capable of easily manipulating Japan's trading partners by the sheer weight and value of its expanding trade, foreign direct investments, overseas lending, and technology licensing.[6]

Is Japan in the throes of genuine domestic change that will significantly alter its international trading position? Facts can support either a positive or negative answer, depending on which event the observer wishes to emphasize. Real change was evidenced by the unprecedented appointment in 1996 of a foreigner as president of Mazda, a major Japanese industrial corporation. A Scottish-born executive was put in charge by Ford Motor Company after it was invited to increase its part-ownership of Mazda in order to effectively take control and then turn around the financially ailing Japanese auto maker. Conversely, the centuries-old

legacy of a strong government and its discomfort with the import of foreign influence was clearly demonstrated in early 1995 when the Japanese
bureaucracy stiffly unreeled reams of red tape to bar the quick entry into
the country of foreign doctors, rescue workers, and relief supplies standing by to assist victims of the Kobe earthquake.

What all this means is that reality is operating on various levels at the
same time. The U.S.-Japanese relationship does not operate on a smooth,
consistent linear basis. Exceptions exist to almost every rule. Interest
groups within each country have conflicting objectives. Paradoxes and
inconsistencies abound. The truth is seldom pure and almost never
simple.

## TWO DISTINCT PROBLEMS EXIST

A critical preface to the integrating thesis spelled out in the next section
is the argument that the tensions generated by bilateral trade frictions and
imbalances are the end-products of two distinct, albeit related, problems.
Failure to disentangle these two economic phenomena is a major cause of
conflicting perceptions of what has occurred over the past three decades.
The first problem is the inability of a wide range of U.S. industrial corporations to maintain or attain competitive parity with, or supremacy over,
their Japanese competition within the United States or in overseas markets. The main sources of weakness internal to the United States are
inadequate corporate performance and the economic and regulatory
environment in which companies operate. Short of unfair trade practices
(dumping [selling below production cost] and illegally obtaining trade
secrets) Japanese industrial exporters owe no apologies for perfecting a
winning formula for a no holds barred, do what it takes, compassionless
strategy to maximize domestic industrial strength and competitiveness.

The second problem originates in Japan: severe market access difficulties encountered by many foreign companies. As the century moves to an
end, foreign companies with the right product and the right strategy for
doing what is necessary to succeed in the idiosyncratic Japanese market
can still run smack into daunting obstacles, direct and indirect, in what
purports to be the world's most open market. The Japanese follow a number of policies and business practices that discourage imports of many
kinds of manufactured goods. A sovereign country is under no obligation
to act in conformity with U.S. standards and wishes. Nevertheless, the
unequalled degree of enmity that Japan's import impediments have
engendered among its trading partners does raise important questions
about its trade policies.

These two otherwise distinct problems are directly linked in cases
where the protected home market has enhanced the ability of a Japanese
manufacturer to penetrate foreign markets. The term "sanctuary profits"

refers to the ability of Japanese companies to maximize prices in a home market relatively devoid of foreign competition. Large profit margins in the large Japanese market could then be used to offset minimal or non-existent profits generated by exporting the same product at rock bottom prices to build foreign market share. The ability to maximize sales volume at home and abroad contributes to economies of scale and reduced per-unit production costs, that is, it increases Japanese competitiveness.

A vivid example of Japan's extraordinary competitiveness is the ability, mostly by Toyota (admittedly one of Japan's very best industrial companies), to continue exporting pickup trucks to the United States. In the five-year period beginning in 1991, the value of U.S. imports of light trucks (up to 2.5 metric tons) from Japan averaged more than $1 billion.[7] According to an early 1996 survey of new motor vehicles being sold in the United States, Toyota's T100 pickup truck (an import) was selling in the same price range as similar U.S.-made models.[8] Even when factoring in Toyota's reputation for dependability, the continued export of pickup trucks to the U.S. market in the 1990s represents an extraordinary accomplishment — one that is inconsistent with what textbooks teach about balance of payments adjustment and with the image of a rejuvenated Big Three in Detroit. First, Japanese exporters of light trucks had to overcome the burden of a seemingly prohibitive 160 percent appreciation of the yen against the dollar from the latter's peak in early March 1985 to mid-1995 (0.0038 to an average 0.01 cents per yen). Once past that formidable hurdle, the manufacturing costs of Japanese pickup trucks had to remain low enough to absorb the stiff U.S. tariff duty of 25 percent imposed in the 1960s as retaliation against European agricultural import barriers.

A striking example of market access difficulties emanated from Japanese officialdom's propensity to put producer interests ahead of consumer welfare. Details of an extraordinary impediment to imports in the mid-1980s belatedly became public in the scandal surrounding the Ministry of Health and Welfare's negligence in stopping the distribution of unsafe blood products used by Japanese hemophiliacs. In agreeing to an out-of-court settlement of the suits filed by hemophiliacs who had contracted the AIDS virus, the ministry tacitly admitted, among other things, that for two years it had failed to act prudently on clear medical warnings that transfusions using untreated blood posed a serious risk of HIV infection. An internal ministry memorandum dated July 4, 1983, suggested approval of emergency imports of safe, heat-treated blood products produced only in the United States. It also said that "consideration should be given to the market shares of unheated . . . products held by Japanese companies." The paper trail indicates that senior ministry officials (possibly in consultation with retired former colleagues who had gone to work for makers of Japanese blood products like Green Cross) delayed the approval of heat-treated blood products in Japan until 1985. It was not until then that domestic companies had perfected their own heat-treated products.[9]

## A COMPREHENSIVE THESIS ABOUT
## THE CAUSE OF THE PROBLEM

Before defining the bilateral problem, it is appropriate to confirm that one exists. This is most easily done by circumventing the inconclusive debate as to whether an economic problem exists (that is, whether bilateral trade deficits are relevant, or whether the United States should delight in being able to import real economic resources in exchange for paper currency). At a minimum, a serious political problem exists. For many years, public opinion polls and U.S. government statements have indicated widespread belief that Japan is inflicting unacceptable injury on the U.S. economy, mostly by means of widespread violations of what they consider to be fair play and proper competition.

An objective overview of U.S.-Japanese trade problems should begin with a unifying thesis that identifies and explains the primary forces behind nearly 30 years of trade frictions and disequilibria. How one defines the problem is of critical importance. All major elements of analysis logically flow from such a definition: causality of trade frictions, significance of Japanese trade surpluses, which country should initiate which changes, and so on.

A synthesis of the dynamics underlying the twin phenomena of superior Japanese industrial competitiveness and relatively vexatious market access difficulties for foreign-made manufactured goods brings us to the integrating thesis. *A managerial, policy, and attitudinal mismatch has shaped U.S.-Japanese economic relations in the three decades beginning in the late 1960s.* The origin and continuation of this mismatch is logically consistent with *dissimilar national priorities.*

The short explanation of bilateral trade frictions and disequilibria is the continuing existence of an underlying asymmetry in the abilities of the two countries to sell manufactured goods in each other's market. The long explanation is that these frictions and disequilibria reflect a systemic problem rooted in sharply divergent trends that emerged in the 1950s in the United States and Japan:

1.     The Japanese consciously adopted a mutually reinforcing mix of highly successful government economic policies, business strategies, and innovations in production technology. This mix was fortified by preexisting, supportive social values, a proven historical formula for achieving relatively quick industrialization, and a unanimous national consensus for the priority of economic growth. The result was extraordinary success

in achieving the sequential objectives of industrial recovery, the prestige and material rewards of industrial strength, and the psychological comfort of increased technological self-sufficiency. Japan's seemingly inefficient pursuit of industrial power mainly through an infant industry strategy that promoted domestic companies and restricted foreign competition was not an impediment to quickly developing world-class manufacturing companies. Japan's historical determination to keep the outside world at arm's length and the intensity of market share rivalry among domestic corporations more than offset potential drawbacks of an exclusionary strategy that effectively shielded targeted industries from import competition.

2.    The United States unconsciously maintained a relatively debilitating mix of official economic policies, outmoded production strategies, predilections for consumption, and social priorities that prevented the U.S. industrial sector from mounting an effective response to the twin challenges of Japan's single-minded export offensive and its inhospitable home market for manufactured goods. The priority of allowing consumers to buy everything at the cheapest possible price and the emphasis on short-term corporate profits impeded efforts to preserve the international competitiveness of U.S. industry vis-à-vis mounting Japanese industrial strength. These shortcomings were magnified by the U.S. government's frequent subordination of international commercial interests to the pursuit of cold war–related political-military goals. Free market ideology and national priorities that lay elsewhere delayed a U.S. sense of urgency that a more forceful, effective response to growing Japanese economic power should be elevated to urgent national priority.

Many things have changed in bilateral trade relations since the late 1960s, but these systemic factors continue. Under such circumstances, a sustained correction in bilateral trade frictions and imbalances presupposes major substantive changes in the economic performance of one or both countries — above and beyond those that have occurred.

The integrating thesis of this book emanates from an intellectual base composed of a broad presumption about the generic nature of foreign trade relations and four premises specifically relating to bilateral relations. All five concepts appear explicitly or implicitly in subsequent chapters of this book.

The generic presumption is that the conduct of foreign trade is ultimately a political process in which trade-offs are inherent and inevitable. Democratic governments must weigh the rights of the relatively few who are losers from import competition against those of the majority of winners from the international flow of goods and services. These governments also must weigh the possibility of undermining the political coalition supporting liberal trade by causing domestic companies and workers to doubt they can get a sympathetic hearing from government officials when they seek relief from injurious foreign competition.

The first bilateral-specific premise is that the U.S. and Japanese economies are not alike in all major ways and that this hypothesis is not some intellectually unsound form of "Japan bashing." (My views might more accurately be dubbed "America bashing" since most of the differences discussed below are complimentary to Japanese industry and critical of U.S. industry.) My approach to bilateral trade relations is based on the conviction that a valid middle ground exists between the academically unsound extremes of being protective of Japan against any and all insinuation that its economic order is subject to different constraints and incentives as those of the United States and branding the Japanese economy and value system as so alien to their Western counterparts that all traditional trade policies are wholly inappropriate for them. The middle ground approach will be validated in later chapters by identifying several important institutional differences between the Japanese and U.S. economies, including the regulatory environment, corporate governance and organization, labor-management relations, and the structure of capital markets. By my definition, the middle ground approach suggests only that a country-specific, modified U.S. trade policy to directly address Japan's unique economic and social factors makes more sense than a universal trade policy mechanically and identically applied to every trading partner.

The second premise asserts that the extent of the structural differences between U.S. and Japanese approaches to domestic and international economics has been badly underestimated. A remarkably consistent but misplaced faith has persisted since the 1970s that bilateral trade problems and disequilibria were on the verge of being solved. Both countries have dealt more with symptoms than structural discontinuities. Both repeatedly have been surprised by the imperviousness of bilateral trade imbalances and frictions to the application of every known adjustment measure over the span of three decades.

In the 1960s, U.S. political scientists belatedly learned from the bitter Sino-Soviet political schism that communism was not monolithic. Even in the late 1990s, prolonged discontinuities in U.S.-Japanese domestic economic and foreign trade performances had failed to convince many Americans that capitalism is not monolithic.

The third premise is that both sides share blame for the unbroken series of trade problems. The official and private sectors in both countries have fallen considerably short of making the structural adjustments needed to correct the aforementioned structural mismatches. Many Americans have demonstrated an "arrogance of weakness" by being quick to blame Japan instead of acknowledging U.S. shortcomings in domestic economic performance and trade policy. Japanese critics of the United States have demonstrated an "arrogance of success" by being quick to become overly defensive, thereby dismissing legitimate complaints about the adverse external impact of some of Japan's economic and business practices. This is not an either-or issue.

The fourth, and final, premise contends that Japan, not the United States, is the independent variable in explaining the trends in bilateral relations since the late 1960s. The United States is only one of a very large group of countries complaining about Japanese export strengths and import disinterest. The often anemic record of U.S. industrial exports to Japan is not widely duplicated in other foreign markets. An additional reason for asserting that Japan is the independent variable is that its characterization of the U.S. industrial sector as a listless, ineffective exporter is not a criticism usually heard from other countries, few of whom have outperformed the U.S. economy. Many of these countries, however, have received exactly the same response from Japan that it has given to U.S. criticism of hard-to-penetrate Japanese markets: an exhortation to try harder and invest more time. Japan's large bilateral trade surpluses in manufactured goods with other countries — even the newly industrialized economies of Southeast Asia — have been as common as foreign complaints about shortfalls in Japanese fairness and reciprocity. The speed and magnitude of Japan's success in attaining industrial superpower status, along with the formidable problems of access to its market by exporters of manufactured goods in all countries, are the defining characteristics of the issues we are examining.

## PROVING THE THESIS

The chapters that follow are designed to defend the thesis that a systemic mismatch between the Japanese and U.S. economies is at the crux of three decades of bilateral trade frictions and disequilibria. The defense is based on a vigorous methodology employing a detail-oriented, cross-disciplinary approach. Only three generalizations are endorsed: an impartial analysis inevitably apportions blame to both sides, all single-factor explanations of bilateral trade problems are incorrect, and all single-factor solutions are inadequate.

A two-pronged effort to explain in detail what happened comprises the rest of Part I. Chapter 2 presents a brief, nonjudgmental history of bilateral trade frictions from the end of the 1960s through 1996. A chronology of bilateral frictions is analogous to inkblots drawn for a Rorschach test: different interpretations of the observed patterns lie at the heart of the debate. Chapter 3 depicts a version of reality that is unequivocally sympathetic to the Japanese viewpoint and critical of the U.S. one. Next, in presenting a brief on behalf of the U.S. case against Japan, Chapter 4 offers a diametrically different version of reality in which blame and praise are allocated in exactly opposite directions. Chapter 5 takes a first step in bridging the perceptions gap by repudiating some of the erroneous and fallacious analyses that have most distorted the debate about bilateral trade strains.

Part II is devoted to a multilevel examination of why a systemic mismatch developed that was strong enough to cause bilateral trade frictions and disequilibria to persist for three decades. The first step in explaining this phenomenon is to assume that a country's international economic competitiveness is primarily an outgrowth of domestic economic, political, and social variables. Chapters 6 and 7, therefore, analyze the Japanese and U.S. economies, respectively, in terms of three key indicators of domestic economic performance and institutions:

history and culture,

business strategies and manufacturing skills, and

government policies.

Part II concludes with separate chapters analyzing two key international phenomena that have contributed directly to the mismatch and that exemplify the sub-theme of different priorities being pursued by the two countries. Chapter 8 examines the substantive gulf between U.S. and Japanese international trade, finance, and investment policies. The second factor external to domestic economics, the political economy that favored Japan in bilateral negotiations, is discussed in Chapter 9.

The final assessments comprising Part III begin with Chapter 10, which synthesizes the valid elements of the conflicting versions of what happened and why in bilateral trade relations. Chapter 11 offers suggestions for diminishing the systemic problem and moving the two countries toward harmony and equilibrium.

## NOTES

1. This term is adapted from "*Rashomon* Mirror," coined by William K. Tabb in *The Postwar Japanese System: Cultural Economy and Economic Transformation* (New York: Oxford University Press, 1995), pp. 21–22.

2. Ivan P. Hall, "Samurai Legacies, American Illusions," *The National Interest* (Summer 1992), p. 22.

3. Osamu Shimomura, "The 'Japan Problem' Is of America's Making," *Japan Echo* (Autumn 1987), p. 26.

4. Laura D'Andrea Tyson, *Who's Bashing Whom? Trade Conflict in High-Technology Industries* (Washington, D.C.: Institute for International Economics, 1992), pp. 66–91; Scott Latham, "Poor, Poor Motorola," *The Wall Street Journal*, March 3, 1994, p. A16.

The alleged victim in the pro-Japanese argument was the private Japanese phone carrier who was forced by a government-to-government agreement in 1994 to invest the equivalent of more than $100 million of its own capital to build relay facilities to enable Motorola's cellular phones to operate in the Tokyo area. Subsequent events reduced the company's martyr status. Senior executives of IDO Corporation later said that the forced marriage with Motorola has been vital to the company's ability to survive in Japan's intensely competitive cellular phone market; see, for example, "Cellular Firm Sees Former Foe as Ally," *Nikkei Weekly*, April 3, 1995, p. 2.

5.  See, for example, David Asher, "What Became of the Japanese 'Miracle,'" *Orbis* (Spring 1996), pp. 215–34; Christopher Wood, *The End of Japan, Inc.* (New York: Simon and Schuster, 1994). For the theory that bilateral problems are being ameliorated by the convergence of the two economic systems, see Michael Armacost, *Friends or Rivals? The Insider's Account of U.S.-Japan Relations* (New York: Columbia University Press, 1996).

6.  Leon Hollerman, "The Headquarters Nation," *National Interest* (Fall 1991), pp. 16–25; Chalmers Johnson, *Japan: Who Governs? The Rise of the Development State* (New York: W. W. Norton, 1995), pp. 8–9.

7.  Unpublished statistics provided to author from the U.S. Department of Commerce.

8.  "Profiles of the 1996 Cars," *Consumer Reports* (April 1996), p. 46.

9.  See *The Wall Street Journal*, October 9, 1996, p. A1; Japan Economic Institute, Report 11B, March 22, 1996, pp. 10–12; *Los Angeles Times*, March 4, 1996, p. D1; and *Washington Post*, March 16, 1996, p. A22.

# 2

# A History of Contemporary Bilateral Trade Relations

Why do other countries view our economic accomplishments with so much hostility?
— Frequently asked Japanese question

The nail that sticks up gets hammered down.
— Traditional Japanese proverb

History is useful in making the present at least a little more understandable. In the case of contemporary U.S.-Japanese trade relations, a knowledge of events occurring from the late 1960s through the mid-1990s is the first step in recognizing the larger forces that shape and sustain this relationship. A misreading of these events has caused history to repeat itself again and again. This chapter summarizes the many recurring events and frictions between the United States and Japan that are manifestations of the larger policy — managerial and attitudinal mismatches that, more than anything else, have shaped bilateral trade relations since the late 1960s. Space constraints require the following chronology to be highly selective.[1]

## BROAD PATTERNS AND RECURRING THEMES

Mutual suspicion has been a fixture in U.S.-Japanese trade relations since they began in the middle of the nineteenth century. Americans have been suspicious of what they see as an inscrutable, reclusive country whose people have a different way of thinking and are not inclined to buy foreign goods. The Japanese have remained suspicious of what they see as a self-righteous, aggressive country whose people have a different way of thinking and are not inclined to let other societies operate their economies as they see fit.

The endless procession of bilateral trade imbalances and frictions since the late 1960s is indicative of a complex systemic problem. The volume of patchwork and short-lived remedies aimed at relieving these problems is symptomatic of the degree to which both countries miscalculated the problem's depth and breadth. Through it all, however, the special nature of the bilateral relationship that developed in 1945 has been subtly demonstrated by the mutual preference (at least until 1996) to deal with virtually all trade problems in bilateral forums closed to interested third countries. The United States and Japan preferred to work out their trade problems privately in lieu of using the General Agreement on Tariffs and Trade, the multilateral venue established for trade negotiations and dispute settlements.

Literally speaking, bilateral trade frictions began with demands initiated by the United States, which has been complaining for 30 years about being victimized by Japan's closed markets, government assistance to industry, and overly aggressive export tactics. The U.S. government has taken the political offensive because the U.S. industrial sector has been on the defensive in head-to-head competition with Japan, has petitioned on numerous occasions for governmental relief from import-induced injury, and has sought Washington's aid in convincing Japan to lower barriers to U.S. exports. Meanwhile, the Japanese would have been delighted to perpetuate the status quo in a trade relationship where Japanese industry was successful in its goals of maximizing trade surpluses and market share. Official Japanese complaints about the United States, its closest ally, have been almost exclusively directed to what they regard as the rudeness, excessive severity, and illogic of incessant demands that Japan stop its unfair trade practices.

Over the past three decades, U.S. tactics to spur Japan to change its ways have been more ad hoc than elements of a grand design. Most U.S. initiatives have been either responses to individual private sector pressures or recycled demands by incoming administrations. What political scientists call a two-level game is at work. On one level, senior officials of the executive branch formulate a trade position deemed responsive to interested domestic politicians and interest groups; on another level, they negotiate the best possible agreement with counterparts in a foreign government. The relatively less accountable senior civil servants in Japan usually operate at two levels as well, although members of the Diet and private sector constituents have less influence on trade policy decisions than their U.S. counterparts.

U.S. policy initiatives seeking to alter Japanese economic behavior have taken four different forms. The first consisted of demands made from the 1950s through the early 1990s for "voluntary" restraints on exports of a number of goods whose rising sales were causing economic dislocations among U.S. producers. The second, more divisive U.S. initiative consists of demands for greater access to the Japanese market — often with the threat of unilateral retaliation if U.S. exports did not increase. The third form of initiative has been the use of the U.S. anti-dumping laws and other statutes against what were deemed unfair Japanese trade practices. The fourth and newest vehicle for U.S. pressures began in the 1960s and consists of demands for internal changes in Japan's regulatory framework and business practices.

The transcendent recurring theme of the past three decades of bilateral relations is escalating frustration and disillusionment accompanied by persistent threat of trade war. Countless economic adjustment measures and liberalization packages by Japan have failed to either defuse frictions or permanently reduce the bilateral trade disequilibrium (see Table 2.1). The United States remains upset with failure to solve what it regards as Japanese reluctance, duplicity, and backsliding in genuinely opening its markets. Japan remains upset with what it sees as unjustified U.S. accusations of unfairness and excessive demands for yet more concessions.

## STARTING OFF ON THE WRONG FOOT

Believers in omens can point to the inauspicious beginning of the U.S.-Japanese trading relationship: a show of raw naval power. Commodore

**TABLE 2.1**
**U.S.-Japan Trade Balances, 1969–1996**
**(in billions of U.S. dollars)**

| Year | U.S. Bilateral Deficit | U.S. Imports from Japan | U.S. Exports to Japan | U.S. Exports to Japan as a Percentage of U.S. Imports |
|------|------|------|------|------|
| 1969 | 1.4 | 4.9 | 3.5 | 71 |
| 1970 | 1.2 | 5.9 | 4.7 | 80 |
| 1975 | 1.7 | 11.3 | 9.6 | 85 |
| 1980 | 9.9 | 30.7 | 20.8 | 68 |
| 1985 | 46.2 | 68.8 | 22.6 | 33 |
| 1990 | 41.1 | 89.7 | 48.6 | 54 |
| 1995 | 59.1 | 123.5 | 64.3 | 52 |
| 1996 | 47.7 | 115.2 | 67.5 | 59 |

*Source*: U.S. Commerce Department. (Imports measured FAS.)

Matthew Perry, who commanded the fleet of "black ships" sent to convince Japan to alter its commercial isolation, was the first in a long line of U.S. officials to confront the Japanese with market access demands. Perry was also the first in a long line of officials to be frustrated with Japan's slow responses to demands for greater hospitality to U.S. goods. The Treaty of Kanagawa, signed in March 1854, was limited to procedural matters, such as protection of ships and crews in distress and the opening of two Japanese ports for purchasing fuel and food supplies.

Another portent was the delay in formalizing commercial relations. The Tokugawa authorities resorted to every possible obstacle, and the people were not enthusiastic about buying strange foreign goods. It was not until 1858 that the first U.S. consul, Townsend Harris, was able to conclude a treaty that officially opened designated Japanese ports to trade with U.S. ships. Edwin O. Reischauer notes that popular opposition to the forced opening of the country gave rise to the rallying cry "honor the emperor and expel the barbarians."[2]

Japan's worst fears about dealing with the West were soon confirmed. After news of the U.S. treaty spread, warships from the European powers arrived, demanding equivalent market access. Imposed in 1866, the so-called unequal treaties forced Japan to limit its tariff levels to a maximum of 5 percent. Japan did not regain autonomy over tariffs until the end of the century.[3]

By the beginning of the twentieth century, Americans already were expressing anxiety over Japan's commercial prowess. The country was characterized by a U.S. writer in 1904 as presenting "the amazing spectacle of an Eastern society maintaining all the outward forms of Western civilization . . . accomplishing by prodigious effort, the work of centuries within the time of three decades."[4] One year later, a New York newspaper described the Japanese worker as "ingenious . . . , industrious and intelligent, wearing almost no clothes and living on less than would support a mechanic's dog in this country."[5]

The spreading global depression and the protectionist trade measures that followed in its wake caused a massive downward spiral in international trade in the early 1930s. Later in the decade, Japan agreed to restrain exports of cotton fabrics and a few other inexpensive consumer goods (matches and pencils, for example) to the United States — harbingers of things to come. U.S.-Japanese trade relations embarked on their most tragic period in 1940. President Roosevelt responded to Japanese military expansion in Asia by gradually restricting exports to that country of such important raw materials as petroleum and scrap metal. In 1941, he froze all Japanese assets in the United States. By angering Japan's military high command, these economic sanctions may have contributed to Japan's decision to attack Pearl Harbor.

After World War II, a radically different, friendly, bilateral, economic partnership was born. It was defined by the Occupation, U.S. efforts to help Japan rebuild its political and economic vigor, and U.S. sponsorship of Japanese membership in the newly created cluster of international economic organizations. U.S. benevolence was first tempered in the late 1950s, when the U.S. government pressured Japan to implement voluntary restraints on the export growth of several labor-intensive, unsophisticated products, most notably cotton textiles, bicycles, flatware, baseball gloves, and ceramics. In 1962, a U.S. economist identified the central dilemma that exists to this day in Western attitudes toward Japan: "The problem is how to integrate Japan's export capability agreeably into the trade pattern of the Free World."[6]

## THE LATE 1960s AND THE 1970s: THE UNITED STATES BECOMES IMPORT-UNFRIENDLY AND JAPAN STARTS SHEDDING IMPORT BARRIERS

Until the mid-1960s, the closed door import policies of Japan and the open-door import policies of the hegemonic United States made excellent economic sense and created no political problems. Structural changes in both domestic economic performances and trade patterns gradually ushered in the era of bilateral trade imbalances and frictions. The first sign that it was no longer business as usual was the Johnson administration's seemingly one-of-a-kind demand in 1968 that Japan (and Western Europe) agree to restrain steel exports to the United States for three years.

The shift to a more contentious phase of bilateral trade relations is more formally associated with the acrimonious dispute, lasting from 1969 through 1971, caused by the Nixon administration's unwavering demand that Japan voluntarily restrain shipments of synthetic (chemical-based) textiles to the U.S. market. For the first time in the postwar era a Japanese government resisted a U.S. trade demand. Months of fruitless negotiations dragged into years of bitter impasse during which a vast amount of political goodwill was exhausted and economic logic was largely ignored (partly because President Nixon thought the Japanese prime minister reneged on a personal promise to resolve the dispute).

In August 1971, the New Economic Policy abruptly imposed shock therapy on the U.S. economy and on global economic relations. President Nixon's decisions to impose a 10 percent surcharge on all U.S. tariffs and terminate the obligation to convert dollars held by foreign central banks into gold ended the initial postwar phase of U.S. trade policy in which foreign policy objectives overwhelmingly had been placed ahead of domestic interests.

Growing U.S. sensitivity to relatively rapid increases in imports spurred Congress to relax the statutory criteria for demonstrating import-induced injury under the so-called escape clause. This measure offers domestic producers the possibility of temporary relief (higher tariffs and/or quotas) from intense, albeit fair, foreign competition if the petitioner can demonstrate that imports are a substantial cause of serious injury, or threat thereof, to the domestic industry. The U.S. International Trade Commission, operating under the relaxed statutory criteria inserted into the Trade Act of 1974, began to find more frequently that domestic petitioners were, in fact, facing economic injury from rising imports. Presidents usually responded to positive findings of injury by seeking a middle ground between unilateral protectionism and no action, negotiating orderly marketing agreements (OMAs) in which exporting countries — Japan, more often than not — agreed to voluntarily keep shipments of a specified product to the United States under an agreed-upon ceiling.

An OMA signed with Japan in 1976 covering specialty steels was followed the next year by an OMA covering color televisions — the response to dramatic surges in Japanese imports. The early impression that this three-year agreement unfairly penalized Japan for producing lower-cost, higher-quality products later gave way to a very different interpretation when it was discovered that Japan's highly successful television export offensive largely reflected predatory dumping based on negotiated price collusion among Japanese manufacturers and illegal kickbacks to large U.S. retailers.[7]

On the other side of the Pacific, the Japanese had begun moving in the opposite direction — shifting priorities from a total commitment to advancing internal interests to addressing some external commercial obligations. By the end of the 1960s, most of Japan's industrial sectors were in a position to withstand gradual dismantling of the vast array of postwar export-promotion and import-retarding programs that had been constructed to accelerate economic recovery. In the absence of any powerful domestic Japanese constituency in favor of exposing industry to increased overseas competition, U.S. government pressure was the critical catalyst in the Japanese government's initiation of a long series of politically painful adjustment measures to stimulate imports and restrain the growth of exports. Actions taken included eliminating most import quotas and easing other nontariff barriers, lowering tariffs, revaluing the yen's exchange rate in 1971, phasing out export promotion incentives, and reducing international capital controls and barriers to inward foreign direct investment.

The bilateral trade negotiating agenda eventually expanded beyond traditional liberalization measures to include use of expansionary macroeconomic policies to stimulate Japanese GDP growth and, therefore, boost demand for imports. The Strauss-Ushiba agreement of January 1978 called for efforts by both countries to achieve higher levels of noninflationary economic growth as well as efforts by Japan to reduce its current account surplus. The latter goal was not met because of the absence in Japan of both a large spurt in GDP growth and an income-elastic demand for imports.

## THE 1980s: JAPAN BECOMES THE FOCAL POINT OF U.S. TRADE ANXIETIES

As measured by its overall impact on the economies of both countries, the most important bilateral export restraint agreement took effect in 1981 when Japanese automobiles were added to the list of Japan's voluntary export restraints. There was no denying a surge of automobile imports from Japan, a trend largely caused by the dramatic shift in U.S. consumer demand for gasoline-efficient cars in the wake of the second oil shock. There was also no denying massive increases in sticker prices of automobiles sold in the United States following the quantitative Japanese automobile restraints, which dampened price competition.[8] Next, successful escape clause petitions filed by the U.S. carbon and specialty steel industries led to successful U.S. overtures to the Japanese in the mid-1980s that multiyear restraints on exports of these products were advisable in order to avoid unilateral import restraints. In what was the last bilateral OMA negotiated as of 1997, the Japanese, in 1987, initiated multiyear restraints on machine tool shipments to the United States.

Announcements of Japanese moves to liberalize import barriers were much in evidence throughout the 1980s. In what might be described as a process of creeping incrementalism, tariffs were unilaterally reduced on a wide variety of products, and partial relaxations were repeatedly made in nontariff barriers, mainly involving Japanese customs procedures, product standards, and testing requirements. In addition, restrictions on foreign direct investment in Japan were further eased, and financial markets were partially liberalized.

Many U.S. government agencies took a cynical view of this procession of import liberalization measures, arguing that, as a whole, they were long on generalities but short on implementation and failed to meet key U.S. market access demands. In some cases, the U.S. government found it necessary to threaten retaliation repeatedly against what it regarded as superficial or disingenuous reductions in import impediments affecting competitive U.S. goods. Among the longer and more important examples of recurring disagreements involved Japanese efforts to improve access to its lucrative public works projects to U.S. construction and engineering firms, to open its markets for telecommunications equipment and cellular telephones, and to change governmental procurement procedures that discriminated against purchases of U.S. supercomputers. Although Japan first eased barriers on imported cigarettes in 1980, it was not until fall 1986 that the U.S. government and industry were satisfied with market access. Japan substantially liberalized cigarette imports at the time mainly to head off impending retaliation by the Reagan administration. U.S. efforts to convince the then government-owned Nippon Telegraph and Telephone Corporation to channel a respectable portion of its multibillion dollar telecommunications equipment contracts to foreign firms commenced in 1980 and continued into the 1990s even after the company was privatized.

Japan dominated U.S. trade policy concerns during the second half of the 1980s. Concerns about declining U.S. competitiveness produced spirited discussions of enhanced science and technology policy, competitive advantage induced by industrial policy, results-oriented trade agreements, and targeting priority foreign trade barriers. Anxiety about Japan's industrial strength and trade surpluses inspired all of the major new concepts introduced into U.S. trade policy debates in the late 1980s.

The mood and economic situation in Japan at this time were radically different. Emboldened by a growing sense of confidence and power, Japan's gratitude for postwar U.S. assistance was turning into irritation and disdain at what it perceived as the strident tones of a declining superpower more inclined to complain than to undertake self-improvement. The Japanese economy was booming, and a seemingly unstoppable growth dynamic had emerged. Corporate profits, land and stock prices, trade surpluses, and corporate investment outlays soared to unthinkable heights.

Conversely, on Capitol Hill, frustrations with the U.S. foreign trade position threatened to boil over. Although dollar overvaluation and the mounting budget deficit caused a deterioration in the U.S. trade deficit with all of its major trade partners, Japan's allegedly adversarial trade policies and performance generated more rancor in the U.S. Congress than the trade practices of all other countries combined. In March 1985, the Senate approved by a vote of 92 to 0 a nonbinding resolution introduced by Senator John Danforth (R., Mo.). It categorized Japan as an unfair trader, one who denied U.S. products fair access to Japanese markets despite its ready access to the U.S. market, and urged the president to be more aggressive and take "all appropriate and feasible action" to rectify the situation. A similarly worded resolution sailed through the House of Representatives a few days later.

Citing increased reasons to doubt the efficacy of opening Japan solely through verbal changes in laws and regulations, hard-liners began urging use of results-oriented market access agreements going beyond circumventable rule changes. Support grew for a policy demanding Japan's acceptance of specific, quantifiable targets for increased imports and then telling them to decide among themselves how these commitments would be met. The concept of "managed trade" was transformed into policy reality when the two countries signed a landmark agreement in 1986 that sought to address two major U.S. complaints involving semiconductors, a critically important high-tech product. Specifically, the U.S. government was energized by the domestic industry's complaints first, that the Japanese were dumping memory chips, and second, that the virtually permanent 10 percent market share in Japan for foreign-produced semiconductors — despite elimination of import barriers and yen appreciation — demonstrated anti-import collusion within the Japanese market.

To prevent imposition of stiff antidumping duties, the semiconductor agreement (renewed in 1991 for a second five-year period) mandated a set of minimum prices on all Japanese chips exported to the U.S. market. It also included an unprecedented agreement-in-kind that foreign-made chips should have a larger market share in Japan. In a secret, still not officially recognized side letter, the Japanese government said that it "recognizes the U.S. semiconductor industry's expectation that semiconductor sales in Japan of foreign . . . companies will grow to at least slightly above 20 percent of the Japanese market in five years [and] considers that this can be realized and welcomes its realization."[9] What the Japanese government viewed as an informal target for increased imports, U.S. officials saw as a binding commitment. When U.S. semiconductor exports increased only slightly and when surveillance detected continued dumping of Japanese chips in third markets, the Reagan administration retaliated on the grounds of noncompliance with the agreement. One hundred percent tariffs were imposed temporarily on $300 million worth of U.S. electronics imports made by other divisions of the diversified Japanese semiconductor manufacturers.

Mounting dissatisfaction over market access in Japan and to a lesser extent elsewhere was the catalyst for a new element in U.S. trade strategy — the congressionally-inspired quest for reciprocity. Advocates of this approach wanted U.S. trade negotiators to present a simple choice to foreign offenders. They could either open their markets to the same degree that the U.S. market was deemed open to them or face the risk of retaliatory restrictions. The main vehicle for pursuing both the principle of reciprocity and the strategy of reducing the mammoth U.S. multilateral trade deficit through export expansion rather than import reduction was Section 301 of the Trade Act of 1974 as amended. It called on the executive branch to seek reduction or elimination of foreign trade measures deemed to be discriminatory, unjustifiable, or unreasonable impediments to U.S. commerce and authorized retaliatory measures if foreign accommodation was not forthcoming. The Omnibus Trade and Competitiveness Act of 1988 took this measure one step further in the form of the Super 301 amendment. It required the president (for two years) to identify priority practices that were major impediments to U.S. exports and to initiate bilateral negotiations with the offending country to reduce or eliminate the designated barriers or distortions. Japan was one of three countries cited under the first Super 301 review for imposing priority trade barriers. Under threat of U.S. retaliation, the Japanese government, in 1990, agreed to reduce impediments to imports in its three designated priority sectors: supercomputers, communications satellites, and wood products.

A significant innovation in bilateral trade relations was the U.S. effort to expand the scope of its efforts to open the Japanese market beyond relatively narrow, time-consuming, product-by-product negotiations. The first incarnation of a more efficient liberalization process was the Market-Oriented Sector-Selective (MOSS) talks that began in 1985. The MOSS talks were designed to address all identifiable trade barriers within a Japanese industry where U.S. companies were demonstrably competitive in the international marketplace but experienced relatively poor results exporting to that country. The Japanese government eventually agreed to take market-opening measures in all four of the originally selected MOSS sectors — electronics, telecommunications equipment and services, medical equipment and pharmaceuticals, and forest products. U.S. trade strategists excluded a number of other unresolved market access issues, such as rice, soda ash, and semiconductors, from the initial Super 301 list — apparently to avert Japanese embarrassment and anger.

The Structural Impediments Initiative, launched in 1989, represented the first potential breakthrough to serious discussion of the underlying structural factors that this book suggests are the principal causes of bilateral disequilibria and frictions. Never before had the governments of two major countries officially probed so deeply and systematically into each other's internal affairs. One of several structural changes in economic policies and business practices requested by the U.S. government sought to reduce Japan's chronic over-saving through increased governmental expenditures on infrastructure and to introduce shorter work weeks (to encourage more leisure-time spending). A second request sought reductions in two forms of alleged discriminatory business practices: the tendency for member companies of *keiretsu* (informal alliances of manufacturing companies owning a significant percentage of each other's shares) to buy from one another and the lack of antitrust enforcement to limit cartels and collusion. Changes also were requested in Japan's complex distribution system to make it more import friendly. More responsive pricing mechanisms were sought to reduce high retail prices in Japan and to assure that future appreciations in the yen's exchange rate would increase Japanese export prices and reduce prices for goods imported from the United States. Finally, the U.S. government suggested reforms in those land-use policies that contributed to inflated prices for commercial property and housing in Japan.

The Japanese government offered a separate list of what they viewed as structural weaknesses in the U.S. economy. They urged correction of the U.S. saving-investment imbalance by reducing the federal budget deficit and increasing saving rates, as well as increased levels of capital investment and adoption of longer-term planning horizons by U.S. corporations. Japan also recommended that the U.S. government increase its funding of non-defense research and development and improve education and training programs.

Few significant changes were implemented as direct outgrowths of the Structural Impediments Initiative talks. Perhaps the most significant change was the relaxation of Japan's Large Scale Retail Store law to ease approval of larger Japanese- and U.S.-owned stores that tend to sell more imports than "mom and pop" shops.

A new variant of strain in bilateral relations emerged in the late 1980s. Many Americans began to resent the sizable capital inflows from Japan despite the fact that they were the natural consequences of the United States needing imported capital to finance large current account deficits and to offset inadequate saving and large Japanese trade surpluses. Wall Street analysts estimated that Japanese institutional investors in the latter part of the decade were buying as much as 30 percent of newly issued Treasury bills and bonds.[10] U.S. Treasury Department officials still turn ashen at the interest rate and borrowing cost implications of Japanese investors halting their purchases of the debt instruments used to finance the U.S. budget deficit or, even worse, selling off existing holdings. Nevertheless, public opinion turned belligerent toward Japanese foreign direct investment and real estate purchases. The vision of the "selling of America" spread as Japanese investors began buying up cultural icons, such as Rockefeller Center and Hollywood movie studios.

The decade ended on a more familiar note when the Japanese government announced in December 1989 its intention to implement an unparalleled import promotion program.

## THE 1990s: THE UNITED STATES STRESSES RESULTS; JAPAN TIRES OF BILATERALISM

Twenty years of dispute settlement practice did not enable the two countries to produce more effective remedies to the bilateral trade problems that emerged in the 1990s. Twenty years of Japanese economic liberalization did not change the opinion of many Americans that credible threats of retaliation elicited far more Japanese responsiveness than expressions of goodwill. Twenty years of trying to accommodate nonstop U.S. demands did convince the Japanese that, at some point, enough would be enough. Japan's multilateral and bilateral trade surpluses hit record levels in the early 1990s after both had increased, on average, twenty-fold since the early 1970s.

The Bush administration's last big Japan initiative was the president's ill-fated visit to Tokyo that is remembered for two things. One is Mr. Bush's collapse at a formal state dinner that drew suggestions from some Japanese that this was an apt metaphor for a tired, sick country. The other is the Global Partnership Plan that included a second instance of results-oriented trade policy — numerical targets of $10 billion in increased purchases of U.S.-made auto parts by Japanese-owned automobile producers located in Japan and the United States.

Japan immediately became a high priority trade issue in the new Clinton administration. Shared skepticism about Japan produced a distinctive bilateral strategy that determined "not just to negotiate the removal of trade barriers, but also to see concrete, measurable results in the marketplace."[11] This strategy led to the agreement in July 1993 between President Clinton and Prime Minister Kiichi Miyazawa on the charter for a "Framework for a New Economic Partnership." Among other things, it was agreed that structural and sectoral market access issues would be conducted with the objective of substantially increasing access and sales of competitive foreign goods and services in Japan. Assessments of progress on these issues would be based on "sets of objective criteria, either qualitative or quantitative or both as appropriate." It was also agreed that the core agenda of the framework talks would consist of five specific categories corresponding to U.S. concerns: government procurement; deregulation; other major sectors, principally automobiles and auto parts; economic harmonization (intellectual property rights and foreign direct investment in Japan); and implementation of existing bilateral agreements and measures.

Market-opening agreements were delayed by a deep philosophical cleavage on the appropriate level of specificity of Japanese compliance indicators, for example, percentage changes in the market share of U.S. goods. The Japanese side argued the need to defend the liberal trade ethic against alleged U.S. efforts to invoke managed trade. Painstaking negotiations eventually produced agreements that relaxed Japanese procurement practices covering telecommunications equipment and services (a process that had started in 1980), reduced collusion in Japan's flat glass sector, and eliminated remaining obstacles to Motorola's access to the cellular telephone market. The Japanese government announced yet another import-promotion program in October 1994.

Following this flurry of progress, only one major framework issue remained unsettled in early 1995: new automobiles and auto parts — the source of more than one-half of the U.S. bilateral trade deficit with Japan. The two countries were so divided on this issue that they marched to the brink of what was arguably the most feared and publicized near trade war in history. Japanese intransigence to U.S. export-enhancement demands, which centered on deregulation of their automobile and auto parts industries, was driven by adamant opposition to any forms of quantitative criteria to certify acceptable rates of increased imports. They believed that the models of U.S.-made cars being exported held very limited appeal to Japanese consumers. Also, it is likely that Japanese trade strategists assumed they had a better chance of winning if the dispute was arbitrated on a multilateral basis in the World Trade Organization. A vaguely worded agreement dealing with market-opening measures and U.S. expectations of enhanced exports was reached in June 1995 — just in time to avert the impending imposition of prohibitive tariffs of 100 percent on imports of Japanese luxury cars valued at about $6 billion annually. (U.S. sanctions were threatened following a Section 301 finding of discrimination against U.S. automobile parts.)

Hopes for a respite in bilateral trade frictions following the end of the automobile ordeal in June 1995 were soon shattered by the endless dispute syndrome. Contentious negotiations dealing with a second extension of the semiconductor agreement produced a diplomatic victory for Japan in the form of a token arrangement devoid of any target for foreign market share or even reference to continuing progress in increasing sales of foreign-made chips. The Clinton administration did slightly better in December 1996, when another approaching deadline for threatened U.S. sanctions inspired the two governments to break a three-year deadlock on liberalization of the Japanese insurance market. Yet another source of protracted friction was the two sides' inability to agree on a schedule of reciprocal air routes and landing rights for both passenger and air cargo flights. In a major example of backpedaling from bilateralism, the Japanese government rejected the Clinton administration's request for consultations on the issues raised in the Section 301 complaint filed by the Eastman Kodak Company. After the Ministry of International Trade and Industry refused negotiations on the grounds that it was an antitrust issue falling solely under the jurisdiction of the Japan Fair Trade Commission, the administration filed a complaint in the World Trade Organization alleging nullification and impairment of trade benefits. It claimed that the Japanese government actively sought to neutralize the liberalization of formal import barriers by encouraging the Fuji Photo Film Company to fashion an anticompetitive stranglehold on the retail distribution of photographic film.

## CONCLUSION

The most significant characteristics of the three-decade history of U.S.-Japanese trade imbalances and frictions are length, magnitude, and durability. One does not associate a 30-year-old problem whose end is not yet in sight with two friendly countries that are both uncomfortable with its continuation and actively committed to its eradication.

The unfolding of events is perfectly clear, but their underlying cause and meaning are not. Was it a story of a U.S. bully in search of a scapegoat or of the Japanese doggedly resisting adoption of a market-oriented, liberal trade policy regime? Each country viewed itself as the protagonist and the other as the antagonist. Each had diametrically opposite views on the legitimacy of Japanese trade practices and of U.S. complaints about them. With the United States alarmed at what it saw as a nationalistic campaign by Japan to maximize its commercial power and with Japan disconcerted at what it saw as a self-indulgent effort by the United States to keep Japan in its place, the systemic nature of the problem was ignored and efforts to correct it were inadequate.

The next two chapters detail the ultimate *Rashomon* lens effect: irreconcilable interpretations of who bears responsibility for the succession of bilateral trade frictions since the late 1960s.

## NOTES

1.  For those interested in historical detail, an excellent source is the U.S. International Trade Commission's annual report on the operation of the Trade Agreements Program. Since 1990, the Japan Economic Institute in Washington, D.C., has published an annual "Look Back" on bilateral economic relations in the previous year. These two publications are the sources of many of this chapter's factual references to the contents and dates of U.S.-Japanese trade agreements.

2.  Edwin O. Reischauer, *The Japanese* (Cambridge, Mass.: Harvard University Press, 1981), pp. 79–80.

3.  Christopher Howe, *The Origins of Japanese Trade Supremacy* (Chicago: University of Chicago Press, 1996), p. 159.

4.  Lafcadio Hearn, *Japan — An Attempt at Interpretation* (New York: Grosset and Dunlap, 1904), p. 501.

5.  Newspaper editorial quoted in William Newman, *America Encounters Japan* (Baltimore, Md.: Johns Hopkins University Press, 1963), p. 22.

6.  Raymond Saulnier, "An Economist's Eye View of the World," *Fortune* (May 1962), p. 159.

7.  See, for example, Kozo Yamamura and Jan Vandenberg, "Japan's Rapid-Growth Policy on Trial: The Television Case," in *Law and Trade Issues of the Japanese Economy*, edited by Kozo Yamamura and Gary Saxonhouse (Seattle: University of Washington Press, 1986), pp. 259–62.

8.  The politically induced shortage of much-in-demand Japanese cars caused a rapid escalation in their sticker prices. Rather than seek to increase their market share, U.S. auto manufacturers opted for repeated price increases. The resulting upward spiral in automobile prices cost the consumer dearly; estimates of the cost per job saved in the U.S. automobile sector (relative to total incremental prices paid by consumers) were in excess of $100,000 annually. See, for

example, Robert W. Crandall, "Import Quotas and the Automobile Industry: The Costs of Protection," *Brookings Review* (Summer 1984), pp. 8–16.

9. Identical texts of the side letter were published in a U.S. newsletter, *Inside U.S. Trade*, and in a Japanese magazine, *Bungei Shunju*.

10. See, for example, R. Taggart Murphy, *The Weight of the Yen — How Denial Imperils America's Future and Ruins an Alliance* (New York: W. W. Norton, 1996), p. 147; "Japanese Pulling out of U.S. Bonds, But the Markets Are Calm," *Reuter Business Report* (October 23, 1990) available from the Lexis/Nexis data base.

11. Jeffrey E. Garten, "U.S.-Japan Relations: Accomplishments, Next Steps, Future Consideration," speech delivered at the U.S. Department of Commerce, December 2, 1994, p. 5.

# 3

# An Uncompromising Japanese Interpretation of Trade Frictions

The United States has continuously refused to admit its declining competitive power as the true cause of the existing trade friction and has continued to maintain that it has been a victim of cheap labor, dumping, and other unfair export practices by Japan.
— Naohiro Amaya, former MITI vice-minister (1980)

The question we should be asking is not what Japan should do but what the United States should do. Americans blame Japan, mistaking the effect for the cause.
— Osamu Shimomura (1987)

Full understanding of the history of U.S.-Japanese trade conflicts requires the subject to be divided into two parts. The first consists of the factual chronology of events recited in the previous chapter. The second part consists of the highly contentious, emotionally charged question of the legitimacy of each country's behavior and accusations against the other. About the only thing on which there is nearly unanimous agreement is that only one country has acted honorably. One viewpoint attributes problems to the insatiable appetite of the United States for ill-conceived, sometimes irrational demands on Japan. The contradictory viewpoint apportions blame to Japan's self-absorbed, nonmarket approaches to industrial organization and trade policy. Given this book's emphasis on the importance of perception, it will avoid the traditional, oversimplified approach of taking sides. The arbitrary assumption that one version of trade frictions is valid and one is misguided has relegated both public debate and scholarly literature to intellectual gridlock. This error has undermined consensus on meaningful policy solutions.

This chapter and the next adopt an unorthodox approach to the perception and communication gaps between the two countries. These gaps are so wide that they have become part of the problem. The two chapters seek to explain — fully, unequivocally, and passionately — the mutually exclusive arguments of the two sides. This chapter is not objective scholarship but is, instead, designed to be the equivalent of a legal brief, unapologetically articulating the Japanese case against the United States. The brief for the U.S. case against Japan unfolds in similar fashion in Chapter 4. The veracity of and the author's opinion on the many arguments presented in these two chapters are irrelevant to an exercise in role-playing. The main objective of the analysis following these chapters is the construction of an analytical framework capable of integrating the seemingly irreconcilable beliefs that comprise the pro-Japanese and pro-U.S. viewpoints.

## THE FRAGILE OUTSIDER

Japan's successful pursuit of industrial power has failed to extinguish the country's historically intense feelings of vulnerability and isolation. Most Japanese perceive their country as a tenuous economic superpower whose position of strength could suddenly be undermined at any time from unforseen internal setbacks or hostile actions abroad. Japan lacks critical natural resources. It has suffered throughout its history from such disasters as earthquakes, tidal waves, typhoons, and attack by atomic bombs. Japan is not part of any formal regional grouping of countries. Its distinctive culture, subject to unwanted dissipation from foreign influences, precludes close bonds of friendship with other societies. The economic stagnation that followed the bursting of the "bubble" boom of the 1980s has been sufficiently serious and long-standing that many Japanese seriously doubt that the rapid growth rates once taken for granted will ever return. Longer-term, economic prospects are clouded by the rapidly aging Japanese population in which rising numbers of elderly, nonworking persons will place substantial financial burdens on the work force early in the next century.

Most Japanese believe that very few foreigners respect their accomplishments or sympathize with their precarious position. Worse yet, actions taken by these physically and spiritually distant foreigners are major variables in Japan's economic destiny. The Japanese are hypersensitive to the possibility that injury from abroad can occur even if they are not an intended target. If asked to provide a brief history of the country's international economic relations since 1969, most informed Japanese would emphasize external shocks, not Japan's export boom. The U.S.

soybean embargo of 1973 is still a vivid reminder of weak links in Japan's external food supply. Given Japan's dependence on foreign oil, the negative economic effects of the two upsurges in oil prices in 1973–74 and 1979–80 provided incontrovertible proof to most Japanese that the continuation of their economic good fortune was far from certain. The two oil shocks hit Japan suddenly and severely with the greatest threats to its economic prosperity and stability since the 1940s. The subsequent slowdowns in economic growth and inflationary surges were seen as a brutally clear signal that Japan's economic miracle would always be at risk from the actions of other countries. Not even the relatively quick economic recovery from the two price shocks of the Organization of Petroleum Exporting Countries could instill a sense of serenity and security in the Japanese psyche.

The uncertain world of the Japanese people suggests that working harder and better is a necessity, not an option. No matter how hard they work, they are a tiny minority on the global scene and are unable to attain the same social status and peace of mind possessed by the white Anglo-Saxon establishment. The cultural and political bonds linking Western Europe and North America are not applicable to a spiritually and geographically distant Japan. The Atlantic Alliance and the Atlantic Community still have no Pacific counterparts. The Western economic powers have never welcomed Japan as a full partner in their elite club. At the back of its collective mind, Japan still worries about the Europeans and North Americans jointly embracing an actively hostile economic posture toward it. Twentieth-century Japan "has stood forlornly out in the cold, selling her wares to passers-by, and peering in longingly through the tightly closed windows of the world councils." Even when the door has been opened to them, the Japanese "have felt that they have not been treated as genuine equals."[1] The Washington Naval Conference of 1922 produced a treaty establishing an unequal 5:5:3 ratio in the number of heavy warships and aircraft carriers allowed for the United States, the United Kingdom, and Japan, respectively. For many Japanese, the onset of "voluntary" export quotas imposed by the West beginning in the 1950s rekindled thoughts of the warship restraints imposed on Japan to keep it in its place.

Sensitivity about outsider status has been magnified by perceptions of an ongoing double standard in trade relations. Americans seem far more tolerant of European imports, and U.S.–Western European trade disputes appear to be settled in a friendlier, more family-like manner that does not portray the other side as an adversarial trader. The European Union's Common Agricultural Policy has cost the United States countless billions of dollars in lost exports over the past three decades. However, the United States long ago resigned itself to its continuation. The U.S. government has not publicly and repeatedly attacked the Common Agricultural

Policy — as it has attacked Japanese import barriers — as a major threat to fairness, the liberal trading system, and domestic economic producers.

Japan thinks that its economic miracle reflected a superior national effort in the universal pursuit of economic prosperity. The acceleration of the Japanese miracle in the 1980s was seen as all the more remarkable in view of rising wages and external problems, such as growing foreign antipathy toward Japanese exports, rapid yen appreciation, and nonstop foreign demands to reduce trade barriers and restructure internal business practices. Less successful countries should view Japan as a role model. Instead, foreigners' jealousy and inability to understand Japan's culture cause it to be wrongly viewed as a predator and threat to the economic stability of other countries, or in more polite academic circles as an outlier, having distinctive trade patterns suggesting a restrictive market.

The Japanese find it galling when trading partners insist that their domestic and international economic successes could only have been achieved by unfair means. Foreign reaction to Japan's miraculous economic performance has been long on dislike and jealousy, short on respect and imitation. The Japanese view Western analysis of this success as consisting mostly of a stream of fatuous accusations involving various forms of cheating: an exploited and workaholic labor force, government subsidies, dumping, a rigged exchange rate, trade barriers, consumer prejudice against foreign-made products, industrial targeting, collusive business practices excluding foreign products, and even an effort to continue fighting World War II through economic aggression. Instead of admitting that the Japanese economy was simply performing better, the United States and Western Europe incessantly demanded modifications in Japanese domestic and international economic behavior to make it more acceptable.

Why, the Japanese wonder, did the world trade community not express outrage at West Germany's surging current account surpluses in the years prior to its reunification with East Germany? While directing bitter criticism to the size of Japan's surpluses, the rest of the world ignored the fact that, from 1987 through 1990, the West German current account surplus, expressed as a percentage of GDP, was well above that of Japan. In 1989, for example, its current account surplus was 4.8 percent of GDP while Japan's was only 2 percent.[2]

By failing to reciprocate, even remotely, the scale of Japanese study of U.S. political, economic, and social trends, the United States consigns itself to a limited understanding of its main Pacific ally. Foreigners' distorted images and ignorance of new trends in Japan allegedly hinder their ability to recognize the extent to which its market has opened to imports and foreign investment.

Although a more accurate external understanding of the new Japan would reduce unfair foreign criticism, it would not eliminate another perceived cause of dislike for Japan: racism. Foreign prejudice causes Japan to be censured for working hard and well. A case in point is the infamous European Union memorandum, leaked to the press in 1979, that branded the Japanese as "workaholics living in what Westerners would regard as little more than rabbit hutches," a people "who have only recently emerged from a feudal society."[3] The controversial right-wing politician Shintaro Ishihara wrote in his widely read book, *The Japan That Can Say No*, that "Caucasians are prejudiced against Orientals," and that "virulent racism underlies trade friction with the United States."[4] He later stated that, despite the U.S. establishment's assumption of racial superiority, "the modern civilization built by whites is coming close to [an] end, and I feel that is adding to the irritation of Americans as the postwar representative of whites."[5] Ishihara adds that the failure of Western societies to recognize the need to learn from the innovations of the Japanese and other nonwhite societies blinds the former to their need to adjust to a new technological era, causing them to fall further behind in the economic race. The 1988 U.S. omnibus trade bill appeared to direct so many provisions at Japan that Ministry of International Trade and Industry Minister Tamura asserted that the legislation was motivated by "anti-Japanese feeling and racial discrimination."[6]

## JAPAN: A CONVENIENT BUT INNOCENT SCAPEGOAT

The Japanese believe that they owe no apologies to the United States. They have conducted trade relations at least as fairly as other countries. It is Japan that is owed an apology for being unfairly made the prime scapegoat for U.S. economic shortcomings. The Japanese most certainly do not believe that they are predatory exporters who indirectly restrict imports through a closed, cartel-ridden, domestic economic system. Most Americans have found it more comfortable to point a finger at foreign duplicity than to admit to internal economic weaknesses, a relative decline in industrial competitiveness, and a growing preference for imported goods. Hostile U.S. accusations of inequitable, unfair, and sometimes illegal trade practices by a conspiratorial "Japan, Inc." are poor substitutes for U.S. acceptance of the need to adopt remedial measures, many of which would be neither simple nor painless. The Japanese would like more Americans to heed a line in Shakespeare's *Julius Caesar*: "The fault, dear Brutus, is not in our stars, but in ourselves."

While admitting a tardiness in liberalizing tariff and nontariff barriers to imports, most Japanese are at a loss to understand why Americans and others refuse to believe the empirical data showing that, by the 1980s, their market was as open to foreign goods as that of any other country. The rest of the world is wrong if it thinks Japan's trade patterns reveal deliberate efforts to maximize exports and to minimize imports. Japan's relative export sector, at 12 to 15 percent of GDP over the past 20 years, is only half as large as those of many West European countries.

Any underperformance on the import side mainly reflects insufficient commitment by foreign business to the hard work, time, and money required to succeed in the Japanese market. In 1981 the Report of the Japan-United States Economic Relations Group noted that "in terms of average tariff levels and quotas on manufactured products, Japan's market . . . will be no more closed than that of the United States. Indeed, given informal U.S. 'quotas' in the form of orderly marketing arrangements, Japan's market may well be less closed." While not denying that a number of informal practices and a bureaucratic legacy of administrative controls still inhibited some imports, the report concluded "Japan appears to be generally meeting its international obligations to provide equal national treatment in those areas where there are treaties or international trade codes, and in this sense, Japan is playing according to the rules."[7] Why, the Japanese wonder, do more foreigners not understand that succeeding in their highly competitive market is difficult for everyone and that new Japanese companies have to fight for acceptance by the entrenched corporate power elite just like foreign companies?

Japanese government officials and business executives deny that the bilateral trade disequilibrium is an outgrowth of the closed nature of the Japanese market, asserting that their tariff and nontariff barriers are among the lowest in the world. Noted liberal trade advocate Jagdish Bhagwati has argued that relatively sophisticated econometric studies do not support the argument that Japan imports too little, nor do they indicate a special and extraordinary effect of informal trade barriers that make Japan a proper target for discriminatory trade treatment.[8] An International Monetary Fund study of the bilateral current account concluded that "From a macroeconomic perspective, there is nothing surprising about Japan's surpluses."[9]

The Japanese discount criticism that its markets discriminate against imported manufactured goods. Charges that imports of manufactured goods are artificially low were addressed in a Japanese government rebuttal to the statistic that Japan's annual imports of manufactured goods in the early 1980s were approximately equivalent in value to those of Switzerland, at that time a country with only one-tenth of Japan's GDP.

Such a comparison is misleading and illogical. Small countries in general are required to specialize in a narrow range of industries. . . . Since they rely upon foreign countries for most of their manufactured goods, they have much higher ratios of [imported] manufactured goods to GNP than do larger nations. . . . If one uses this sort of twisted logic, then it would seem that the United States does not import enough manufactured goods, when compared with Belgium, for instance. America's GNP is 22 times larger than Belgium's, yet U.S. manufactured imports ($137 billion in 1980) are only about twice the value of Belgium's manufactured

imports ($60 billion). Does this imply that the United States has a restrictive poli-
cy toward manufactured imports?[10]

The Japanese believe that the United States falsely accuses them of
trade transgressions because Americans work too little at being competitive and spend too much time complaining and making demands on others. It was inexcusable that the United States (and Europe) sat idly by and
took no remedial action as imports from Japan gained increasingly large
market shares. As Japan lowered its mask of politeness, it increasingly
chastised Westerners on their relative lack of commitment to industrial
excellence, their loss of work ethic, their emphasis on self-gratification,
and so on. The Japanese have adopted the attitude typical of countries
with a structural current account surplus: the responsibility for restoring
equilibrium rests principally with deficit countries. Just as the surplus
West European countries lectured the United States in the 1960s on the
need to adjust, Japan believes that countries with trade deficits are under-
performing and they should take the bitter policy medicine needed to
return to equilibrium.

Japan and its supporters reject the thesis that its export success is a
function of government subsidies, predatory dumping, a free ride in the
international arena, or any other insidious or unfair practice. Japan dismisses as untrue the popular U.S. conception that its industry has been
victimized by a conspiratorial, export-at-all-costs Japan, Inc. whose vastly different institutions shut out foreign-made manufactured goods.

The Japanese attribute their success to their own economic and social
virtues as well as to weakness in the United States, Europe, and elsewhere. They earned their international success from hard work, endless
innovations, and a lot of saving and investment channeled into plant
capacity, capital equipment, and research and development — for which
they should not be ashamed. The results are Japanese products of high
quality that have garnered large market shares in the United States and
elsewhere. Nobody is holding a gun to the heads of consumers in other
countries, forcing them to buy Japanese goods. In fact, a large percentage
of Japanese exports to the United States is bought by U.S. companies. The
attractiveness of Japanese capital goods was spelled out by a Korean jour-
nalist: "Korean factory owners believe Japanese products offer the best
price, fastest delivery and most efficient after-sales service. The standard
line for Korean businessmen when asked why they prefer Japanese
machinery to quality products from the U.S. or Europe is, 'When the
equipment breaks down, it will take weeks for a U.S. or European maker
to fix it, or supply spare parts. A Japanese technician will be in the factory within hours of the telephone call.'"[11]

The role of scapegoat is also galling because so much of Japan's industrial success can be attributed to a brilliant track record of converting basic

technologies — for example, the transistor and the video cassette recorder — into successful commercial products. "Turning technology into products is where Japan is number one in the world," wrote Akio Morita, founder of Sony Corporation.[12] Conversely, a staff member of the Congressional Office of Technology Assessment argued in 1982 that the United States "is an underdeveloped country when it comes to getting useful, proven technologies transferred to business and industry."[13]

One of the leading U.S. academic advocates of a pro-Japanese point of view, Gary Saxonhouse, has argued that historical data suggest its extraordinary industrial performance does not rest on a few distinctive institutional arrangements and that Japan has changed without forfeiting its superior economic performance. "The economic facts remain that since the second half of the nineteenth century, Japan's productivity growth and structural transformation have outstripped every other major industrialized economy. . . . Japan's economic performance has been far too successful for far too long under far too many different contexts for its growth to be attributable to any one particular configuration of its economic institutions."[14]

The government and business leaders of postwar Japan have, until recently, all belonged to the generation that surrendered to the United States, felt gratitude for one of history's most benevolent military occupations, and continued to look to the United States as a source of both economic inspiration and political stability. Expectations that one more concession would put trade frictions to rest turned to despair in the 1980s. It seemed the United States would remain mired in a state of self-pity rather than get its economic house in order. Each passing year brought new complaints and intimidation, all based on failure to understand that Japan's comparative advantage is based on its skilled, dedicated managers and workers and a national work ethic fostered by the need to import vast quantities of natural resources. The result is a distinctive, logical foreign trade structure based on relative factor endowments: importing raw materials, adding value to them, and exporting finished goods.

For much of the past three decades, the United States has allegedly acted in a manner unbecoming a political and economic superpower. Japan was resented for practicing many values it learned from Americans, such as hard work, saving, and risk taking. Perhaps worst of all, the United States was suddenly given to extreme, erratic actions as exemplified by the Nixon shocks of 1971. As U.S. behavior became more bizarre, the U.S. government began making nonsensical recommendations, most notably urging the Japanese not to act like Japanese. While Secretary of Commerce, the late Malcolm Baldrige declared that because Japanese cultural traditions were a major cause of their trade surplus, they "simply have to be changed because . . . Japan now has the second largest economy in the free world."[15] Incessant demands for trade concessions were viewed as an inscrutable form of confrontation that threatened Japan's sovereignty and dignity. As one Japanese observer summed it up, "Many in the United States insist on attacking Japan's identity — its society, its economic structure, its political system, and its language. Yet the U.S. refuses to recognize the internal roots of its own failure."[16]

Until the Japanese perceive that U.S. companies are investing the same amount of time and resources in penetrating their market as Japanese companies invest in developing export markets, there will be little sympathy for foreign complaints about a closed market. Most criticism of Japan is based on outdated information and lack of insight into the extent that business conditions are changing dramatically in Japan. Japan's economy has shifted from one that is export-driven to one based on domestic expansion, a shift necessitated by rising foreign protectionism. At the same time, the number of foreign firms successfully selling in the Japanese market also has grown rapidly.

In Japanese eyes, the United States is a lazy bully. It needs to stop acting like a crybaby and start repairing its deteriorating social and economic order. The Japanese are incorrectly indicted by Americans as the source of the problem. There is nothing in foreign trade theory that says Japanese officials are obliged to establish export advisory facilities in the United States to offset the lack of effort by most U.S. companies. Some Japanese officials continue urging accommodation through additional market-opening measures despite the dubious legitimacy of U.S. insinuations that widespread import impediments remain. They believe their scapegoat status requires them to appease misinformed foreign critics in order to avoid arbitrary foreign retaliation against Japanese exports.

## SHORTCOMINGS OF U.S. ECONOMIC POLICIES AND BUSINESS PRACTICES

The Japanese are proud of their competitive accomplishments, but they would not deny that the self-destructive bent of their biggest trading partner has contributed to their success. During the 1970s and 1980s, Japan presumed the United States did not realize or did not care that it was in serious economic decline. The positive qualities that had made it a great nation were dissipating. A decline in its manufacturing prowess and technological leadership was accompanied by epidemics of violent crime, drugs, deteriorating inner cities, illiteracy, homelessness, single parent families, and racial strife. The growing emphasis on immediate personal gratification and the mindless 1980s fad of mergers and acquisitions that treated corporations like tradeable commodities further hindered the efforts of the United States to keep pace with the drive and excellence of Japan's industrial sector.

The advent of the Structural Impediments Initiative in 1989 gave the Japanese a long-awaited opportunity to vent their disdain for a wide array of U.S. domestic economic and business policies. Having made the discussion of U.S. structural impediments a quid pro quo for discussing Japanese impediments to balanced trade, the Japanese wasted no time in cataloguing instances of mismanagement in the U.S. official and private sectors. They argued that the U.S. government needed to reduce the federal budget deficit, increase saving, encourage corporations to increase investment in plant and equipment and research and development outlays, ease export restrictions, improve its educational system, and so on.[17] Among other things, corporations were criticized for excessively short time-horizons for planning as well as for inadequate worker training programs.

Corrective actions taken solely by the Japanese will not suffice to restore equilibrium to the U.S. trade account — no matter how often Japan capitulates to U.S. demands. A large part of the bilateral problem is that the United States buys too much, not that the Japanese sell too much. The Japanese cannot compensate for the United States maintaining one of the lowest saving rates among major industrial countries. Also they cannot compensate for the fact that, in the 25-year period beginning in 1968, the United States did not once invest, as a proportion of GNP, as much as Japan.[18] Japanese deregulation and easier market access cannot fully compensate for the continually strong U.S. demand for Japanese products, many of which are not available elsewhere. It certainly is not Japan's fault that the United States has an unusually high income elasticity of demand for imports.[19]

Despite corporate America's vociferous complaints about Japan's trade practices, many of them are major importers of Japanese-made components. For example, Japanese sources estimated that one-third of the U.S. deficit in auto parts was because of purchases from the Big Three producers in Detroit.[20] "Therefore, unless the U.S. begins to produce more goods that can compete against Japanese products, no matter how much effort is made by Japan to promote a restructuring and reduce the imbalance, such efforts will not be sufficient."[21] More U.S. consumers need to be attracted to U.S.-made goods. A U.S. automobile specialist colorfully argued that "While Detroit flogged away at the bankrupt notion that Americans could be bamboozled into buying oversize, outdated, cheaply built cars covered with a layer of vinyl and chrome glitz, the Japanese recognized that technology was the key to future sales."[22]

As seen in Table 2.1, U.S. bilateral deficits with Japan were relatively modest until the early 1980s when "Reaganomics" generated massive changes within the U.S. economy. The most important of these changes were massive tax cuts, more than a tripling of the federal budget deficit, a lower saving rate, a saving-investment imbalance, and an overvalued exchange rate for the dollar. Quite independent of any Japanese actions, claimed a former Ministry of Finance official, "Reaganomics turned America from a country with a manageable budget deficit into one burdened by enormous budget and trade deficits. This and this alone is the source of the economic problems now plaguing Japan-U.S. relations."[23] Lest one suggest bias in this assessment, a research analyst with the International Monetary Fund concluded that "Whatever the causes of the U.S. current account deficits and Japanese surpluses, it is clear that the explanations must be specific to the 1980s because these sustained . . . imbalances are not in evidence before the early 1980s. It seems very difficult to argue that Japanese trading practices explain these current account patterns since such an explanation would require a large increase in Japanese barriers to imports or subsidies to exports, which is contrary to all available evidence."[24] Economic theory suggests that until the internal U.S. macroeconomic disequilibrium is corrected, that is, until the federal budget deficit is reduced sufficiently to allow domestic saving to finance domestic investment, the U.S. trade deficit will persist.

The shortcomings of the U.S. government's economic policies have been replicated in underperforming managers, especially in basic industries. By Japanese standards, U.S. industrial companies demonstrate a self-defeating fixation with short-term profits, fail to invest adequately in expanded capacity and new machinery, undervalue and squander the talents of production line workers, and are obsessed with balance sheet juggling through mergers and acquisitions rather than increasing sales volume and making things better. In addition, they have a propensity to drop a product line prematurely because it is not generating sufficient profits or to abandon product development if research and development outlays go too high. Senior corporate executives are often grossly overpaid. Chief executive officers of large U.S. corporations on average earn more than $1 million annually in salary alone, two to three times the rate of their Japanese counterparts. (Stock options for U.S. executives can dramatically increase amounts of total compensation; for example, the *New York Times* calculated that the value of salary, bonuses, and grants of common stock bestowed on the chief executive of the Coca-Cola Company from 1979 through 1996 exceeded $1 billion.)[25] Press reports calculated that Michael Ovitz was getting a $90 million package for leaving the number two position at the Walt Disney company in 1996.

The Sony Corporation's Morita spoke for the many Japanese who see a strong industrial sector as the foundation of a strong nation when he decried growing U.S. indifference to the manufacturing process: "when people forget how to produce goods, and that appears to be the case in America, they will not be able to supply themselves even with their most basic needs."[26] Writing in the 1980s, Mr. Morita argued that "Real business entails adding value to things by adding knowledge to them, but

America is steadily forgetting this. . . . America no longer makes things, it only takes pleasure in making profits from moving money around."[27] Hajime Ohta, an economist with Japan's Federation of Economic Organizations (Keidanren) provides another view of the down side of U.S. business culture: "Ideally, corporate profits should be the direct result of risk taking, efficient management of production and administration, technological innovation and investment in research and development. One gets the impression, however, that these characteristics of American business are on the decline, and instead ingredients for an American success story today — particularly over the short term — are effective lobbyists, lawyers, public relations and advertising agencies."[28]

## THE HYPOCRISY OF U.S. TRADE ACTIONS

The oft-repeated U.S. claim of being the world's most open market is greeted with undiluted skepticism in Japan and many other countries. Viewed from the other side of the Pacific, there is a large gap between the rhetoric and the reality of U.S. trade policies, a situation that undermines U.S. critics of Japan. The United States preaches the virtues of a liberal trade policy, emphasizing reliance on free market forces. It does practice such a policy, but only up to the point where imports start to cause serious domestic disruption. The market mechanism is allowed to function in the United States only as long as it is politically convenient; then government intervention begins. This qualified free market philosophy was responsible for U.S. demands that Japan voluntarily restrict exports of cars, steel, color televisions, machine tools, textiles, and so on.

U.S. economic dissatisfaction with Japan centers on a statistic that most economists believe is devoid of much economic significance: the bilateral trade balance. It is inevitable that a country will run surpluses with some countries and deficits with others. What matters is the sum total, or multilateral trade balance. Thirty years of U.S. efforts to force Japan to restrict exports and increase imports ignore this basic international economic concept.

Japan perceives that the U.S. government wants to change international trade rules whenever necessary to defend its own interests. In the words of a former chairman of Honda, "What started with complaints about textiles and other manufactured goods turned into antidumping laws, escape clauses and attacks on Japanese culture. It seems the Americans feel they can no longer win in the marketplace — so they have to attack in other ways."[29] One Japanese scholar argued: "In some ways current U.S.-Japanese relations . . . resemble a card game where one player wins continuously. The loser, unwilling to accept the full blame for a poor showing, asserts that the rules of the game are unfair, while the winner is intent on explaining why the old rules are reasonable. Obviously, if it is mutually beneficial to continue the game, the rules will have to be changed with mutual agreement."[30]

There are numerous anecdotes to support Japan's contention that the alleged U.S. open door to imports has repeatedly been slammed in its face. No Japanese company has ever sold a supercomputer to a federal U.S. agency. Given the experience of the NEC Corporation in 1996, it is not likely to happen soon. The company's proposed long-term lease of four supercomputers to the University Corporation for Atmospheric Research (an academic organization whose acquisition of the computer network was to be largely funded by the National Science Foundation) immediately triggered cries of unfair trade by a U.S. company, Cray Research, and the U.S. Commerce Department. The latter, in an unprecedented move, mailed an intimidating "predecisional" memorandum to the National Science Foundation in which it outlined the reasons it presumed the existence of dumping margins of 163 percent to 240 percent. The memo was sent before a dumping complaint was even filed.[31] Counsel for NEC petitioned the U.S. Court of International Trade to enjoin an allegedly prejudiced, predisposed U.S. Commerce Department from investigating the subsequent dumping petition and to appoint independent, objective arbiters in its place.[32] This episode was largely a case of history repeating itself. In 1987 the Massachusetts Institute of Technology broke off negotiations to acquire a Japanese-made supercomputer when warned by a senior U.S. Commerce Department official that the university would be liable for serious dumping duties if a subsequent investigation determined that the computer had been sold at less than fair value and that the domestic industry incurred material injury.

Another example of highly discriminatory U.S. action was Fujitsu's encounter with "America, Inc." In 1981, congressional and corporate pressure persuaded the American Telephone and Telegraph Corporation to reject the Japanese company's low bid and accept a domestic bid on a major optical fiber telephone cable link between the major cities of the northeastern United States. Similarly, the Japanese were confused about U.S. government protestations of national security concerns in 1987 that were serious enough to convince the Fujitsu Company to voluntarily withdraw its offer to buy the troubled Fairchild Semiconductor Company. At the time of the fuss, Fairchild was controlled by a French company.

The Japanese think they are more than justified in declaring the U.S. market considerably more closed than the U.S. government has claimed. They are far more aware than the average American of various statutory measures that the U.S. government has employed to attack the majority of Japanese products gaining a significant market share in the United States. U.S. trade statutes are so numerous and arbitrary that they collectively amount to a nontariff barrier. As a people uncomfortable with the uncertainties of legal technicalities, the Japanese believe the intricate web of U.S. trade laws imposes far more impediments and costs to their exporters than anything encountered by U.S. companies trying to sell in their market.

It is not by choice that Japanese corporations have enriched the large cadre of foreign trade lawyers who ply their trade in Washington. As the number one exporter of goods competing directly with U.S.-made products, Japan's industrial sector has been forced to defend itself over and over again in Washington's various trade tribunals. U.S. producers have sought relief from Japanese imports under all of the standard import relief laws. These laws include the escape clause in cases of alleged injury from fair foreign competition as well as the antidumping law (when imports are alleged to be priced at less than fair value) and the countervailing duty statute (when imports are alleged to have received subsidies from the exporter's government) used in cases of charges of unfair foreign competition. The Japanese also have found their exports threatened by innovative legal maneuvers, such as Houdaille Industries' unsuccessful effort under the Revenue Act of 1971 to deny investment tax credits to U.S. purchasers of Japanese-made machine tools.

The uncertainties and imprecision of U.S. trade statutes are viewed as de facto trade barriers because foreign exporters and local importers can be intimidated by the mere threat of legal action. Responding to an accusation of dumping has become such a long and costly process that only the very rich, brave, or foolish ignore the prospect that an antidumping complaint will be filed. Even if the importer wins the proceeding, the bill can run into many millions of dollars for legal fees and administrative costs, such as data preparation, document translation, and travel by corporate executives to the United States. According to a U.S. lawyer who mainly represented importers,

The uncertainty of the trade laws, and in particular of the dumping standard, is itself a significant trade barrier. The fact that importers generally cannot know what prices or practices will be condemned as unfair naturally tends to inhibit price competition and thereby to serve a protectionist interest. In addition the multiplicity and overlap of the trade laws, combined with various substantive and procedural features of the law, tend to create incentives for domestic firms to use strategies of legal harassment to impose costs, delays or penalties on their foreign competitors. As a result, the perception is spreading in Japan and elsewhere that the United States market, though basically "open," has become a hazardous and hostile environment in which to do business. [33]

Legal costs aside, initiation of antidumping proceedings can temporarily impose a chilling effect on imports regardless of the final decision on whether sales were made at less than fair value. Once a preliminary determination of dumping is made, importers must post bonds or cash deposits with the U.S. government. These would defray potential antidumping duties that would be assessed retroactively (to the time of the initial complaint) to offset underpriced imports. The final margin of dumping determined by the U.S. Commerce Department is based largely on arbitrary guesswork and maximum discretion. The percentage of dumping duty that can be imposed is open-ended; for example, if an imported good is estimated to be selling at only one-third its cost of production, a dumping duty of 200 percent would be applied to assure a fair price. Imposition of onerous dumping duties could exceed the importer's profit margin and create financial hardship. Cautious importers, therefore, will cease or reduce importing, at least until the dumping case is resolved. Even U.S. specialists have difficulty making sense of the law, and foreign corporations are hard pressed to assemble the profusion of data demanded by government investigators. Lawrence Walders, a Washington-based lawyer who often represents Japanese clients in antidumping cases, once told me that "the hardest thing for me as a lawyer is to explain to my client why the U.S. government is doing this to them."

As the number one target of U.S. allegations of import barriers hindering U.S. exports, the Japanese industrial sector has been threatened repeatedly with unilateral retaliation if they do not implement liberalization measures acceptable to Washington. The Section 301 and Super 301 provisions of U.S. trade law demonstrate hubris and a dangerous disregard for established international procedures to resolve trade disputes. Japan considers it unfair for the U.S. government to perform the roles of prosecutor, judge, jury, and executioner in determining what is acceptable trade behavior by other sovereign countries. If Japan had not bowed to repeated U.S. threats, the latter would have severely restricted market access in the name of pursuing freer trade. U.S. trade hypocrisy arguably hit its zenith when it rejected the use of the newly established World Trade Organization's improved multilateral dispute settlement mechanism, the creation of which was championed by the United States. The entire international trade community sided with the Japanese government when the Clinton administration summarily rejected its request to have the World Trade Organization appoint a panel of third country experts to resolve the 1994–95 dispute on access to the Japanese automobile and auto parts markets. Yet another form of perceived U.S. intimidation has been the occasional Justice Department threats to apply antitrust laws on an extraterritorial basis to punish allegedly collusive Japanese domestic business practices impeding U.S. exports.

Sometimes the Japanese get caught between U.S. trade officials' demands for organized export restraint and Justice Department enforcement of antitrust legislation. For example, in early 1982, U.S. semiconductor manufacturers of random access memory (RAM) devices accused the Japanese of aggressive pricing actions to obtain worldwide market dominance in 64k RAMs. Shortly thereafter, Japanese exports of these RAMs slowed and prices rose. A few months later, to the surprise of almost everyone, the Justice Department announced that it was formally investigating the marketing practices of six major Japanese semiconductor producers to determine whether they had conspired to fix prices or impose supply restrictions on 64k RAMs exported to the United States. Coincident with rising U.S. worries about predatory pricing, the Japanese 64k RAM producers apparently were confronted with genuine shortages that led to higher prices and fewer exports. The Japanese vendors blamed the shortfall on their lack of capacity to meet a sudden spurt of demand from Japanese and U.S. computer manufacturers, not an effort to mute accusations of dumping by raising prices. This explanation of why the 64k RAM market shifted almost overnight from a buyer's market to a seller's market apparently did not ring true to antitrust lawyers in the Justice Department, even though it was supported by market conditions.[34] (The department closed the investigation two years later after finding insufficient evidence to warrant prosecution.)

Although some Japanese acknowledge in principle that external pressure from Washington is often an essential catalyst forcing their government to accelerate market-opening measures, they deplore the extremes of U.S. demands. The negotiating cycle typically begins with a single industry's complaint about market access but regularly escalates to a high-stakes issue declared by U.S. negotiators to be vital to the national interest, at which time they demand a Japanese response "or else." A Japanese version of U.S. negotiating excesses puts it this way:

In response to [market opening] demands, Japan's reaction usually takes the form of a pledge to "try our best. . . ." When Japan comes up with what it thinks is an adequate step toward improvement, these measures are evaluated by American negotiators as but a first step toward the ultimate goal. One after another, demands have been introduced in a similar pattern . . . on beef, citrus, leather, tobacco and government procurement. While there may have been some slight improvement in the bilateral trade figures as a result of American pressure on these items, many of them are of peripheral importance. Yet the political manner in which they were raised and the attention they received from the media gave the impression to the U.S. public that Japan is a closed market, and that the Japanese are the prime cause of the deficit in the American balance of payments figures. Neither Japanese nor American officials should view these problems as fundamental economic issues between the two countries.[35]

The Japanese case also argues that U.S. demands for export restraints have had the regrettable effect of resurrecting abandoned efforts at tight government-business cooperation. To minimize dumping accusations and disruptions of U.S. markets, the Ministry of International Trade and

Industry occasionally has felt compelled to exert influence on export pricing decisions. A more formalized business-government relationship becomes necessary whenever Japanese exporters, such as automobile makers, must apportion overseas market share among themselves for products covered by orderly marketing agreements.

## JAPAN'S RAPIDLY CHANGING TRADE POSITION

The perspective on bilateral trade frictions that is favorable to Japan states that use of up-to-date trade data demonstrates that the Japanese market is open and that the country does not exhibit an abnormal import pattern. Statistics in the mid-1990s show a normalization in Japan's import flows as well as a slowdown in export growth. Rapid rises in imports have not erased Japan's trade surpluses because exports have continued to increase in dollar terms, albeit at a relatively slower rate. This situation can be explained by unassailable economic factors, not by an export conspiracy or by closed markets. First, Japanese exports appear artificially high when measured in dollars because the yen appreciated significantly in value against the dollar in the early 1990s. The slow-down in the volume of Japanese exports is more than offset by the increased dollar value of these shipments. Second, Japan's high rates of saving relative to investment outlays makes inevitable a multilateral current account surplus. Third, the rapid rise in imports would have been far greater had Japan's overall economy not stagnated since the onset of the 1990s. Fourth, the rest of the world has not lost its appetite for unique and well-made Japanese goods, even at higher prices.

A close look at the statistics overwhelmingly suggests to the Japanese that the more recent the data cited, the more accurate is the measure of their country's accommodating trade behavior. Expressed in yen terms, Japan's exports in 1995 (41.5 trillion) were exactly the same amount as they were in 1990 (exports in 1996 rose to a record 44.7 trillion yen).[36] Manufactured goods accounted for 68 percent of U.S. exports to Japan in 1995, up from 45 percent in 1982.[37] Japan's export volume between 1986 and 1991 grew at rates below the industrial country average, except in 1990 when they were equal. Conversely, in each of these years, Japan's import volume grew at a rate that exceeded the average of the industrial countries.[38] In another quantitative indicator of Japan's changing trade patterns, the average annual percentage growth of real imports of goods and services in the United States and Japan during the 1970–87 period was 5.7 and 4.1 percent respectively; a different situation existed between 1988 and 1995, when average import growth rates were 6.1 percent in the United States and a robust 8.2 percent in Japan.[39] Furthermore, as seen in Table 3.1, Japanese market-opening measures and yen appreciation have

**TABLE 3.1**
Manufactured Goods as a Percentage of Total Japanese Imports

| Year | Percent |
| --- | --- |
| 1980 | 22.8 |
| 1985 | 31.0 |
| 1990 | 50.4 |
| 1995 | 59.1 |

*Source*: Official Japanese Ministry of Finance data provided by the Japan Economic Institute. Calculations were based upon imports expressed in U.S. dollars.

caused dramatic increases in the percentage of total imports accounted for by manufactured goods.

Statistics and anecdotal evidence also demonstrate widespread U.S. export sales successes in Japan. Between year-end 1993 and April 1996, U.S. exports of goods to Japan increased more than 85 percent in those sectors covered by bilateral trade agreements and the multilateral Uruguay Round agreement. This rate of increase is well above comparable figures for U.S. exports to Japan not covered by these agreements and overall exports to the European Union.[40] The pattern of sizeable surges in U.S. exports following market-opening agreements refutes the revisionist argument that traditional liberalization efforts produce minimal results. It also repeats the same cause and effect pattern found when the Congressional Research Service measured increased U.S. exports to Japan in sectors liberalized in the second half of the 1980s.[41]

By setting up their own distribution system and selling at prices well below their local competitors, Compaq and Apple quickly grabbed sizeable shares of Japan's personal computer market. The assertion that the Japanese customer will not buy foreign-made goods has been further undermined by reports in the business press of runaway retail successes in Japan by Toys-R-Us stores. The total number of stores jumped from one at the end of 1991 to 51 five years later, while total sales jumped from about $80 million at year-end 1992 to an estimated $750 million at year-end 1996.[42] Other notable retail successes included Tower Records (the company's managing director for the Far East said that, despite a number of obstacles, he believed that Japan "is the easiest place in the world to do business"[43]), and appliances made by General Electric and Maytag. Mail-order sales by U.S. catalogue companies have surged to the point that Tokyo's international post office had to hire additional staff and clear a floor to accommodate merchandise valued at an estimated $750 million in 1995 arriving from the United States.[44] As for the list of alleged impediments to Japanese imports published annually by the United States Trade

Representative, the Japanese government argues that it "appears to be little more than a compendium of U.S. industry complaints, without evaluation against any objective of internationally recognized standards."[45]

Increased reliance on offshore production to service the U.S. and other foreign markets further mitigates against a return of the large Japanese trade surpluses of recent years. Not only should exports be displaced but also imports into Japan will increase from foreign subsidiaries. (This trend is already evident in rising exports to Japan from Honda's U.S. automobile assembly plants.)

## CONCLUSION

The Japanese view their trade success vis-à-vis the United States with feelings of pride and persecution. They feel they worked smarter and more diligently than their U.S. competition, but received in return only criticism, scorn, and threats. Uncle Sam's paternalistic attitudes in the immediate post–World War II era were replaced by a self-centered, "What have you done for me lately?" mentality. The Japanese think they had a good response, but it fell on deaf ears: "We have repeatedly restricted our exports to a country with a self-proclaimed open market and repeatedly bowed to your pressures to liberalize our import practices." Instead of respecting and emulating Japan's extraordinary successes, the United States blamed its own shortcomings on Japan. Shamelessly, the United States treated Japan as a whipping boy, punishing it if it did not behave according to U.S. standards. The Japanese people felt they had been put in a false, distorted light by foreign critics who were not above using racist slurs.

Even the prized trait of stoicism could not prevent Japan from gradually revealing its growing contempt for what it perceived as serious shortcomings in U.S. economic policies and business strategies. The list of U.S. demands was endless, but Japanese patience and generosity were not. Shedding the role of quiet, deferential junior partner in the bilateral relationship, the Japanese did nothing more than echo many U.S. voices that the United States should do less whining and expend more energy addressing home-grown, self-inflicted problems. The United States eventually did address many of these shortcomings, as seen in the revival in the 1990s of the U.S. high-tech sector. However, the U.S. industrial turnaround, the reality of a relatively open Japanese market, and an enhanced multilateral dispute settlement mechanism have not yet convinced the U.S. government to rise above unilateral demands and threats of retaliation.

## NOTES

1. Michael Blaker, "Japan, 1982: The End of Illusion?" *Washington Quarterly* (Spring 1982), p. 86.

2. Federal Reserve Bank of St. Louis, "International Economic Trends," July 1996, p. 12.

3. As quoted in *Financial Times*, March 30, 1979, p. 1.

4. Shintaro Ishihara, *The Japan That Can Say No* (New York: Simon & Schuster, 1991), pp. 27–28.

5. *New York Times*, January 18, 1990, p. D8.

6. *Washington Post*, April 23, 1988, p. B1.

7. Japan–United States Economic Relations Group, "Report of the Japan–United States Economic Relations Group," January 1981, pp. 55–56.

8. Jagdish Bhagwati, "Samurais No More," *Foreign Affairs* (May/June 1994), p. 10.

9. Stephen S. Golub, "The United States–Japan Current Account Imbalance: A Review" (Paper on Policy Analysis and Assessment, 94/8) (Washington, D.C.: International Monetary Fund, 1994), p. 23.

10. Consulate of Japan, *Twenty Questions and Answers on Japan-U.S. Relations* (New York: Consulate of Japan, 1982), p. 14.

11. Jie-Ae Sohn, "Japan and Korea: Too Close for Comfort," *Business Korea* (February 1992) available from Lexis-Nexis data bank.

12. Ishihara, *The Japan That Can Say No*, p. 27.

13. John A. Alic, "Industrial Policy: Where Do We Go From Here?" paper presented at the Conference on Corporate Strategy and Structure, Chicago, April 30, 1982, p. 18.

14. Gary R. Saxonhouse, "What Does Japanese Trade Structure Tell Us about Japanese Trade Policy?" *Journal of Economic Perspectives* (Summer 1993), pp. 22, 39.

15. U.S. Department of Commerce, press release, December 8, 1981, pp. 4–5.

16. *Asahi Journal* (March 26, 1982), as cited in Kent E. Calder, "Opening Japan," *Foreign Policy* (Summer 1982), p. 29.

17. "Japan, Weary of Barbs on Trade, Tells Americans Why They Trail," *New York Times*, November 20, 1989, p. A1.

18. Kenneth S. Courtis, "U.S. Transition as Golden Opportunity in Japan," *International Herald Tribune*, December 24–25, 1992, p. 12.

19. Statistical studies have determined that, when the U.S. GDP grows, Americans divert a larger percentage of their additional incomes to foreign-made goods than do other large industrial countries. This means that if the U.S. economy is growing at least as fast as those of its main trading partners, the U.S. trade balance is likely to deteriorate. See, for example, Robert A. Blecker, *Beyond the Twin Deficits* (Armonk, N.Y.: M. E. Sharpe, 1992), pp. 62–65.

20. "At the Roots of the U.S.-Japan Trade Gap," *The Wall Street Journal*, October 10, 1994, p. A6.

21. Takashi Eguchi, "The U.S.-Japan Trade Imbalance: Causes and Remedies" (Occasional Paper 88-05 of the Program on U.S.-Japan Relations), Harvard University, 1988, p. 54.

22. Brock Yates, "American Taste, Made in Japan," *Washington Post Magazine*, September 3, 1989, p. 29.

23. Osamu Shimomura, "The 'Japan Problem' Is of America's Making," *Japan Echo* (Autumn 1987), p. 25.

24. Golub, "Account Imbalance," p. 3.

25. *New York Times*, October 13, 1996, p. 36.

26. Ishihara, *The Japan That Can Say No*, p. 8.

27. As quoted in "A Japanese View: Why America Has Fallen Behind," *Fortune* (September 25, 1989), p. 52.

28. Hajime Ohta, "Recent U.S.-Japan Economic Relations: A Japanese View" (report). Washington, D.C.: U.S.-Japan Trade Council, 1979), p. 5.

29. "A Rising Tide of Protectionism," *Newsweek* (May 30, 1983), p. 27.

30. Toshikazu Maeda, "Japanese Perception of America: Evolution from Dependency to Maturity," in *U.S.-Japan Relations in the 1980s: Towards Burden Sharing* (program on U.S.-Japan relations) (Cambridge, Mass.: Harvard University, Center for International Affairs, 1982), p. 24.

31. The text of this memorandum and a covering letter from the U.S. Commerce Department is attached to the complaint filed in the U.S. Court of International Trade by the law firm of Paul, Weiss, Rifkin, Wharton, & Garrison on behalf of the NEC Corporation and HNSX Supercomputers, Inc., dated October 15, 1996, Exhibits A and B.

32. Ibid., pp. 16–17.

33. Carl J. Green, "Legal Protectionism in the United States and Its Impact on United States-Japan Economic Relations" (study prepared for the Advisory Group on United States-Japan Economic Relations) (Washington, D.C.: Advisory Group on United States-Japan Economic Relations, 1980), p. 267.

34. See, for example, Susan MacKnight, "Justice Department Looking into Sales of Japanese-Made 64K RAMs" (Japan Economic Institute report, August 6, 1982), p. 2.

35. Ohta, "Economic Relations," p. 3.

36. Japan Economic Institute, various reports.

37. Calculated by the author from trade statistics published by the U.S. Department of Commerce.

38. Golub, "Account Imbalance," p. 8.

39. Calculated from data in Annex Table 10 of the *OECD Economic Outlook* (June 1996), p. A13.

40. The President's Council of Economic Advisers and the U.S. Treasury Department, "U.S. Trade with Japan: Addressing the Record," April 10, 1996, p. 2.

41. "Japan-U.S. Trade: U.S. Exports of Negotiated Products, 1985–1990," *Congressional Research Report*, November 26, 1991, pp. 4–7.

42. Data provided to the author by a corporate representative.

43. As quoted in *Washington Post*, January 23, 1996, p. A10.

44. "Japanese Do Buy American: By Mail and a Lot Cheaper," *New York Times*, July 3, 1995, p. A1.

45. Japan Ministry of International Trade and Industry, "Comments on the 'USTR 1996 National Trade Estimate Report on Foreign Trade Barriers' with Regard to 8 Sectors Relevant to MITI," press release, May, 1996, p. 1.

# 4

# An Uncompromising U.S. Interpretation of Trade Frictions

How courteous is the Japanese;
He always says, "Excuse it, please."
He climbs into his neighbor's garden,
And smiles, and says, "I beg your pardon";
He bows and grins a friendly grin,
And calls his hungry family in;
He grins, and bows a friendly bow;
"So sorry, this my garden now."
— From *Verses From 1929 On* by Ogden Nash.
Copyright 1935 by Ogden Nash.
By permission of Little, Brown and Company
and Curtis Brown Ltd.

The objective of this chapter is the same as the one that preceded it: to articulate an aggressive, unqualified viewpoint of one of the two conflicting explanations of what has occurred in contemporary bilateral economic relations. The author considers neither chapter to be definitive. As two extremes of a larger whole, neither should be read or judged in isolation from the other.

A large number of non-Japanese observers of bilateral trade problems completely and adamantly disagree with the accuracy and relevance of any effort to exonerate Japanese behavior. A second, completely different perspective holds the chauvinistic, antimarket Japanese mentality responsible for three decades of bilateral trade disequilibria and frictions. This second viewpoint does not deny Japan's efforts to moderate its allegedly aggressive export drive and its determination to protect favored industries from import competition, yet it dismisses change in Japan's economic policies as mere window-dressing that is too little, too late. From this perspective, Japan's thousand-year effort to keep the rest of the world at arm's length continues to injure the commercial interests of its trading partners.

Once again, the methodology here is to present a multifaceted indictment of one country's motivation and actions that does not necessarily reflect what all Americans or the author believe to be fair or accurate. When read together, Chapters 3 and 4 illustrate the *Rashomon*-lens syndrome: two logical, defensible interpretations of the dynamics of bilateral trade frictions that are diametrically different. Chapter 3 told one side of bilateral frictions; this one tells the other side.

## A UNIQUELY SELF-CENTERED AND INSULAR VALUE SYSTEM

If there is one thing worse than a bad loser, it is an ungracious winner. The Japanese seem to be arch-mercantilists with an insatiable drive to maximize their overseas market shares and trade surpluses — goals matched in intensity only by their determination to minimize dependence on imports for sophisticated manufactured goods. Japan's single-minded pursuit of its commercial goals often seems "more appropriate to an international trading firm than to a nation-state." The cold war enabled it "to rely on the United States to guarantee its security and at the same time to maintain the international free trade order, while Japan was free to follow policies of economic nationalism."[1]

Japan has acquired the reputation of the global economic order's most conspicuous outsider because the world's trading rules are products of Western ideology. Advocates of this approach would agree that the opening lines of Ruth Benedict's now classic 1946 study of Japanese culture, *The Chrysanthemum and the Sword*, remain applicable to Japan's aberrant international economic behavior in the 1990s: "The Japanese were the most alien enemy the United States had ever fought in an all-out struggle. In no other war with a major foe had it been necessary to take into account such exceedingly different habits of acting and thinking."[2]

Henry Kissinger made a similar argument in his diplomatic memoirs: "Two peoples could hardly be more different than the pragmatic, matter-of-fact, legally oriented, literal Americans, and the complex, subtle Japanese, operating by allusion and conveying their meaning through an indirect, almost aesthetic sensitivity rather than words. . . . Japan's achievements . . . have grown out of a society whose structure, habits, and forms of decision-making are so unique as to insulate Japan from all other cultures."[3]

Japan remains unable or unwilling to discard the feelings of exclusiveness that peaked in the Tokugawa period of enforced isolation (from 1600 until the mid-1800s). Fear of outside influence; the domination of special interests; and impermeable, interlocking social networks are cultural traits inherited from Japan's unique historical circumstances. "Totally rejecting and repelling outsiders — whether from another country or another 'fief' — is an old trait inherited from the . . . enclosed village society, where it was the main means of self-defense. Even today, if you enter a farming village, you will feel the full force of this utter exclusivity in operation."[4]

Japan's differences could be viewed from afar as quaint only until the 1970s, when it simultaneously acquired the twin reputations of being the world's most successful, aggressive exporter of manufactured goods and of having the most protected market. Japan's political leaders, senior bureaucrats, and business leaders were slow to recognize the legitimacy and intensity of warnings from foreign friends and foes alike that token concessions alone would not alter the Western perception that Japan posed a major threat to the international trading system.

Critics emphasize Japan's failure to exercise responsible, visionary, or benevolent international leadership commensurate with its expanding economic power. It has yet to heed its "call to leadership" as the United States did in the late 1940s, when, virtually overnight, it abandoned its isolationist foreign policy in favor of global responsibility. The United States assumed unprecedented burdens to help create a postwar international order compatible with its political and economic values. Winston Churchill once said "the price of greatness is responsibility." Two decades after the full blossoming of their economic miracle, the Japanese still seem to equate greatness with protecting and enhancing their own economic interests. They still are unable to generate "universalist" values. Ivan Hall, a U.S. academic teaching in Japan, argues that, despite technological sophistication and talk of globalizing their economy, the Japanese "are still in the thrall of a resolutely defensive insularity, neither the depth nor the rationale of which we fully understand." In any event, "This insularity is the main source both of its trade 'frictions' and of its hesitation in playing a more active world role."[5] Internationalization may be a fashionable term in Japan, but it has yet to be genuinely implemented.

The Japanese are survivors, not visionaries. Critics argue that Japan coldly views other countries in terms of export markets and sources of raw materials. If a given country is not buying cars from Japan or selling it petroleum, "that society does not interest us at all," said a Japanese intellectual. "The rest of the world is interesting only as it affects Japan."[6] The typical Japanese citizen is unmoved by the economic plight of foreigners and severely limited in the ability or desire to see situations from others' points of view. Parochial Japanese policymakers surely dream of finding a magic formula for achieving economic self-sufficiency. If they could somehow free themselves of dependence on foreigners for raw materials and export markets, the rest of the world could be reduced to an idle curiosity. As a second-best, more realistic alternative to autarky, it is likely that the xenophobic Japanese would embrace the self-centered scenario of future international economic specialization articulated by a Japanese businessman: "Australia will be our mine and America will be our grain bowl . . . [and] Europe will be our boutique."[7]

Probably the outside world will always be regarded by the Japanese as threatening and unpleasant. It cannot be organized and regulated by the uniquely intricate discipline of obligations and intensely personal loyalties that keeps Japan running smoothly and consistently. Most Japanese would still agree with their countryman's recommendation "to conclude friendly alliances, to send ships to foreign countries everywhere and conduct trade, to copy the foreigners where they are at their best and so repair our own shortcomings, to foster our national strength . . . and so gradually subject the foreigners to our influence until in the end . . . our hegemony is acknowledged."[8] The contemporary tone notwithstanding, these suggestions were made in 1857.

Critics assert that the Japanese do not make concessions to assure international trade equilibrium and harmony because they view themselves as totally different from, and superior to, every other nationality and race. "What makes Japan fundamentally different is that its racially based national consciousness and exclusivity, far from being the objects of attack, disdain, and efforts at amelioration, are openly sanctioned by the intellectual establishment, public consensus, and government policy."[9] When he was prime minister, Yasuhiro Nakasone suggested that racial diversity was a source of U.S. weakness. His statement was translated in the U.S. press to the effect that blacks and Hispanics lowered the U.S. literacy level.[10] A mid-level official of Nippon Telegraph and Telephone claimed in 1983 that Japan "can manufacture a product of uniformity and superior quality because the Japanese are a race of completely pure blood, not a mongrelized race as in the United States."[11]

Such a flippant remark may have been a careless personal indiscretion, but it illustrates the animosity with which the Japanese historically have viewed foreigners, that is, as "barbarians who smell of butter." In the seventeenth century, Japanese fishermen who had been shipwrecked and rescued by foreign ships were forbidden to return to Japan; they were tainted by the foreign contact.[12] Even today, should a Japanese citizen return from a stay abroad with "an un-Japanese-like aura about him or her, the group resorts to bullying tactics in order to purge the individual of alien influence."[13] Japanese children returning home after attending

schools abroad face extraordinary problems of reassimilation and criticism by teachers and fellow students for "foreign" behavior (including
speaking English too well).

Japanese often link their views on the purity and supremacy of their
race and land with rejections of imports. In 1986 their government
justified imposition of extraordinary safety specifications for imported
skis, above and beyond accepted world standards, on the grounds that
Japanese snow was "different."[14] Two years later, a Japanese politician
attributed low meat imports to Japanese people having longer intestines
than others and, therefore, having more difficulty in digesting beef.[15] The
Japanese justified refusing to buy European pumps on the grounds that
their water was "softer" and, therefore, "slightly different."[16] Exclusion of
foreign contracting firms in receiving major contracts to build the new
Osaka airport was justified on grounds that Japanese soil is different from
that in other countries. Shortly before becoming minister of the Ministry
of International Trade and Industry (MITI) in 1985, Michio Watanabe
publicly announced he saw nothing in the United States that anyone in
Japan would want to buy.[17]

Japanese culture allegedly has spawned an economic ideology so dissimilar to that of the United States that the world's two greatest capitalist
powers do not really speak the same language. The late Senator John
Heinz (R., Pa.) stated that completely different national experiences
meant that the United States cannot understand Japan's "closed society
any more than they can understand our open one."[18] Japan has agonized
over reductions in barriers to imports and inward foreign direct investment, viewing them as sacrifices required to avoid anger and retaliation
from trading partners. They have not made these concessions to serve the
principle that economic liberalization is a virtue in itself. In the words of
former Senator John Danforth, "What sets Japan apart is this: No other
nation contributes so little to the open trading system of the world, in proportion to what it gains."[19] The normally free trade-oriented editorial
page of the *Washington Post* lamented the sad familiarity of U.S. efforts to
push Japan into opening up a sector to trade or investment: "Japan resists,
complaining bitterly of American high-handedness, even though the market-opening would benefit Japan most of all. Finally, in the face of mid-
night threats and brinkmanship, Japan more or less gives way, doing
what it should have done in the first place."[20] Someone who served in the
U.S. embassy in Tokyo in the 1990s privately complained that Japan's
"denial of problems, rigid resistance, strong rhetoric, vigorous PR efforts
abroad, minimal concessions, and weak implementation of agreements
are familiar patterns going back more than 30 years."

Reliance on the invisible hand of the marketplace is not high in the
hierarchy of Japanese values. As Karel van Wolferen argued:

Freedom of the market is not considered a desirable goal in itself, but only one of several instruments for achieving . . . effects that are totally subordinated to the ultimate goal of industrial expansion.[21]

The USA stresses that Japan itself stands to gain from free trade and open markets, but what it means by this — greater choices for the Japanese consumers — is not at all what the Japanese administrators understand by gain. A truly open market would undermine the domestic order, so how, in their eyes, could this ever be considered a gain for Japan?[22]

George Soros, a U.S. investment manager with considerable international experience, flatly asserted "The Japanese treat markets as a means to an end and manipulate them accordingly."[23] When British brokerage firms demanded that seats on the Tokyo Stock Exchange be open to foreign firms, the Ministry of Finance did not need to discuss abstract criteria; it only wanted to know what number of seats would mollify the British.[24] Those who perceive a perversity in Japan's approach to market economics were not surprised when a major Japanese consumer organization expressed regret over a bilateral agreement in 1988 to relax Japanese import barriers on citrus fruit and beef. Their reasoning may have been influenced by concern that such an action would harm the economic well-being of fellow Japanese, namely relatively inefficient farmers. In the late 1980s the Consumers Union of Japan was headed by a former senior official of the highly protectionist Agriculture Ministry, which may explain why the union opposed removal of agricultural trade barriers as well as relaxation of product standards that would have facilitated imports of consumer goods.

Critics of Japanese trade actions and attitudes tire of listening to seemingly endless counterarguments and excuses. In defending the trees, Japan and its apologists have lost sight of the forest. Individual issues have now been swamped by the negative foreign perception generated by the totality of its behavior. Even if some Japanese rebuttals are logical,

It is also reasonable to regard each of these arguments as simply self-serving, as a rationale advanced by a nation that defines its self-interest narrowly and takes selfish advantage whenever and wherever it can. All of Japan's interactions with the rest of the world in trade, investment, aid, and defense can be interpreted as those of a country acting purely in self-interest, with regard only to consequences for itself. Japan seems to change its international policies only in response to threats, and thus appears to the rest of the world to act in a defensive and ungenerous manner.[25]

Individual anecdotes about extraordinary problems encountered by foreigners exporting to Japan became too numerous to be accepted as aberrations that can be dismissed. These incidents cumulatively portray in a "meaningful way the operative Japanese policy towards foreigners in

Japan. The anecdotes *are* Japanese policy. Japan is restrictive; it is a difficult place for foreigners to do business."[26]

## ADVERSARIAL TRADE: BEYOND EXPORT ZEAL

Peter Drucker, one of the most respected U.S. management scholars
and consultants, dubbed Japan an "adversarial" trader. This term came to
epitomize the school of thought that Japan's import and export policies
are so extreme as to put them in a league of their own. Instead of healthy
competition for profits, adversarial trade seeks to achieve "market control
by destroying the enemy," methodically driving competitors out of the
market. Drucker went on to say that "When the attacking country is still
closed to imports — or at least severely restricts them — the competitor
under attack cannot effectively counterattack. It cannot win; it will at best
not lose everything."[27] "Adversarial investment" often occurred when
MITI's industrial policies encouraged expansion of production capacity
so far beyond domestic demand that increased exports were axiomatic.
The noted historian Arthur Schlesinger, Jr., categorized Japan as being
"even more mystical [and] humorless in its hypernationalist traditions
than Germany and far more scornful of other countries."[28] Other
observers have accused it of practicing "technoeconomic Prussianism"
and of being the only country to attack U.S. industries "as a matter of
national policy."[29]

The viewpoint critical of Japan perceives a country exhibiting a double
standard and much hypocrisy in its conduct of trade relations. To them,
it is inconceivable that Japan would allow its bilateral trade deficit in
manufactured goods to balloon from $2 billion in 1965 to $123 billion in
1995, as did the United States. While the Japanese were sparing no effort
to publicly criticize the United States for trying to "manage" trade, their
government was discretely practicing it on a grand scale: using massive
intervention in the foreign exchange market to weaken the yen's
exchange rate against the dollar from what market forces would have otherwise dictated. The effort to stabilize the dollar resulted in a $145 billion
increase — more than a tripling — in Japan's publicly reported holdings
of foreign exchange reserves between the end of 1992 ($62 billion) and
year-end 1996 ($207 billion).

The excellence of Japanese industrial corporations was responsible for
only part of Japan's superb trade performance; the remainder was a result
of unfair, antimarket tactics, such as limiting price competition in the
home market. Some express gratitude for Japan's long effort to liberalize
its import sector. Others mourn the many U.S. companies that have been
decimated or destroyed by Japan's militaristic fixation with export expansion and its determination to restrict access to imports until key industries
had become world-class competitors. Japan's belated moves to "normal"

trade behavior is meager consolation to foreign companies and workers already harmed by adversarial trade.

The "Ten Percent Rule" memorandum, apparently written by Hitachi's semiconductor division and distributed in the United States, provided a rare smoking gun substantiating the charge that Japanese export aggressiveness embraces dumping. Leaked to and then released by U.S. trade officials in the 1980s, the memo instructed Hitachi's U.S. semiconductor distributors to "Quote 10% below competition; if they requote . . . bid 10% under again; the bidding stops when Hitachi wins." Price quotes were to be reduced as many times as necessary: "Don't quit till you win!" The memo also assured U.S. distributors they need not worry about the financial impact of unlimited price cutting because Hitachi guaranteed a 25 percent profit margin for specified semiconductor models.

Pro-Japanese observers branded as overly quick the U.S. Commerce Department's judgment in 1996 that the NEC company intended to dump supercomputers. The department's actions can be better described as a fully justified and accurate warning of predatory dumping of massive proportions. The losing U.S. corporate bidder, Cray Research, argued that its continued financial solvency required stopping its Japanese rival's flagrant attempt to gain a foothold in the U.S. market by submitting a bid that could not recoup production costs. According to Cray, the published cost of leasing, in Japan, the same network of supercomputers for the comparable length of time NEC was proposing to lease them to the University Corporation for Atmospheric Research was about $150 million. NEC's apparent winning bid to the U.S. group was a mere $35 million, which allegedly equates to a dumping margin of about 330 percent.[30] Cray further argued that, given the relatively small global market, high development costs, and relatively short product cycle of supercomputer models, as well as the company's lack of income from other product lines, it would have been seriously injured by a loss of market share in the United States brought on by sales at less than fair value by a large, diversified electronics firm.

## THE MYTH OF THE OPEN DOOR

Three decades of liberalization efforts cannot obliterate the perception of Japan as the master of discouraging unwanted imports. A two-tiered "chrysanthemum curtain" to this day deliberately and inadvertently discourages imports. This section summarizes the first level of protection: relatively low tariffs and a variety of non-tariff barriers of various gradations of subtlety. The next section argues that internal domestic factors — government regulations, administrative guidance, and exclusionary business practices — constitute de facto trade barriers.

Japan may be changing, but only at the margin. Because traditional priorities and values still apply, its market cannot be open in the U.S. sense of the term. Japanese government officials and industrialists think of openness as removing restrictions case by case and providing bureaucratic permission for a specific change. A senior economist at the Nomura Research Institute (hardly a Japan basher) stated in late 1994 that "virtually every arm of the Japanese government is still geared toward increasing exports and finding domestic substitutes for imports. One is hard pressed to find any group within the government that does not subscribe to these two goals."[31]

For many years, Japanese economic policymakers have viewed the absence of local production of an important new product or technology developed overseas as a sign of weakness needing urgent correction. This is, perhaps, an instinctive reflex in a country that traditionally has acted to minimize its dependence on and vulnerability to the outside world. This attitude, together with Japan's excellence in process technology, makes it the world's number one locale for the "disappearing market" phenomenon. Once a comparable or improved domestically produced version of a foreign innovation comes to market, imports of that product can dry up almost overnight. For example, Japanese orders for the U.S.-made 8080-type microprocessor quickly dropped to zero in late 1979, when adequate supplies of Japanese-made equivalents became available.[32] (Sales of this chip declined worldwide but at a much slower rate.)

The plural of "anecdote" is not data. Even if one discounts the presumption that happy exporters are quieter than unsuccessful ones, the sheer number of frustrating and painful experiences by would-be exporters to Japan suggest it harbors a pervasively antagonistic attitude toward imports. A definitive list of efforts and circumstances inhibiting access of a broad array of foreign-made manufactured goods to the Japanese market would be long enough to comprise a book. So many formal trade barriers remain that Japan still has, by a wide margin, the most pages devoted to it in the annual survey of foreign trade barriers issued by the U.S. Trade Representative's office — 40 pages in the 1996 edition covering some 50 contentious issues.

The propensity for Japan to drag its feet in improving market access for U.S. supercomputers, construction services, telecommunications equipment, cellular phones, and other sectors was discussed in Chapter 2. The first section of this chapter discussed import barriers justified by supposed physical differences of Japanese anatomy and terrain. Chapter 8 will discuss the role of minimal foreign investment in limiting imports. These examples barely scratch the surface of Japanese impediments to imports. What follows is another sampling that purports to accurately depict the larger reality.

Japan is the only country accused of systematically seeking to undermine the effects of import liberalization measures with indirect impediments so that imports cannot enlarge their market share after formal barriers are eased. The U.S. government filed a complaint with the World Trade Organization reiterating Kodak's charges of government-sanctioned collusion in the distribution of photographic film. The complaint details the nature of Japan's "liberalization countermeasures" and quotes a 1967 Japanese cabinet meeting at which it was decided that "it would be necessary to restrain foreign enterprises coming into Japan after liberalization from disturbing order in domestic industries by resorting to the strength of their superior power."[33]

On the eve of liberalizing the computer sector in 1976, the Japanese government announced it would "cherish" the domestic industry's "independence and future growth" and would "keep an eye on movements in the computer market so that liberalization will not adversely affect domestic producers nor produce confusion" (officialdom's code word for intense price competition that could lead to unsettled business conditions). The government subsequently increased contributions to research and development in the computer sector and invoked administrative guidance to tighten "buy Japan" procurement practices by all official agencies and government-owned corporations.[34] When the automobile market was first liberalized, Japanese tax officials frequently audited local buyers of foreign-made cars.[35]

In some instances, Japan does not need countermeasures to foil the effects of removing formal trade barriers — it can fall back on indirect, informal barriers. Import liberalization measures do not terminate the corporate propensity to buy from *keiretsu* partners or trusted suppliers. Nor do they end the distribution *keiretsu* whereby small retail stores, most notably those selling consumer electronics, carry only a single Japanese brand. Furthermore, statutory changes do not terminate the extreme reluctance of Japanese trading companies to import large volumes of those goods that would displace output of their *keiretsu* partners.

Many U.S. trade officials were furious in 1996 at what they regarded as the Japanese government's misrepresentation of the purposes of two planned communication satellites in order to exploit a loophole in the bilateral 1990 satellite procurement agreement that would allow them to buy from domestic sources.[36] Japan's health care system has been systematically reducing reimbursements to patients receiving "special treatment materials," for example, pacemakers. This category of treatment appears to have been drawn up to coincide with sectors where U.S. medical technology companies have a relatively high market share. In other words, budgetary cutbacks in this area would not seriously hurt sales by Japanese companies.

U.S. companies have often been unable to discover what ingredients and specifications are acceptable in Japan. As late as the early 1980s, U.S. makers of cosmetics and data communications machinery were merely told yes or no as to whether their products could enter the Japanese market. The Japanese government refused to disclose the criteria on which the rejections were based. Vigilant customs officials reportedly rejected a container of pineapples arriving from the Philippines because the name of the fruit was incorrectly spelled with a hyphen separating the words pine and apple.[37]

A Japanese citizen ran into difficulties in early 1982 when he tried to import two Mercedes-Benz cars from Germany. Customs officials at Narita Airport told him the first aid kits and fire extinguishers in the cars did not comply with government drug laws and high-pressure-gas control regulations. When these officials refused to open the first aid kits to see that no illegal drugs were present, the would-be importer was so outraged that he became the first Japanese to file a complaint with the Office of the Trade Ombudsman.[38] A U.S. company encountered a bizarre rejection in 1989 of its bid to export wood treated with a fire-resistant coating that foams on contact with flames. Japanese product standards require that wood withstand exposure to fire for an unspecified minimum time period. The new product failed to meet the standard because it was too good: by so quickly extinguishing flames applied to it, the coated wood failed to demonstrate that it could withstand fire for the required minimum length of time.[39]

Several years ago one MITI official boasted — or let slip — to a visiting scholar the protocol for imposing administrative guidance on a Japanese construction company importing so much Korean cement that local companies were complaining. Any of several contingencies might be presented to the company to "help" it see that its interests lay in cooling its purchases of imported cement. It could face major problems getting contracts in the future for government-financed construction; it could find its corporate tax returns more closely examined; and it might be shut out of any future MITI support programs for the industry.[40]

The Lions Oil affair of the mid-1980s began with the seemingly admirable effort by the company's president to import a small amount of relatively inexpensive gasoline from Singapore so that a limited number of gasoline stations could sell it at a modest discount below the fixed prices imposed by the major petroleum refiners. Although MITI lacked direct authority to prohibit the proposed gasoline imports, it apparently responded with a classic example of the unofficial power of administrative guidance. Hardly by coincidence, the bank financing the gasoline imports suddenly canceled the loan, and the discount gasoline proposal folded.[41]

Letters of complaint sent by U.S. companies to the U.S. Commerce Department during the 1980s reveal a wide range of problems encountered in exporting to Japan. For example, a leading producer and exporter of airport baggage handling equipment learned that a Japanese competitor had been awarded a large airport contract without price competition. The letter of complaint included this revealing quotation from Nissho-Iwai, the trading company with which the U.S. company had contracted to enter the Japanese market: "Frankly speaking, we still have difficulty selling the high quality, less-expensive foreign made products for Japanese public projects."[42]

South Korea epitomizes the export success of the newly industrialized countries (NICs) of East Asia and is geographically close to Japan. However, Japan's pseudo–open door also finds ways to inhibit South Korean exports. While it was running surpluses with virtually all of its other trading partners in the mid-1980s, Korea incurred a deficit with Japan. Several anecdotes suggest reasons for this singular deficit. Korean steel shipments had to be all but smuggled into Japan (at least through the 1980s). Clandestine operations reportedly were necessary because the trading companies importing the steel were fearful of angering large Japanese steelmakers who would not hesitate to refuse to do business with anyone importing cheaper products.[43] Prior to discrete importing, stories circulated in the Washington trade community that trucks delivering Korean-made steel in Japan were regularly tailed to determine who was buying it. (There was a presumption that customers identified in this way had their arms twisted to buy domestic steel.)

Japanese trade officials, arriving in Seoul in late 1984, just days after the first deliveries of South Korean exports of cement, demanded informal, voluntary export restraint, even though the shipment in question amounted to a minuscule 0.3 percent of Japanese cement consumption. When South Korean officials refused, all outstanding orders from Japanese wholesalers were "abruptly and mysteriously canceled."[44] Hyundai quickly developed a niche market in the United States for its relatively inexpensive automobiles, but it has never exported cars to Japan — for foreigners "the most severe and complicated battlefield" — and has no plans to try to do so.[45]

## NONMARKET MARKET AND COLLUSIVE
## BUSINESS PRACTICES

Getting past barriers at the border is the first of many major hurdles exporters must clear if they are to gain a foothold in contemporary Japan. Success is still not assured. Even if a foreign company has a better product, it must then deal with publicly and privately administered systems of internal discrimination against foreign-made manufactured goods. A stifling regulatory system, widespread business collusion, an industrial structure often contemptuous of unrestrained competition, and a preference for maintaining existing domestic business relationships over maximizing profits all represent potential quicksand for even the best of foreign companies.

More than 10,000 regulations cover every aspect of commercial activity, from entry into business to the impact of corporate activity on health, safety, and the environment. The myriad licenses, approvals, and authorizations needed from various ministries "can be, and have been in the past, arbitrarily enforced against foreign companies," the American Chamber of Commerce in Japan asserted in 1995.[46]

The trade complaint filed with the U.S. government in early 1990 by the Allied-Signal Corporation exemplifies Japan's desire to squelch imports of goods that would adversely affect a high-tech industry targeted for domestic development. Amorphous metals, first developed in the 1970s by Allied-Signal, have an enormous array of potential commercial applications in reducing energy loss in electrical devices such as power lines. Despite sales success in the United States and other foreign markets, Allied-Signal got nowhere, either exporting to or producing in the Japanese market. MITI's tactics appeared to encourage would-be domestic producers and potential customers to wait while the government attacked on the patent front. As a result of delays of up to twelve years on patent applications, Allied-Signal's protection expired in Japan in 1993. (The exclusionary period starts when a patent application is filed, not granted.) Meanwhile, through a publicly-owned corporation, MITI organized a 34-company group to develop an indigenous amorphous metals industry. Allied-Signal claimed that the Tokyo Electric Power Company, Japan's biggest public utility, admitted that its strategy was to postpone purchases of amorphous metals until after the expiration of Allied-Signal's patents.[47] (Japan's very different philosophy and laws affecting patents have been a bone of contention with U.S. companies for years. The latter have contended that protection of their intellectual property has been inadequate. Many foreign companies have been victims of Japanese businesses engaging in "patent flooding" in which they file dozens of narrow patents that relate closely to a competitor's invention so that the competitor will be open to charges of patent infringement.)

Allied-Signal does not appear to have been lazy or inefficient in its efforts to sell amorphous metals in Japan. Its resident representative at that time, Dr. Ryusuke Hasegawa, a Cal Tech Ph.D. with numerous publications on amorphous metals, was born and reared in Japan before emigrating to the United States. When he asked why his sales efforts were being rejected, he often got this blunt answer: "You're destroying our harmony. Everything was harmonious until you came along."[48]

Relatively lax enforcement of antitrust laws is the major exception to the rule of blanket business regulation. The Japanese government's preference for concentrated markets dominated by oligopolies provides a license for business executives to engage in self-serving, nonmarket behavior that discriminates against newcomers who might challenge the status quo — actions that would not be tolerated in the United States. Cartel behavior involving price fixing, market share allocation, and bid rigging is openly practiced in many sectors, including glass and paper production, petroleum refining, construction, and breweries. Consumer electronics companies compete on price, but not for retail outlets, most of which are allowed to carry only a single brand. "The result is a frenzied contained competition."[49]

The soda ash cartel has been a prime case study of collusion designed to protect a relatively inefficient Japanese industry from the fate of many U.S. import-impacted industries. Prior to 1983, lower U.S. prices were negated by a comprehensive market-fixing scheme. The major Japanese producers of soda ash (a chemical used in various manufacturing processes, such as making glass, which is represented by yet another cartel) regularly consulted with each other on domestic production levels and prices under the auspices of the Japan Soda Ash Industry Association. Also, because they were all members of *keiretsu*, each was linked to one of the five large trading companies that handled virtually all imports of the product. Each trading company was specifically assigned to one of five U.S. exporters of soda ash, and each had an informal quota of 12,000 tons annually. All of the imported soda ash (about 5 percent of Japanese consumption at that time) was purchased directly from trading companies by the major Japanese soda ash producers and resold domestically at prevailing local prices.[50] When U.S. producers of the chemical tried to expand sales by selling more product to their assigned trading company or directly to Japanese users, they were rebuffed because "delicate relationships" would be upset.[51]

The violations of Japan's antimonopoly law by the soda ash cartel were so egregious that the Japan Fair Trade Commission issued a cease and desist order in 1983 and a follow-up warning in 1987. U.S. shipments did increase rapidly beginning in 1984, but they peaked in 1990. Efforts to bypass the cartel by using a Japanese trading company (Sumitomo) with no soda ash producers in its group eventually resulted in the company's being pressured to limit imports. A MITI vice minister subsequently informed the head of the U.S. soda ash exporters association that, with the Japanese industry operating well below full capacity, imports from the United States had grown enough. Japanese customers later rejected offers by U.S. producers of deep discounts in exchange for increased market share, citing their purchasing policies that are not subject to market-based changes.[52]

Cartel-like behavior that frequently discriminates against the imported goods and local activities of U.S. subsidiaries is fostered by the enormous power granted to Japanese trade associations. Quasi–governmental authority makes them far more powerful than their U.S. counterparts. The typical trade association coordinates exchanges of data on production, sales, prices, customers, and technology among its members; it sets product standards; and it might arrange joint manufacturing, sales, purchasing, research and development, and so forth among its members. The result is an advanced form of self-regulation by the major companies in most sectors. The propensity of trade associations to constrain competition is suggested by the high frequency with which they have been cited for violating the antimonopoly law.[53] The relatively few foreign corporations admitted as members of a Japanese trade association rarely are allowed to participate fully and equally in the group's committees and activities.[54]

Japanese companies — as opposed to Japanese consumers — have purchasing criteria that clearly differ from those of most Western companies. Preserving personal relationships in "network capitalism" is more important than buying from the vendor that is quoting today's lowest price. Import flows in Japan are as likely to be determined at the microeconomic level by "the concrete relationships among the firms that actually make buying and selling decisions" than by macro factors like exchange rates and import barriers.[55]

Buying decisions are heavily influenced by the fact that most major Japanese industrial companies participate in horizontal (corporate alliances) and vertical (suppliers and end-users) keiretsu groups. "Densely linked and strongly preferential trading systems, such as that found in the Japanese keiretsu, are likely to be less sensitive to fluctuations in exchange rates or to government liberalization efforts than more arm's-length market ties. Allied firms, quite rationally, base their purchasing decisions on relationships in their entirety rather than on a transaction-specific pricing calculus."[56]

A survey by the Japan Fair Trade Commission determined that, in the early 1990s, the big six horizontal keiretsu made 68 percent of their purchases from other Japanese companies within their group (or those they had an equity interest of at least 10 percent), but only 5 percent of their purchases came from unrelated foreign companies.[57] A study by Richard Z. Lawrence found "statistically significant evidence that keiretsu do reduce imports." In sectors where keiretsu firms dominate the market, they "typically cut the import share of consumption in that industry by half."[58] Furthermore, all major trading companies belong to a keiretsu, and seldom, if ever, have they inflicted financial harm on associated manufacturing companies by aggressively importing goods that compete with the latter's output.

A Japanese company's most likely response to a foreign proposal to supply goods at a lower price or with advanced technical features is not to sign a contract but to urge its current supplier to match, at least partially, the foreigner's offer, or risk losing both contract and face. Japanese contractors and subcontractors are more likely than not to rise to the occasion. They are accustomed to meeting their main customer's onerous demands to improve price, quality, and product specifications. The pressures on contractors to avoid becoming a financial burden on long-term customers are as intense as the pressure on large manufacturing companies not to abandon Japanese suppliers for a foreigner. This pattern only infrequently causes total exclusion of imports. Many foreign companies, especially those based in the United States, are allocated minor market shares in Japan because not every model of every product is made there, because imports can reduce average costs of Japanese manufactured goods, and because of the public relations value of being able to demonstrate that U.S. companies can make money in Japan.

As a result of the many roadblocks faced by a foreign company, the price advantage or technical superiority of foreign-made goods must be substantial. A documented study of the Japanese distribution system, prepared by the professional staff of the U.S. International Trade Commission, made one of the rare public references to the usually muted suspicion that Japanese trading companies follow an informal "10 and 20 rule." The latter allegedly limits foreign suppliers' shares of the Japanese market for a given product to about 10 percent unless they have a 20 percent or greater price advantage over domestic competitors.[59]

Arguably, it is not a coincidence that, in the past, foreign companies' market share in Japan for a number of high-tech capital goods was clustered around a fixed percentage. To bolster its contention that managed trade was the best way to deal with Japan, the U.S. semiconductor industry circulated its "worm chart" in the 1980s. A nearly straight horizontal line showed import penetration of Japan's semiconductor market hovering at around 10 percent market share over a 13-year-period beginning in 1973, progressive market liberalization and yen appreciation notwithstanding.[60] Simply put, the Japanese electronics industry reserved the bulk of the local market for these devices for domestic producers.

Attributing the fixed-market-share syndrome to natural market forces becomes all the more difficult when glaring differentials exist between foreign companies' experiences in global markets and Japan. One of Silicon Valley's premier firms, Hewlett Packard, reported a high-tech product having a market of 60 percent in the United States, 90 percent in Europe, but only 1 percent in Japan.[61] A Siemens–Corning Glass joint venture in optical fiber had about half of the world market outside Japan, but after 16 years of effort in Japan, the market share there remained minor.[62] Similarly, the market share of U.S. semiconductor companies selling chips to Japanese automakers prior to the 1986 agreement was a tiny fraction of what they were recording in other export markets.[63]

Foreigners are sometimes totally excluded from the market. The Japanese affiliate of a U.S. land development and construction company saw one of its rural building projects halted when subcontractors begged off after being warned by major regional contractors that it would never again hire them if they went ahead with the job for the U.S. company. Efforts by the same company to build its own headquarters met an identical fate: intimidated subcontractors forced the company to work with the *dango*, the entrenched construction bid-rigging cartel.[64]

Japanese distributors interested in adding imports to their sales lines often are threatened with a supply shutoff or with demands by Japanese manufacturers and distributors for immediate payment. It is not unusual for small-scale retailers to face an ultimatum from their chief domestic supplier: choose between carrying the supplier's goods on an exclusive basis or depend entirely on imports. Japan's largest agricultural cooperative once threatened to withhold subsidy payments if farmers purchased foreign feed or fertilizer.

In what other country would a local distributor for imported goods bristle at the exporting company's plans to increase its local market share? When the Japanese distributor of European telecommunications equipment was told of plans to try to double market share to 20 percent, he expressed concern. Despite the prospect of higher earnings for himself, he argued to the manufacturer that they had done well to achieve the 10 percent share, and he spelled out the difficulties of seeking an increase.[65] The same telecommunications corporation lost a sale to a Japanese bank because — the bank later admitted — it favored a slightly less competitive bid from a Japanese company that the bank had helped to go public several years before. The local distributor for a U.S. sporting goods company fought against the company's plan to increase market share in Japan through price reductions, claiming that such actions would "disrupt the marketplace" (the euphemism for avoiding price competition).[66]

## PECULIAR TRADE PATTERNS

By every conventional statistical measure, Japan is an outlier. Its trade patterns have deviated from those of other industrial countries. Although past trends are not necessarily accurate guides to the future, critics suggest that empirical data irrefutably support the thesis that the Japanese market has consistently presented extraordinary direct and indirect impediments to the importation of manufactured goods that compete with Japanese products. Even if these impediments are significantly relaxed in the future so that Japan's trade patterns move closer to the norm, there can be no retroactive cancellation of the benefits received by Japanese companies that matured in a closed home market.

Japan has enjoyed the world's largest trade surpluses on a consistent basis since the late 1980s. Although quality goods and a relatively high saving rate are important explanations for the surplus, they are not sufficient to convince Japan's trading partners (some of whom have higher saving rates) to shrug off the persistent failure of the adjustment process to restore equilibrium. The logic of a resource-poor country mainly exporting manufactured goods to pay for food, fuel, and raw materials is incontestable. However, relative factor endowments cannot explain why Japan's total exports must consistently exceed by a huge margin its import bill for primary products. There is nothing in trade theory to ameliorate the seething discontent with Japan's bulging surpluses in manufactured goods that averaged $215 billion annually in the 1990–95 period, peaking at an astonishing $250 billion in 1993. Japan cannot be expected to have the same proportion of manufactured goods imports with respect to total imports as the relatively resource-rich United States. Yet, there is no obvious reason for Japan to exhibit a significantly lower ratio than other industrial countries having a moderate to low natural resource base. Manufactured goods (by dollar value) as shares of the total imports of the United States, Great Britain, and Germany were about 75 percent during 1991 and 1992. Manufactures as a percentage of Japan's imports in these two years averaged only 45 percent.[67]

Japan's ratio of total imports to GDP is by far the lowest among the major industrial countries (Table 4.1). Moreover, Japan is unique among industrial countries in possessing a declining ratio since the 1970s. The same statistical profile appears if imports of manufactured goods are measured as a percent of GDP. Japan not only scores lowest among the major industrialized economies but also is unique in not experiencing an increase in this ratio during the 1980s.

**TABLE 4.1**
**Ratio of Imports to Gross Domestic Product**
**(in percent)**

|                              | 1956 | 1970 | 1994 |
| ---------------------------- | ---- | ---- | ---- |
| Japan                        | 12.3 | 9.3  | 5.5  |
| United States                | 3.3  | 4.2  | 9.6  |
| Federal Republic of Germany  | 14.1 | 16.2 | 20.4 |

*Sources*: International Monetary Fund, *International Financial Statistics Supplement on Trade Statistics, 1988* (Washington, D.C.: International Monetary Fund, 1988), 1956 was the earliest year for which import ratio data were available); International Monetary Fund, *International Financial Statistics Yearbook, 1996* (Washington, D.C.: International Monetary Fund, 1996).

A precise way to measure the distinctive resistance of the Japanese market to foreign-made goods is to calculate imports of manufactured goods as a percentage of total consumption of manufactures. Japan again scores well below average. The import share of its total domestic consumption of manufactures in 1990 was 5.9 percent as compared with the United States (15.3 percent), Germany (15.4 percent), and Great Britain (17.7 percent).[68] Intra-European Union trade was not included in the calculations for Germany or Great Britain; if it had been, imports as a percentage of manufactured goods consumed would probably have been in the range of 30 to 40 percent.[69]

To the extent that increases in Japanese imports of manufactured goods are recorded in the future (in absolute or relative terms), the significance of this trend will need to be discounted as partly reflecting the recent sharp increases in exports of labor-intensive goods and components to Japan by the foreign subsidiaries of Japanese companies. Such imports demonstrate the desire of these companies to retain sales in the Japanese market, not a genuine opening of Japan to goods manufactured abroad by foreign-owned companies.

Another statistical anomaly is Japan's unusually low rate of intra-industry trade, a measure of a country's imports and exports of similar manufactured products. Because of increasing product differentiation, most industrialized countries now experience extensive two-way trade in different models or types of such goods as cars, electronics, chemicals, machinery, and office equipment. Japan's intra-industry trade index for manufactured goods through the mid-1980s was dramatically below average, being less than one-half that of the other major industrialized countries. Japan once again was the only major industrialized country demonstrating no increase in such trade between 1970 and 1985.[70] "When Japan chooses to engage in major exports of a product, it imports very little." Its "pattern of behavior is seriously at odds with all the expectations generated by intra-industry theory," concluded Edward Lincoln of the Brookings Institution.[71] Robert Lawrence, using an econometric model, found that Japanese manufactured goods in the mid-1980s were about 40 percent lower than what should be expected. If Japan traded as other countries did, he concluded, it would generate considerably more intra-industry trade.[72] Sales of goods in Japan by foreign-owned firms (1.2 percent in 1990) is a minute fraction of the comparable figure for the United States and the large European economies.

When all the statistical evidence is considered as a whole, Robert Lawrence has argued, "These data are . . . consistent with claims that the Japanese market remains relatively closed to foreign trade and investment; that firms producing close substitutes for domestic products are denied entry; that foreign investment is still discouraged and thus foreign firms with know-how are induced to license and engage in joint ventures rather than to set up majority-owned affiliates."[73]

Another indicator of peculiar Japanese trade patterns is associated with a major global economic trend beginning in the late 1970s: the emergence of the East Asian NICs — Hong Kong, South Korea, Singapore, and Taiwan — as hugely successful exporters. The NICs' success in exporting to the U.S. and European markets, however, has been vastly different from their trade experiences with Japan. Despite their proven export skills, relatively close geographical proximity to Japan, and understanding of Asian business mentalities, considerable statistical and anecdotal evidence exists that the NICs have encountered extreme difficulties, similar to those experienced by the United States and Europe, when trying to sell in the Japanese market. This apparently universal experience is further proof that Japanese actions have a much greater impact upon the structural bilateral trade disequilibrium than inept U.S. marketing skills. When citizens of the NICs lambast Japanese import practices, they cannot be dismissed as racist or as sore losers seeking a scapegoat for their country's economic shortcomings.

The relative openness of the U.S. market to the goods of the East Asian countries is easily demonstrated statistically. In absolute terms, the United States accounts for a much higher dollar value of exports *from* most Asian countries than does Japan. The NICs' exports to the United States almost quadrupled between 1982 and 1995, a year in which the United States incurred over $11 billion in cumulative trade deficit with the four NICs. Conversely, Japan accounts for a much higher value of exports *to* these countries than the United States. The former enjoyed large surpluses with all four NICs that in 1995 totaled $70 billion (Table 4.2). Market share data further demonstrate the wholesale dissimilarity between U.S. and Japanese trade relations with the four Asian NICs. Out of the latter's total 1994 exports ($762 billion), 21 percent were shipped to the United States and 12 percent went to Japan.[74] The greater receptiveness of the United States to manufactured goods imported from the East Asian countries is further documented in Table 4.3. U.S. government officials in the late 1980s calculated that the United States was taking more than 50 percent of all developing countries' exports of manufactured goods, compared to only 9 percent for Japan, and 26 percent for the European Union.[75] In recent years, Japanese imports of manufactured goods from most of these countries have accelerated in dollar amounts but not fast enough relative to the United States to significantly alter relative market share numbers.

A final quantitative illustration of Japan's peculiar trade patterns is evident in Korean trade statistics detailing exports of manufactured goods to the Japanese and U.S. markets. As seen in Table 4.4, Japan seldom accounts for a larger or even comparable outlet for Korean goods than the

**TABLE 4.2**
**U.S. and Japanese Trade with the Asian NICs**
**(in billions of U.S. dollars)**

| | Exports to | | Imports from | | Balance with NICs | |
|---|---|---|---|---|---|---|
| | 1982 | 1995 | 1982 | 1995 | 1982 | 1995 |
| *U.S. Bilateral Trade* | | | | | | |
| Hong Kong | 2.5 | 14.2 | 5.9 | 10.7 | −3.4 | 3.5 |
| South Korea | 5.5 | 25.4 | 6.0 | 24.9 | −0.5 | 0.5 |
| Singapore | 3.2 | 15.3 | 2.3 | 18.9 | 0.9 | −3.6 |
| Taiwan | 4.4 | 19.3 | 9.6 | 30.2 | −5.2 | −10.9 |
| *Japanese Bilateral Trade* | | | | | | |
| Hong Kong | 4.7 | 27.8 | 0.6 | 2.7 | 4.1 | 25.1 |
| South Korea | 4.9 | 31.3 | 3.3 | 17.3 | 1.6 | 14.0 |
| Singapore | 4.4 | 23.0 | 1.8 | 6.8 | 2.5 | 16.2 |
| Taiwan | 4.2 | 29.0 | 2.4 | 14.3 | 1.8 | 14.7 |

*Source*: Compiled from International Monetary Fund, *Direction of Trade Statistics Yearbook* (Washington, D.C.: International Monetary Fund, 1989, 1996) (imports measured on "c.i.f." basis).

**TABLE 4.3**
**U.S. and Japanese Shares of East Asian Exports of Manufactured Goods**
**(in percent)**

| | 1980 | | 1990 | |
|---|---|---|---|---|
| Exporter | United States | Japan | United States | Japan |
| Hong Kong | 34 | 3 | 31 | 5 |
| South Korea | 29 | 13 | 32 | 15 |
| Singapore | 21 | 8 | 28 | 6 |
| Taiwan | 38 | 7 | 40 | 9 |
| China | 9 | 11 | 23 | 9 |
| Malaysia | 32 | 6 | 28 | 5 |

*Source*: John Ravenhill, "The 'Japan Problem' in Pacific Trade," in *Pacific Economic Relations in the 1990s: Cooperation or Conflict?* edited by Richard Higgott, Richard Leaver, and John Ravenhill (Boulder, Colo.: Lynne Rienner, 1993), p. 128.

**TABLE 4.4**
**Korea's Total Exports of Selected Commodities**
**Going to the United States and Japan**
(in percent)

|                                         | Japan | United States |
|-----------------------------------------|-------|---------------|
| Clothing                                |       |               |
| 1986                                    | 20.1  | 45.6          |
| 1993                                    | 33.5  | 40.0          |
| Household Appliances                    |       |               |
| 1986                                    | 0.2   | 67.3          |
| 1993                                    | 2.5   | 40.0          |
| Electric Motors and Generators          |       |               |
| 1986                                    | 50.2  | 19.5          |
| 1993                                    | 29.4  | 36.6          |
| Automatic Data Processing Machines      |       |               |
| 1986                                    | 0.41  | 55.5          |
| 1993                                    | 1.5   | 56.8          |
| Telecommunications Equipment            |       |               |
| 1986                                    | 1.9   | 84.6          |
| 1993                                    | 4.5   | 20.6          |
| Passenger Cars                          |       |               |
| 1986                                    | 0.05  | 71.2          |
| 1993                                    | 0.2   | 17.4          |
| Vehicle Parts                           |       |               |
| 1986                                    | 12.4  | 55.3          |
| 1993                                    | 9.9   | 37.9          |

*Source*: Calculated from data in Korea Customs Research Institute, *Statistical Yearbook of Foreign Trade — Republic of Korea* (Seoul: Korea Customs Research Institute, 1986, 1993 editions).

United States. The bottom line is that the NICs' global export triumph stops at the Japanese border.

An important question remains: what is the relevance of all this empirical proof of peculiar data patterns when Japan's trade statistics for the mid-1990s clearly show at least a temporary surge in imports of manufactured goods. There are several reasons to believe this trend does not demonstrate categorically the emergence of a truly open Japanese market. First, part of this correction is the lag effect of extensive yen appreciation in the early half of the decade. In the past, the corrective impact of yen appreciation has been limited in both scope and duration, in part because the yen occasionally experiences periods of weakness, that is, depreciation. There is no reason to doubt history will repeat itself. Second, a disproportionately large percentage of these incremental imports consists of shipments of industrial components and labor-intensive consumer electronics from Japanese-owned subsidiaries in Asia. A MITI survey indicates Japanese imports of manufactured goods from foreign direct investments in Asia, North America, and Europe increased from about $7 billion in 1986 to just over $30 billion (of which Asia accounts for $20 billion) in 1994.[76] Although this trend suggests that intra-company trade is on the upswing in increasingly high-cost Japan, it does not necessarily signal the emergence of a market that is genuinely open to foreign companies in the U.S. sense of the expression.

The Japanese market is, indeed, relatively open to imports of labor-intensive, low-tech goods that have become prohibitively expensive to produce in Japan and to luxury goods that appeal to affluent Japanese consumers. The problem for the United States is that it is not a significant producer of either of these categories of goods (for example, radios, electric fans, designer clothes, and high-performance automobiles). In addition to agriculture, U.S. export strength is concentrated in high-tech, high value added capital goods — the sector most susceptible to the exclusionary buying habits of the horizontal and vertical *keiretsu*.

## JAPAN'S HIGH PRICES: IMPLICIT
## PROOF OF LIMITED MARKET ACCESS

Japan's distorted import patterns cited above might be explained away by factors other than restricted market access, for example, relative factor endowments and uncommonly competitive Japanese manufactured goods. Individual case studies of Japanese import impediments cannot scientifically demonstrate an unusually serious market access problem. However, a Japanese research economist has admitted that significant and consistent cross-national price differences indicate that "de facto trade barriers" exist in Japan.[77] To quote Professor Robert Lawrence again:

If the Japanese market is contestable, we should see the potential for entry keeping Japanese prices in line with those in other markets. If the same product sells for different prices in different locations over long periods of time, however, it seems reasonable to infer the existence of barriers to arbitrage. . . . The inefficiency in the Japanese distribution system is [only] partly to blame for higher Japanese retail prices. Japanese manufacturers appear (on average) to charge prices in Japan that are higher than those in world markets.[78]

The fact that Japan is a capitalist economy does not mean that its price mechanism functions exactly as does the U.S. price mechanism. This statement is self-evident to anyone who has observed the common sight in international air terminals of Japanese travelers, about to board a flight home, clutching bags overflowing with what were, for them, bargain-priced goods.[79] Retail prices tend to be much higher in Japan than in the United States because of the former's relatively lax enforcement of antitrust legislation, corporate priorities, and marketing strategies; consumers' relatively high tolerance levels; and a relatively inefficient distribution system.

The existence of significant differentials has been confirmed in numerous price surveys conducted in the late 1980s and early 1990s.[80] For example, the Organization for Economic Cooperation and Development estimated prices for goods and services in Japan in 1988 to be 60 percent higher than in the United States.[81] A sample taken in the same year by Japan's Economic Planning Agency found prices of comparable goods and services in New York and Hamburg to be 72 percent and 68 percent, respectively, of Tokyo levels.[82] A joint government survey involving exact brand and model comparisons found that two-thirds of the 112 products examined (30 percent of which were made in Japan) were, on average, 37 percent more expensive in Japan than in the United States.[83]

During the U.S.-Japanese automotive dispute, U.S. trade representative Mickey Kantor provided specific examples of U.S.-made auto parts that were relatively cheap, but, nonetheless, unable to increase market share in Japan. He compared a U.S. retail price of $228 for U.S.-made shock absorbers to the equivalent of $605 for Japanese-made shock absorbers in their home market; U.S. alternators priced at $120 cost $600 in Japan; and U.S.-made mufflers and tailpipes at $82 cost $200 in Japan for the same domestically produced parts.[84] Higher prices "expose the constipated nature of Japan's distribution systems and supplier-buyer networks, which were designed to digest only established Japanese goods, not new goods and especially not those of foreign origin."[85]

Persistence of large price discontinuities for a wide range of goods has major implications for the competitiveness of Japanese exports. To the extent that Japanese producers can maintain unusually high profit margins in their home market, they can slash export prices to break-even levels (or lower) in order to seize market share abroad in an adversarial manner. Critics of Japan cite the resulting ability of many Japanese producers to "price to market" as a major reason they have been able to beat their U.S. competition and to hold onto market share in the United States despite the challenges of yen appreciation, rising competition from the East Asian NICs, and so on.

The data also suggest that many imported products have been subjected to higher markups than domestically-made products. (This process may become less frequent with the spread of discount chains in Japan that appeal to value-conscious consumers.)

Large markups on foreign-made goods are caused, to some extent, by the relatively high share of Japanese imports that have been accounted for by Japanese-owned firms, mostly trading companies and overseas affiliates. This is especially true of exports from the United States, where the data also show an unusually low share of shipments to Japan being made by U.S. firms.[86] The reluctance of Japanese joint venture partners and distributors to aggressively market foreign-made manufactured goods on the basis of low prices is an important impediment to imports. Many U.S. companies find that getting imported products to Japanese consumers can be a "daunting and expensive proposition." If they do make their way through the distribution maze, "prices for their goods will likely be pushed 50% to 250% higher" than in the United States.[87] Elimination of Japan's trade impediments and restrictive business practices would reduce the relatively high prices of internationally traded goods in that market — with the likely result of a significant increase in manufactured imports.

To critics of Japan, comments by foreigners living and working there concerning real-life business experiences are far more credible than Japanese government officials pleading the openness of the market or U.S. academics waving statistical models purportedly showing that Japan's trade surpluses and patterns are completely normal. Of particular importance, therefore, is the American Chamber of Commerce in Japan's assertion in a trade white paper that: "once having overcome the initial entry barriers, the ongoing cost of doing business in Japan is significantly higher than anywhere else in the world. . . . The cost of doing business in Japan is extremely high because of structural impediments, unnecessary and protective regulations, exclusionary business practices, keiretsu (affiliated companies), multi-tiered distribution systems, and other non-market pricing mechanisms."[88] This passage lends credence to the alleged "cost protectionism" syndrome. Imports and inward foreign direct investment are discouraged in part by extraordinarily high prices. The latter are triggered in part by deliberate Japanese government policies affecting such key sectors as real estate and distribution.[89]

Japan's price structure is so skewed against consumer interests that it is common for Japanese-made goods to be sold at lower prices in overseas markets — even if its less efficient distribution system is factored in.[90] In the absence of a formalized "gray market" to exploit the opportunities presented by large, company-mandated price differentials between markets, Japanese entrepreneurs and consumers use ad hoc measures. Considerable publicity and some red faces were generated by the revelation, in 1988, that a small trading company was re-importing cordless telephones made in Japan by Panasonic and exported to the United States. It bought these phones for approximately $60 each in the United States and then retailed them in Japan for the yen equivalent of $152. Sales were both brisk and profitable because all other Japanese-made cordless phones were selling for four times that amount, that is, over $600. This exercise in unleashing the invisible hand abruptly ended when Panasonic hurriedly bought up the re-imported phones, huffing that they were not built to meet higher Japanese telecommunications standards.[91]

Residents of Japan sometimes find it cheaper to have overseas friends mail them Japanese-made goods rather than to buy them locally. One person reported that he received Japanese floppy disks from the United States for one-fourth the price charged in Japanese stores, even after paying air parcel post charges.[92]

Foreign companies offer sharply discounted long distance telephone calls in Japan through a convoluted "callback" service. Callers phone a U.S. number, hang up, and are then called back by a computer that connects them to a line on a U.S. telephone network.[93] To cite a personal experience, I looked at automatic-focus cameras during a visit to Tokyo in the late 1980s. Knowing about price markups, I deferred making a purchase until returning home. After waiting a couple of weeks for the model I wanted to go on sale, I paid about one-half the price quoted in Tokyo.

Japan's unique pricing system is also visible in the apparent double standard in government policy response when yen appreciation threatens to change prices of imports and exports. Priority is given to protecting the competitive position of Japanese goods in foreign markets. Efforts to assure that Japanese consumers reap the benefits of lower yen-based import prices are very low on the list of official priorities. Yen appreciation typically produces minimal price increases for the country's exports as well as minimal decreases in import prices. The Japanese government did not contest U.S. complaints in the late 1980s that prices of U.S. goods in Japan had not been reduced to reflect the depreciation of the dollar with respect to the yen. Conversely, after 1985, the Japanese government did seek to minimize dislocations to producers from *endaka* — the strong yen. Subsidized loan programs supported corporate attempts to frustrate precisely what yen appreciation is supposed to do: encourage Japanese imports and dampen exports.

Comparing Japanese input prices, wholesale prices, and export prices, Congress' Joint Economic Committee concluded that "Japanese manufacturers have not been passing on import cost savings fully to Japanese customers. At the same time, export prices have risen much less than either unit labor costs or wholesale prices. . . . The profits made from keeping the gains from cheaper imports and not passing them on to domestic customers may be subsidizing lower prices on exports."[94] A study by the Federal Reserve Bank of Chicago concluded that "Japan passes on far less of its currency-induced cost increases than any of the other" major industrial countries.[95]

The situation today in Japan is just slightly better than this mid-1980s assessment by a British industrialist: "I do not believe that selling in Japan is a matter of price. . . . If you sell into Japan, by and large Japanese will only buy from you if there is no Japanese alternative. If there is a Japanese alternative, they will match you on price, no matter what. It's a matter of national pride."[96]

## A GLOBAL CHORUS OF CRITICISM

Japan does not have a trade problem with the United States; it has a trade problem with the world. The complaints against Japan voiced by its major trading partners in Europe and Asia are similar to those made by the United States. Also similar is the gist of Japan's responses to other countries' complaints: "You need to try harder to increase your exports to our market. You should accept the facts that our successful export sector and relatively low levels of imported manufactured goods reflect our hard work and lack of raw materials, not aggressive trade behavior."

There is no good reason to believe that the rest of the world is misguided and the Japanese are being wrongfully persecuted by a vengeful international community. More likely, Japan's trade practices are out of touch with the needs and desires of its trading partners. This would explain why many countries have felt compelled to act against Japanese goods after their complaints about market access difficulties and excessive Japanese exports fell on stubbornly deaf ears in Tokyo.

In 1982, the European Union (EU) became so incensed over market access problems that it filed an extraordinary complaint in the General Agreement on Tariffs and Trade (GATT). It alleged that Japan's import practices taken as a whole were so restrictive that the country effectively had nullified its agreements to reduce trade barriers, that is, it effectively had violated its obligations to GATT. As an apparent quid pro quo for increased Japanese willingness to voluntarily restrain exports of a number of goods to the EU (including steel, automobiles, ships, consumer electronics, and machine tools), the complaint was later withdrawn.

Over the years, the EU has issued a steady stream of criticism about Japan's aggressive trade policies that is fully comparable with U.S. complaints. The EU asserted in 1985 that "Japan continues to remain out of step with her trading partners in terms of propensity to import manufactures."[97] "Like Japan's other partners," the EU stated in 1989, it "has continually insisted that Japan should reduce its export dependency and move towards an economy based on domestic demand, with all the structural reforms, market liberalization and internationalization which this requires."[98] A senior EU Commission official said in 1992 that "Passivity and fatalism are no response to the damaging consequences of an economic system in Japan and a business culture, which serves — whether by accident or design — largely to exclude exports except in certain niche luxury markets."[99] Even in 1996, Europeans remained skeptical of the Japanese economy's supposed internationalization: the EU saw its "chronic" bilateral trade deficits being caused by the "relatively closed nature of the Japanese market."[100]

The suggestion that U.S.-European criticism is a function of racism or second-rate export capabilities collapses in the face of the uniform criticism of Japan coming from the four East Asian NICs.

To reduce its large and growing bilateral trade deficit with Japan, Taiwan, in 1982, temporarily banned imports of more than 1,500 Japanese-made consumer goods, buses, and trucks. The Republic of Korea, in its 1982–83 Annual Trade Plan, announced measures to diversify the market for several imported products and reduce the severe Korean trade imbalance with one unnamed country. A December 1981 report of the Asian trade mission of the U.S. Congress' House Ways and Means Committee, covering Hong Kong, Singapore, Malaysia, and Thailand, found "Without exception, leaders in these countries said Japan was an unfair trader, that trade was a one-way street, and that the Japanese simply do not want to import."[101]

Singapore's Department of Trade complained that

Commercial practices, many unique only to Japan, had severely inhibited the ability of companies wishing to enlarge their share of the market. For example, it is virtually impossible to sell to Japan without having an affiliate company doing the marketing and distribution. . . . The structure of Japan's distribution network is a major impediment to our exporters gaining a bigger share of the market. The distribution network is so complex that the imported product becomes very expensive by the time it reaches the consumer.[102]

Lee Kuan Yew, former prime minister of Singapore, called on Japan, in 1995, to take the lead in regional initiatives but said that "before Japan can lead, it must set the example and open up its markets."[103]

The Hong Kong Department of Trade once stated that Japan's testing and certification procedures were "generally considered as a non-tariff barrier to exports to Japan."[104] In a 1989 interview with the author, a Hong Kong trade official suggested that market access improved only after the appreciation of the yen in 1985 made clear to the Japanese their diminishing future in domestic production of the labor-intensive goods in which Hong Kong specializes. Prior to reading the handwriting on the wall, the official said, the Japanese had a bad "attitude problem" toward imports, looking first and foremost to their own manufacturers.

An article in a Taiwanese magazine complained of Japanese insensitivity to Taiwan's economic problems and their desire to sell as much as they can and import as little as possible.

If a product can be made in Japan, it is, and the Japanese people must pay through the nose to buy it. The Japanese have been clever in concealing this. They look up innocent-eyed and say their market is "open to all." If anyone knows the Japanese market, our traders do. And almost to a man, they attest that it is nearly impossible to do business in most of the Japanese market. All the regulations favor Japanese products, no matter how inefficiently these are produced. . . . Our government has been appealing to the Japanese for years to give us a better chance. The Japanese smile, say they will and do nothing.[105]

## CONCLUSION

The attitudes of U.S. critics of bilateral trade relations with Japan are dominated by feelings of victimization and alienation. Most Americans feel that they have asked Japan merely to play by the same market-oriented economic and trade rules that are followed by all other industrial countries but that Japan has responded with delays, obfuscation, and deceit. Critics believe that the country whose export sector has benefitted the most from a liberal trading order and whose import sector has discriminated the most against foreign-made manufactured goods deserves frequent and severe criticism for its uniquely ethnocentric behavior. Japan appears to have reduced its trade barriers mainly to preempt retaliation from the United States, not because it believed in an international division of labor dictated by comparative advantage.

Things are changing for the better in Japan. Foreign jealousy does color attitudes toward Japan. Nevertheless, an overwhelming case can be made for demonstrating Japan's pattern of internal business and trade policies that methodically discriminated against foreign companies and contributed to their industrial miracle. Nothing can alter the historical record of bankrupt U.S. companies victimized by aggressive Japanese exporting. Nothing can restore the revenues, operating efficiencies, and jobs that were lost because of export opportunities denied to U.S. producers. There is no reason for an outpouring of U.S. gratitude for Japanese magnanimity. Dispassionate observers have ample reason to characterize Japanese trade behavior as still operating on a double standard between minimal willingness to accept foreign competition in Japan's home market and maximum expectation that the rest of the world should welcome unlimited Japanese exports and investments. Reminiscing about his mid-1980s assignment in Japan, a *Washington Post* reporter wrote of the factories he visited "where managers were quite open about their goals. It was to ship the maximum number of the plant's products to foreign countries and make a substitute for everything that those . . . countries might want to sell to Japan."[106]

The hard-line assessment of Japan finds the evidence overwhelming that, despite an unprecedented three decades of non-stop unilateral liberalization measures, the Japanese market — deliberately and inadvertently — still is without peer in causing problems for foreign exporters. The reason is simple: Japan's model of capitalism is different. It reflects a uniquely strong sense of national identity and an equally strong determination to protect the "essence of Japaneseness" against dilution from excessive foreign influences. U.S. critics of Japan suggest that Americans who defend Japan's actions should be closely screened. Too many of them allegedly either are free-market ideologues ignorant of the Japanese system or have a personal financial stake in promoting nonprotectionist U.S. policies.

This concludes the recitation of the charges and countercharges — offered without judgment as to accuracy or fairness — that comprise the public debate on bilateral trade frictions. The next chapter is designed to provide a reality check. It seeks to debunk the more egregious distortions embedded in the mutually exclusive analysis articulated by dedicated, uncompromising advocates of the pro-Japanese and the pro-U.S. perspectives.

## NOTES

1. Kenneth B. Pyle, *The Japanese Question: Power and Purpose in a New Era* (Washington: The AEI Press, 1992), pp. 3–4.

2. Ruth Benedict, *The Chrysanthemum and the Sword* (New York: Meridian Books, 1972), p. 1.

3. Henry Kissinger, *White House Years* (Boston: Little Brown, 1979), pp. 321–22.

4. Mitsuyuki Masatsugu, *The Modern Samurai Society* (New York: American Management Association, 1982), p. 91.

5. Ivan P. Hall, "Samurai Legacies, American Illusions," *The National Interest* (Summer 1992), p. 16.

6. Quoted in James Fallows, "Containing Japan," *Atlantic* (May 1989), p. 48.

7. William Chapman, "Now the Japanese Are Acting as if They're Number One," *Washington Post*, July 15, 1984, p. B1.

8. Masayoshi Hotta, as quoted in Steven Schlossstein, *Trade War* (New York: Congon and Weed, 1984), p. 104.

9. Hall, "Samurai Legacies," p. 17.

10. See, for example, *New York Times Magazine*, August 28, 1988, p. 74.

11. As quoted in *The Wall Street Journal*, November 19, 1982, p. 33.

12. Jared Taylor, *Shadows of the Rising Sun* (New York: William Morrow, 1983), p. 35. Another example of Japanese attitudes toward foreigners during the Tokugawa period was Dutch traders who were allowed to live on an island in the port of Nagasaki and were barred from being buried on Japanese soil if they died there.

13. Masao Miyamoto, *Straitjacket Society — An Insider's Irreverent View of Bureaucratic Japan* (Tokyo: Kodansha International, 1994), p. 143.

14. See, for example, *Financial Times*, September 4, 1986, p. 48.

15. See, for example, *New York Times*, March 6, 1988, p. IV-4.

16. Interview with European Union Commission official, November 1995.

17. "Flippant Remark Haunts Japanese Official at Meeting," *Washington Post*, January 19, 1986, p. C1.

18. Office of Senator John Heinz, press release, July 10, 1989, p. 3.

19. Office of Senator John Danforth, press release, January 13, 1986, p. 1.

20. "The Japan Trade Drama," *Washington Post*, December 22, 1996, p. C6.

21. Karel van Wolferen, "The Japan Problem," *Foreign Affairs* (Winter 1986–87), p. 293.

22. Karel van Wolferen, *The Enigma of Japanese Power* (New York: Alfred A. Knopf, 1989), p. 420.

23. George Soros, "After Black Monday," *Foreign Policy* (Spring 1988), p. 77.

24. Fallows, "Containing Japan," p. 51.

25. James C. Abegglen, "Narrow Self-Interest: Japan's Ultimate Vulnerability?" in Diane Tasca, ed., *U.S.-Japanese Economic Relations: Cooperation, Competition, and Confrontation* (New York: Pergamon, 1980), p. 27.

26. Dan Henderson, as quoted in Bela Balassa and Marcus Noland, *Japan in the World Economy* (Washington: Institute for International Economics, 1988), p. 215.

27. Peter F. Drucker, *The New Realities* (New York: Harper & Row, 1989), pp. 130–31.

28. "Our Problem Is Not Japan or Germany," *The Wall Street Journal*, December 22, 1989, p. A6.

29. Charles H. Ferguson, "America's High-Tech Decline," *Foreign Policy* (Spring 1989), p. 125; House Ways and Means Committee, *Statement of American Motors Corporation, Testimony before the House Ways and Means Committee*, September 29, 1982, p. 1.

30. Data from the law firm of Wilmer, Cutler, and Pickering, counsel to Cray Research. Some would argue that if a Japanese company can legitimately underbid an efficient U.S. supercomputer producer in the U.S. market, the yen is undervalued and should appreciate considerably.

31. Richard C. Koo, "The Yen's Appreciation and the Nature of Policy Debate in Japan" (paper, November 17, 1994), p. 4.

32. U.S. Semiconductor Industry Association, "The Effect of Government Targeting on World Semiconductor Competition," 1983, p. 82.

33. U.S. Trade Representative, "Japan — Measures Affecting Consumer Photographic Film and Paper," press release, February 20, 1997, p. 2.

34. House Ways and Means Committee, *High Technology and Japanese Industrial Policy: A Strategy for U.S. Policymakers*, October 1980, p. 13.

35. Eamonn Fingleton, "Japan's Invisible Leviathan," *Foreign Affairs* (March-April 1995), p. 78.

36. Interviews, November 1996. By declaring the satellites to be for "research," the bidding process did not have to be fully open to foreign companies.

37. "Be Patient and Industrious, West Told," *Financial Times*, December 18, 1984, p. 6 (special section on Japan).

38. *London Sunday Times*, February 21, 1982, n.p.

39. "Wood Products Enter the Trade Battle," *The Wall Street Journal*, June 15, 1989, p. A10.

40. Interview, June 1989.

41. "Japan's Oil Import Argument," *New York Times*, January 21, 1985, p. D10.

42. Letter from BAE Automated Systems Inc. to the deputy assistant secretary of commerce for Japan, October 27, 1988.

43. *Japan Economic Journal*, December 6, 1981, as reproduced in Thomas R. Howell, William Noellert, Jesse Kreier, and Alan Wolff, *Steel and the State* (Boulder, Colo.: Westview Press, 1988), p. 210.

44. "Symbiotic Relationship in Danger," *Financial Times*, May 15, 1985, p. iv (special insert).

45. Correspondence from an executive at the Hyundai Motor Company, December, 1996. Hyundai at one point did export a limited number of special 1988 Olympics commemorative cars to Japan.

46. The American Chamber of Commerce in Japan, "United States-Japan 1995 Trade White Paper," p. 4.

47. Section 301 Petition filed by Allied-Signal Inc. in the Office of the U.S. Trade Representative, March 5, 1990, vol. I, pp. 20, 31, 45.

48. Fred Hiatt, "Hidden Wall: A Native Son Battles Japan's Trade Barriers," *Washington Post*, June 23, 1989, p. G1.

49. R. Taggart Murphy, *The Weight of the Yen — How Denial Imperils America's Future and Ruins an Alliance* (New York: W. W. Norton, 1996), p. 58.

50. William V. Rapp, "Japan's Invisible Barriers to Trade," in Thomas A. Pagel, ed., *Fragile Interdependence* (Lexington, Mass.: Lexington Books, 1986), p. 28.

51. Ibid.

52. U.S. Trade Representative, *1994 National Trade Estimate Report on Foreign Trade Barriers*, p. 182.

53. Mark Tilton, *Restrained Trade — Cartels in Japan's Basic Materials Industries* (Ithaca, N.Y.: Cornell University Press, 1996), pp. 22–24.

54. John P. Stern, "Between Bureaucrat and Buyer: The Role of Japanese Nonprofit Industry Groups in Braking Market Forces," 1995, p. 18, photocopy.

55. Michael Gerlach, "*Keiretsu* Organization in the Japanese Economy — Analysis and Trade Implications," in C. Johnson, L. Tyson, and J. Zysman, eds., *Politics and Productivity — How Japan's Development Strategy Works* (New York: Ballinger Publishing Co., 1989), p. 165.

56. Ibid., p. 166.

57. Dick K. Nanto, "Japan's *Keiretsu*: Industrial Groups as Trade Barriers," report for the Congressional Research Service, January 30, 1994, pp. 15–16.

58. Robert Z. Lawrence, "Japan's Different Trade Regime: An Analysis with Particular Reference to *Keiretsu*," *Journal of Economic Perspectives* (Summer 1993), pp. 13–14.

59. U.S. International Trade Commission, "Phase I: Japan's Distribution System and Options for Improving Its Access," June 1990, p. 36.

60. The Semiconductor Industry Association's graph is reproduced in Stephen D. Cohen, *Cowboys and Samurai — Why the United States Is Losing the Industrial Battle and Why It Matters* (New York: HarperCollins, 1991), p. 58.

61. *The Wall Street Journal*, April 2, 1993, p. A6.

62. Clyde Prestowitz, Jr., "Set Guidelines for Export Market Share," *New York Times*, December 11, 1988, p. III-2.

63. Only the most naive believed one Japanese explanation for this situation: because Japanese automobiles are smaller than U.S. models, fingernail-sized U.S. chips would not fit properly.

64. Interview with U.S. embassy official, Tokyo, April 1989.

65. Interview with a European business representative in Tokyo, April 1989.

66. Interview with U.S. embassy official, Tokyo, April 1989.

67. Calculated from data in The World Bank, *World Tables 1994*.

68. Council of Economic Advisers, *Annual Report, 1994* (Washington, D.C.: U.S. Government Printing Office, 1994), p. 216.

69. This is an estimate based on the 1986 ratios for these two countries as contained in "Analysis of the U.S.-Japan Trade Problem" (Report of the Advisory Committee for Trade Policy and Negotiations), February 1989, p. 56.

70. Edward J. Lincoln, *Japan's Unequal Trade* (Washington, D.C.: Brookings Institution, 1990), p. 47.

71. Ibid., p. 60.

72. Robert Z. Lawrence, "Imports in Japan: Closed Markets or Minds?" *Brookings Papers on Economic Activity* (2:1987), p. 523.

73. Lawrence, "Trade Regime," p. 7.

74. Calculated from data in International Monetary Fund, *Direction of Trade Statistics Yearbook, 1995*.

75. Carla Hills, "The United States, Japan, and Trade Policy in the Twenty-First Century," Office of the U.S. Trade Representative press release, October 13, 1989, p. 7.

76. MITI report on the overseas business activities of Japanese corporations, March 1996, as reproduced in Nomura Research Institute, "The Impact of the Yen's Appreciation on the Asian Economies," July 1996, p. 13.

77. The quote of Hidehiro Iwaki of the Nomura Research Institute was provided to the author without a formal source by Marcus Noland of the Institute for International Economics.

78. Robert Z. Lawrence, "How Open Is Japan?" in Paul Krugman, ed., *Trade with Japan — Has the Door Opened Wider?* (Chicago, Ill.: University of Chicago Press, 1991), pp. 25, 28.

79. Responding to Japan's structure of high prices, the Organization for Economic Cooperation and Development, in its 1989 annual economic review of Japan, urged this fabulously successful country to expend a greater effort to raise the country's living standards. "There is still a substantial discrepancy between the country's economic strength and the relatively poor quality of life," the report concluded, noting that the country ranked fifth among industrial countries in per capita income, but tenth in purchasing power. ("OECD Calls on Tokyo to Lift Living Standards," *New York Times*, December 27, 1989, p. D2.)

80. For a more complete listing of these surveys, see Marcus Noland, "Why Are Prices in Japan So High?" *Japan and the World Economy* 7 (1995), pp. 255–56.

81. Lawrence, "How Open Is Japan?" p. 26.

82. Japanese Economic Planning Agency, "Price Report, 1989."

83. Council of Economic Advisers, *Annual Report, 1994*, p. 219.

84. Transcript of speech delivered by Ambassador Mickey Kantor to the Economic Strategy Institute, March 30, 1995, n.p.

85.   Hugh Patrick, "Crumbling or Transforming? Japan's Economic Success and its Postwar Economic Institutions," Working Paper No. 98 (New York: Columbia University, Columbia Business School, 1995), p. 15.

86.   See, for example, U.S. Department of Commerce, *Survey of Current Business*, May 1995, p. 77; Lawrence, "How Open Is Japan?" pp. 15–17.

87.   The American Chamber of Commerce in Japan, "United States-Japan 1995 Trade White Paper," p. 46.

88.   Ibid., pp. 68–69.

89.   U.S. House of Representatives Wednesday Group, "Beyond Revisionism: Towards a New US-Japan Policy for the Post–Cold War Era," March 1993, p. 17, photocopy.

90.   A dual-pricing phenomenon could not exist in the United States because entrepreneurs would seize the opportunity to re-import U.S.-made goods sold more cheaply abroad. Discount chains would gladly buy all such merchandise, and antitrust laws would deter manufacturers from interfering with the retail process.

91.   "Now Japan Is Feeling the Heat from the Gray Market," *Business Week*, March 14, 1988, p. 51.

92.   *Japan Times*, June 18, 1986, n.p.

93.   See, for example, "AT&T Unveils New 'Callback' Service in Japan," *The Wall Street Journal*, November 29, 1996, p. A4.

94.   U.S. Congress, Joint Economic Committee, *Restoring International Balance: Japan's Trade and Investment Patterns*, staff study, July 1988, p. 62.

95.   Federal Reserve Bank of Chicago, "Chicago Fed Letter," October 1989, p. 3.

96.   John Harvey-Jones, as quoted in *Japan Times*, June 17, 1986, n.p.

97.   "Council Declaration on EC-Japan Relations," European Community document, June 18, 1985, p. 1.

98.   "EEC-Japan Relations," European Community document, June 2, 1989, p. 1.

99.   Text of speech delivered by Sir Leon Brittan, January 16, 1992, p. 1.

100.   European Commission, "Frontier-free Europe (Supplement)," April 1996, p. 1.

101.   U.S. Congress, House Ways and Means Committee, Subcommittee on Trade, "Report on Trade Mission to Far East," December 1981, p. 17.

102.   Balassa and Noland, *World Economy*, p. 236.

103.   "For East Asia's Sake, Japan Should Open Up," *New Perspectives Quarterly* (Summer 1995), p. 51.

104.   Balassa and Noland, *World Economy*, p. 221.

105.   "ROC Battles Trade Deficit with Japan," *Free China Review* (April 1982), p. 55.

106.   John Burgess, "Signs of Change at Japan, Inc.," *Washington Post*, July 6, 1997, p. C2.

# 5

# How Not to Explain Bilateral Trade Problems: Myths, Distortions, and Half-Truths

Whatever is only almost true is quite false, and among the most dangerous of errors, because being so near truth, it is the more likely to lead astray.

— Henry Ward Beecher (1977, p. 192)

The public debate on the causes of bilateral trade imbalances and frictions has been distorted by an abundance of economically inaccurate and logically fallacious arguments. More than a case of different perceptions is involved. Conclusions frequently are based on situations or trends that never existed, that are no longer in existence, or that exist now in different forms than in previous years. This chapter seeks to narrow the gap between the arguments defending the Japanese viewpoint and those defending the U.S. viewpoint by discounting what I consider to be the smoke-and-mirrors element of bilateral relations. The critique that follows is aimed at what are arguably the major myths, distortions, and half-truths that have been advanced, deliberately and innocently, by both U.S. and Japanese observers.

## THE BILATERAL TRADE BALANCE IS THE TRUEST MEASURE OF BILATERAL RELATIONS AND BILATERAL TRADE BALANCES ARE COMPLETELY IRRELEVANT

The large, chronic U.S. trade deficit with Japan has long been the symbolic lightning rod attracting emotional reactions from both sides of the bilateral trade controversy. This is an unfortunate situation. Excessive attention has been lavished on the bilateral trade numbers, giving rise to exaggerated claims and marginal remedies. One side has used it as an empirical measure of the "Japan problem." The opposing viewpoint has dismissed it as utterly irrelevant.[1] The truth lies in between. The arithmetic of the U.S.-Japan trade imbalance can provide a potentially useful snapshot of relative macroeconomic conditions, corporate competitiveness, and consumer preferences at a moment in time.

Analysts with a positive perception of Japanese trading practices assert that bilateral merchandise trade deficits are not important. They contend that only a country's total, multilateral trade balance is significant (and the balance in goods and services is even more significant). This school of thought states that the United States does not and should not feel guilty about its individual bilateral surpluses and neither should Japan. Inevitably, trade surpluses will be recorded with some countries and deficits with others. Although this argument appears sound, it excludes some important issues. The size and longevity of Japan's surpluses raise some very interesting questions about why they exist. The "bilateral deficits don't matter" argument ignores the possibility that, if unusually large and persistent, the imbalance can signal that something is amiss in the underlying economic policies and trade practices of one or both countries.

Some justifications of Japan's trade surpluses do not hold up well under close scrutiny. The argument that it must massively export manufactured goods to finance its heavy dependence on imports of raw materials and fuels does not explain why manufactured goods exports need to exceed total imports by well over $100 billion annually. Defenders of Japan also note that it imports more U.S.-made goods (raw materials and manufactured goods) on a per-capita basis than the other way around. However, they never compare exports on a per-capita basis because it would show that Japan is far ahead.

A diametrically different interpretation of the bilateral disequilibrium is offered by Americans who believe that they are being victimized by the treachery of an adversarial trader. They cite large, chronic bilateral deficits as proof that the status quo in bilateral relations is unsatisfactory. Angered by Japan's long-running status as the source of the largest U.S. bilateral deficit, most of these critics would define a return to equilibrium as a long-overdue victory for U.S. trade policy and attainment of the elusive level playing field. This, too, is a distortion.

The main flaw in blaming the deficit for what is wrong in the bilateral relationship is that it implies that an end to the deficits would signal an end to all serious bilateral trade problems. This would not necessarily be the case. For example, the deficit may have temporarily dissipated because of a deep, prolonged recession in the United States that depressed import demand. The continued existence of serious market access issues, especially for sophisticated, high value-added U.S. goods, is of greater economic importance than whether the United States moves into equilibrium, or even a trade surplus, with Japan. A move toward bilateral equilibrium based solely on a volume surge in Japanese purchases of U.S. waste paper, cigarettes, coal, cotton, and other low value-added goods might boost Americans' morale, on the one hand. On the other hand, such a change would cause a deterioration in the U.S. terms of trade (average export prices relative to import prices), and, for reasons explained below, would keep the more important U.S. high-tech sector at a serious disadvantage.

In short, the sources of the imbalance and the reasons for its permanence are more significant than its size in economic terms. The deficit's longevity, despite three decades of being the target of every known conventional economic adjustment measure found in the economic policymaker's toolbox, reinforces the thesis that a systemic problem exists.

## U.S. TRADE DEFICITS WITH JAPAN ARE THE INESCAPABLE OUTGROWTH OF MACROECONOMIC TRENDS

Sophisticated defenses of Japanese trade practices invariably assert that the structural U.S. trade deficit with that country is the inexorable outgrowth of macroeconomic trends. The gist of this argument is that Japan's high rate of saving is the ultimate cause of its structural trade surplus. Likewise, too much consumption and insufficient saving are seen as the ultimate causes of the U.S. structural trade deficit. When U.S. tax rates were slashed by the introduction of Reaganomics in the early 1980s, low saving rates and a soaring budget deficit — not sudden changes in the Japanese economy — resulted in a massive increase in the U.S. trade deficit. A country whose pool of private and governmental saving is greater (or less) than the value of its outlays for domestic investment will have a surplus (or deficit) in its current account, that is, its balance of trade in goods and services, of approximately the same magnitude as the saving-investment discrepancy. A statistical identity makes a country's current account balance equal the sum of private saving and net government saving (tax revenues less spending), minus expenditures for domestic investment.

The macroeconomic arguments most often employed in the bilateral trade debate constitute a misrepresentation of an economic truism. A relatively high rate of saving does not automatically correlate with a merchandise trade surplus. Singapore's very high saving rate in the early 1990s, averaging about 45 percent annually, was significantly higher than that of Japan, but Singapore still imported more goods than it exported.[2]

When carried one step further, the popular macroeconomic argument claims that the relatively low rate of U.S. saving and its large federal budget deficit automatically and irrevocably impose a current account deficit on the United States, while Japan's high rate of saving makes inevitable a Japanese trade surplus. This claim leads to the erroneous policy conclusion that *only* internal macroeconomic changes — an increase in private U.S. saving and/or a decrease in the federal budget deficit — can reduce or eliminate U.S. trade deficits with Japan.

This line of reasoning ignores the fact that the statistical identity refers to only the state of a country's multilateral balance of goods and services. Increased U.S. saving would not necessarily cause any improvement in its bilateral deficits with Japan. It is possible (but not probable) that the United States could experience sufficient improvement in its saving-investment imbalance to generate a multilateral equilibrium in its current account composed of continued massive merchandise deficits with Japan that are offset by larger surpluses with the rest of the world.

More importantly, there is nothing in the saving-investment imbalance relationship to indicate causality. Only a statistical identity is implied. Declining strength in a country's export sector associated with a competitiveness problem could, in theory, cause a downturn in aggregate saving and an increase in the government's budget deficit.[3] This means that it is possible that an autonomous upsurge in the ability of U.S. industry to sell its goods overseas — through some combination of lower production costs, reduced foreign trade barriers, accelerated product innovations, and exchange rate depreciation — could initiate a sustained reduction in the U.S. current account deficit. It is erroneous to assert that, excluding greater U.S. saving or a reduced budget deficit, increased U.S. exports to Japan would automatically have to be offset by an equivalent increase in U.S. imports.

A sizable increase in U.S. exports to Japan and elsewhere, other things held constant, would reduce (but probably not eliminate completely) the saving-investment imbalance. Increased foreign sales would lead to higher rates of employment. This change would increase the pool of individual and corporate saving by an indeterminate amount, and reduce the government budget deficit through increased tax revenues and decreased outlays for unemployment and welfare benefits. By increasing U.S. national income, however, an export boom would also stimulate growth in imports; hence, elimination of the U.S. current account deficit is unlikely unless total U.S. saving also increases.

Nothing in this loosening of the "iron laws of macroeconomics" causing U.S. trade imbalances should be construed as a denial of the inherent desirability of enlarging the pool of U.S. saving and further shrinking federal budget deficits. Both changes would be healthy in the long-term for the U.S. economy, but they are not the only vehicles for improving the

U.S. international trade balance. The continuation of very large U.S. trade deficits in 1996 and 1997, despite the near elimination of the budget deficit, is empirical proof of this assertion. The bottom line is simply that the United States has a relatively painless, export-led option to reduce the saving-investment imbalance that would also induce adjustment in the overall U.S. current account deficit and possibly reduce the bilateral trade deficit with Japan.

## JAPAN IS THE MOST OPEN MARKET IN THE WORLD

If measured solely by overt, conventional, at-the-border trade barriers, Japan's market is relatively open to imports. The average rate of tariffs is among the world's lowest, and the number of goods subject to quantitative quotas compares favorably with other countries. Claims that serious market access problems in Japan do not exist are fallacious; the reason lies in what is excluded from this overly narrow measure of protectionism. Some politically sensitive goods are still protected by high tariffs (averages can hide a multitude of very high individual tariff rates) or quotas. Moreover, serious impediments remain despite relatively low tariff and nontariff trade barriers. Congressional Research Service analyst Dick Nanto states that some regulatory gates "are narrow and only slightly ajar or lead to lengthy passageways which can take the neophyte nowhere." The Japanese bureaucracy's broad regulatory and discretionary powers are a particular problem in a country where domestic interests can "capture the government regulatory process" relatively easily.[4]

The declaration of an open market in Japan is also fallacious to the extent that it ignores the import-discouraging nature of purely domestic economic policies, such as tolerance of cartels, and of business practices that favor entrenched domestic companies. Group members of so-called horizontal *keiretsu* tend to do business with one another whenever possible, while vertical *keiretsu* demonstrate the importance attached to preserving long-term business relationships between suppliers and customers. (Chapter 4 contains a more detailed discussion of market access problems.)

## THE JAPANESE MARKET IS CLOSED, AND CONSUMERS ARE PREJUDICED AGAINST IMPORTED GOODS

Japan's relatively small amount of imported manufactured goods is often cited as proof that it is still a highly protectionist country. This is a gross overgeneralization. Japan could not have become the world's third largest importer if it was a closed market. Furthermore, given its relative lack of natural resources, it is to be expected that a relatively high percentage of Japan's imports will be primary products, that is, raw materials, fossil fuels, and food. Japan's comparative advantage lies in adding value to primary products in the manufacturing process. Most market access problems in Japan are a function of degree and persistence, not the result of an outright closed door. Very difficult and unique would be more accurate descriptions of exporting problems encountered by foreign companies.

By the mid-1990s, data suggested that a disproportionate number of market access problems in Japan affected exporters of components and capital goods (for example, machinery sold to companies for use in producing other goods or to government agencies for use in providing official services). These exporters continued to face frequent discrimination from companies refusing to change suppliers and from governmental preference to procure domestically produced goods.

One market access grievance that is no longer valid is the generalized assertion that the Japanese public is reluctant to buy imported consumer goods, either out of a sense of national obligation or a chauvinistic feeling that domestically-made goods are of higher quality and better tailored to the special needs of Japanese people. Trade statistics and reports in the business press suggest that most foreign producers of high quality, competitively priced consumer goods can cultivate a responsive and increasingly profitable market there as long as they are prepared to make a major commitment of time, energy, and money. Several factors seem to be responsible for transforming Japan into a reasonably accessible market for most imported consumer goods. First, Japanese shoppers have become more price conscious, especially during the prolonged period of slower income growth in the post-bubble 1990s; discount stores featuring price-competitive imports have proliferated. Second, tariffs and many nontariff barriers have been reduced. Third, for an increasing number of low-technology goods, consumers have no choice but to buy imports. Rising wages and yen appreciation have brought to Japan the same phenomenon experienced earlier by the United States: shifting production of labor-intensive and mature technology goods (for example, apparel and radios) to lower-wage countries.

As for the external factors boosting imports of consumer goods, the quality of many foreign-made goods is at least equal to their Japanese competition, and more foreign producers are willing and able to provide the meticulous marketing and after-sales service needed to please Japan's demanding consumers. The most successful exporters of consumer goods tend to be those who have established their own distribution network, thereby leapfrogging Japan's notoriously byzantine system.

## ONLY THE VENGEFUL, PREJUDICED, OR MISGUIDED ASSERT THAT JAPAN IS SIGNIFICANTLY DIFFERENT FROM THE UNITED STATES

Some observers reject the premise that the Japanese economy is significantly different from the U.S. economy. Conservative U.S. economists and Japanese analysts argue that the basic laws of capitalism are universal and inviolable, that is, the inflexible rules of the marketplace impose the same discipline and rewards on the private sector in every capitalist country. The Japanese economy, according to this view, has thrived simply because it embodies the standard criteria of success: a policy environment fostering private enterprise and price stability; relatively high rates of saving and investment; innovative and bright management; skilled, disciplined workers; and so forth.

Another reason for declaring that Japan's economic order is not different is a calculated effort to provide support for the position that U.S. trade policy should impose no demands on Japan that differ from those made on all other trading partners. If Japan is viewed as being merely a better practitioner of traditional U.S. values, such as hard work, the whole panoply of aggressive U.S. trade policies aimed at Japan is discredited. Accusations that Japan is an adversarial trader, continuous demands for liberalization of the Japanese economy and for changes in business practices, threats of unilateral retaliation if U.S. demands are not met, use of results-oriented trade policies to ensure Japanese compliance with trade agreements, and so on make no sense if directed to a replica of the U.S. economy. Ardent free trade advocate Jagdish Bhagwati brandished the classic argument for a soft line in bilateral U.S. trade policy when he expressed "serious problems" with the notion that Japanese institutions are so "different" that they "effectively impede imports."[5]

The "no big difference" approach is of dubious substantive validity. Calling Japan unique is neither inaccurate nor insulting. It merely restates what the Japanese say about themselves, and it states the obvious: all countries are unique. (Arguably, the United States and Japan are two countries that are "uniquely unique.") In the highly charged debate about U.S.-Japan trade problems, Americans who describe Japan as being different risk being labeled by the opposing viewpoint as "bashers," "revisionists," or even worse, "racists." Those who emphasize differences between the countries might better be dubbed "realists." They say the same thing as the growing ranks of Japanese public officials and scholars who publicly affirm, and often revel in, the distinctive qualities of the Japanese economy.

Markets in individual countries behave differently because the regulations and institutions that set the standards for buying and selling vary from country to country. Society shapes economic goals and activities; the economic order serves social desires. I do not share the tendency of "pure" economists to discount a nation's history and institutions in determining its economic performance. Two conclusions follow from the underlying assumption that a country's beliefs and history influence the nature and performance of its economic system. First, significant social differences between the United States and Japan were responsible for dissimilar evolutions in their domestic economic orders. Second, these domestic differences contributed directly to dissimilar international trade policies and performances.

Economic differences begin with differences in national experience and values. A Japanese political scientist concluded that theories emanating from extensive self-examination of *Nihonjinron* (the theory and study of Japanese-ness) for the most part "have concluded that Japan simply is different from the rest of the world."[6] Central to what sets Japan apart have been two millennia of determination and success in protecting its political independence and in preserving its "distinctive" culture. Many other great cultures have existed throughout history, a Japanese historian observed, but none of them is part of a single web that has "survived intact to become part of the modern life of a nation, to be absorbed into its industrial, scientific, and artistic strength, as is the case with Japan. In that sense, Japan seems a country filled with a strange wonder, at once ancient and new. There is not another case like it in the history of the world."[7]

Centuries of isolation and borders closed to foreigners have created a "cultural self-colonization" in Japan, allowing its racial and ethnic homogeneity to remain intact and permitting it to modernize its society while preserving a sense of its own special identity. The Japanese possess a "distinctive ethos in which both tradition and modernity coexist without contradiction."[8] In sum, "The genius of Japan's response to the challenges of modernity has been its ability to adopt foreign forms but to render them Japanese in substance, to become modern without becoming Western."[9]

The United States is a country that never passed through a feudal tradition. It is richly endowed with land and natural resources, and collectively views the economic order as a means to maximize consumption and expedite the achievement of the good life. Western values are centered on individual rights and self-fulfillment. We expect to create rather than to inherit our own individual social and economic relationships and assume they ultimately will be protected by explicit contractual rules.

A socialization process is at work in both countries, but it offers disparate definitions of proper behavior in social and business situations. Peer group pressure affects human behavior in both countries, but it distributes rewards and penalties for different sets of actions and attitudes. Americans and Japanese are very much alike in pursuing self-interest as they understand it. Bombarded by different societal cues, they use dissimilar criteria in determining "rational" economic behavior. Japanese

people would respond to the same incentives the same way Americans
do if "they saw themselves in the same situation faced with the same
choices; however, they often are not. The context of decision making in
Japanese society is different. The constraints within which choices are
made are not the same. The institutions that constrain behavior may have
the same labels — 'corporation,' 'labor union,' 'democratic political system,' — but those words represent different phenomena in Japan."[10]

Different conceptions of self in the two societies are manifestations of
differing emphases on "rights versus obligations, on autonomy versus
interdependence, on the pursuit of happiness versus personal sacrifice,
and on the priority of the individual versus that of the group — differences that have broad ramifications for the structure of political, economic, and social institutions."[11]

Different societal values and history do not necessarily mean that
Japan's economy functions in a substantially different manner from that
of the United States. It is necessary for economic institutions (capital and
labor markets, corporate structure, government regulation, and so on) to
differ, and they do. Corporations and labor must respond to economic
forces in different ways, and they do. Because it was forced to play catch-
up with the West to avoid colonization and because it views the economic order as a means to encourage social stability and enhance national
security, Japan developed an economic order tailored to its distinct needs.

Japan's acceptance of a major role for government in managing the
economy and its preference for group collaboration over arms-length
competition guided solely by market forces have directly contributed to a
producer-oriented economy in which consumers' interests are of secondary importance. Among the major features of Japan's economic landscape are corporate alliances known as *keiretsu*. Formed around a bank
and a trading company, the horizontal variant of these groups is comprised of a number of manufacturing and service companies that collectively own most of each others' stock, coordinate management strategy,
and are naturally predisposed to procure goods and services from one
another. Bankruptcies of *keiretsu* companies are virtually unknown.

Government officials tolerate and sometimes encourage collusion
among industry cartels, insider trading in the stock market, and bid rigging in the construction industry. Such activities are illegal in the United
States. Corporate executives, in turn, have infinitely higher tolerance levels than their U.S. counterparts for direct government regulation and
indirect regulation through administrative guidance — in part because
Japan's major economic ministries have sought to reduce corporate risk.
In a pure market economy, errant industrial and banking corporations
face the threat of bankruptcy and the need to lay off workers, "But these
things are not supposed to happen in Japan, and in the end it is up to the
Finance Ministry to ensure that they don't."[12]

The views of several influential Japanese policymakers and opinion makers lend further credence to the argument that the Japanese and U.S. economic systems function in fundamentally different ways. Eisuke Sakakibara, a senior Ministry of Finance official and scholarly author, denies that Japan's economy belongs to the same regime as Western capitalism "just because it uses market mechanisms extensively and exists side by side with a democratic political system." Japan, in his words, "has developed a somewhat unique model of a mixed economy" and has established a "non-capitalist market economy." The Japanese economic system "is not capitalist" because 60 to 70 percent of the equity of most corporations is owned not by individuals but by other corporations, principally banks and affiliated companies of the *keiretsu* group. Because the "core of the Japanese private sector" is composed of major corporations whose "interlocking share holdings keep them independent from capital" markets, corporate executives are mainly responsible to their employees.[13] Sakakibara is quite happy with these differences, suggesting that proposals to impose U.S.-style deregulation on the Japanese economy represent "nothing but an act of barbarism against our national cultural values."[14]

The "Japan is not different" school of thought has been further undermined by the public campaign of officials in Japan's Ministry of Finance urging developing countries and countries in transition from central planning to pay closer attention to its distinctive development experience. They are not pleased that the United States has imposed its free-market ideological convictions on the World Bank and the International Monetary Fund with the result that their lending strategies center on privatization and laissez-faire economic policies in borrowing countries. Senior Japanese civil servants have informally advised countries like Russia and Vietnam to incorporate into their long-term development plans Japan's unique blend of private markets and industrial policies that target key industries for official nurturing.[15]

The late Naohiro Amaya, who rose to the vice-ministerial position at the Ministry of International Trade and Industry, wrote: "Postwar Japan defined itself as a cultural state holding the principles of liberalism, democracy, and peace, but these were only superficial principles (*tatemae*); the fundamental objective (*honne*) was the pouring of all our strength into economic growth."[16] Amaya is quoted elsewhere as asserting that postwar Japan "did the opposite of what the American economists said [to do]. We broke all the rules."[17]

Ichiro Ozawa, leader of the New Frontier Party (presently Japan's largest opposition party), approached the issue of Japanese uniqueness from a different direction. He became the most visible advocate for economic deregulation as a way of making Japan a "normal nation," defined as one that assumed political and economic "responsibilities regarded as natural in the international community."[18] Another of his suggestions is the "third opening of Japan," which, unlike its predecessors in 1853 and 1945, would be a voluntary, self-initiated effort to make the country more accessible to foreign goods.[19]

Three important caveats must accompany this assessment of significant differences existing between the U.S. and Japanese economic systems. First, no specific set of "appropriate" U.S. trade policies — aggressive, soft-line, or neutral — inevitably follow; domestic economic differences are only one part of the larger context of bilateral relations in which optimal international economic policy should be determined. Second, a distinctive Japanese economy does not dictate a bilateral trade surplus or deficit of any particular size with any given country. Finally, claiming major differences exist between the two countries in no way constitutes a value judgment that one economic system is better than the other or that Japan is an expansionist, predatory trading country that needs to be contained.

## THE WORLD SHOULD WELCOME THE JAPANESE SURPLUS IN GOODS AND SERVICES BECAUSE IT NEEDS JAPAN'S HIGH RATE OF SAVING AND CAPITAL OUTFLOWS

The deficit in the overall U.S. balance of payments in the 1950s and early 1960s was a major catalyst in financing postwar reconstruction in Western Europe and, to a lesser extent, in Japan. A large surplus in goods and services trade was offset by a larger deficit in the capital account caused by U.S. capital outflows exceeding inflows. Other countries recognized the benefits of accumulating dollars, and they made no complaints. In accounting terms, the same situation exists at present in Japan's balance of payments. Instead of graciously accepting the inflow of capital from Japan needed to offset their inadequate saving, however, other countries have been relentless in their demands that Japan reduce its current account surplus (even though this would reduce Japan's net outflow of capital — the offset to its current account surplus). In the 1990s, critics, rightly or wrongly, focused less on the positive aspects of Japan's capital account deficits and more on Japan's paucity of imports relative to exports as a "significant drag on world growth."[20]

At first glance, Japan's high rate of saving seems essential for financing investment in a world in which most countries prefer consumption over capital formation. However, there is a more attractive alternative: let Japan provide capital to other countries in the form of payments for increased imports. This kind of economic transaction immediately stimulates economic activity, and it does not have to be repaid with interest or in the form of repatriated profits from incoming foreign direct investment. Furthermore, there is no fixed correlation between changes in a country's current account position and outflows of long-term capital. Even after Japan became the world's largest aid donor, in some years its overall long-term capital flows declined. During the early 1990s, the lion's share of its capital outflows took the form of less-desirable (from the borrowers' viewpoint), short-term capital flows, mainly short-term lending by Japanese banks.[21] Another reason for questioning whether Japan necessarily plays the role of optimal saver for the world is the fact that the final destination of all its considerable capital outflows during the bubble years is unknown. Much of the increase in capital outflows took the form of Japanese investors buying convertible bonds floated by Japanese companies in the Eurobond market; how these corporations then disposed of dollars received outside of Japan is not recorded on Japanese balance of payments tables.[22]

Foreign gratitude for Japanese capital outflows is tempered further by perceptions of a fundamental difference between its contemporary trade surpluses and those of the United States in the early postwar period. During the 1950s, foreign complaints about impediments to U.S. market access were negligible. This is not the case with Japan today. In pursuit of foreign policy goals, the United States readily accepted discrimination against its goods (as seen, for example, in the provisions of the European Payments Union created in 1950) and multilateral tariff-cutting agreements in the General Agreement on Tariffs and Trade that were more favorable to exports from other countries.

## AMERICAN COMPANIES FINDING IT DIFFICULT TO PENETRATE THE JAPANESE MARKET SHOULD CONCENTRATE INSTEAD ON FASTER GROWING ASIAN MARKETS

With dozens of countries experiencing higher growth rates as their governments increasingly rely on market-driven economic policies, the United States is sometimes charged with being fixated on improving market access in Japan. East Asia's unprecedented economic boom has created a fast-rising demand for foreign goods. China seems to have an almost unlimited potential for increased imports of goods and services. On the surface, it would seem logical for U.S. corporations that complain about securing little or no market share in Japan, to shift personnel and financial resources to maximize allegedly better business opportunities in more open countries. A deeper scrutiny of the situation, however, suggests the Japanese market is simply too big and important to justify perfunctory marketing efforts. In the first place, it is not an either-or situation. Most dynamic, export-oriented corporations of at least medium size can invest resources in most, if not all, potentially lucrative overseas markets.

For at least five reasons, a collective drift of U.S. industry into "Japan fatigue" would be a dangerous, costly scenario that should be strongly discouraged:

Japan is the world's second largest market for most manufactured goods and the largest for some products, notably semiconductors. As such, the ability to cultivate Japan as a successful export market is an important means to the critical goal of maximizing sales volume. The latter is essential to achieving the economies of scale necessary to amortize high, fixed production costs of high-tech goods and thereby minimize unit production costs. Maximizing sales volume also generates the profits that encourage expenditures for research and development and for outlays on new plant and capital equipment — two more business strategies essential to retaining global competitiveness in high value-added industrial goods.

Experience suggests that it is unhealthy or fatal for foreign manufacturers to allow their Japanese competitors to operate in a protected home sanctuary. The absence of foreign competition seems to facilitate the recurring pattern of using high prices within the Japanese market to offset rock bottom prices of exported goods.

If a foreign company can succeed in the country with the harshest combination of government regulation, collusion among entrenched corporate interests, and finicky consumers, it can succeed anywhere. Japan, in some ways, is the ultimate testing ground for all aspects of the marketing process.

A full-scale business presence is essential for assuring a quick, complete knowledge and understanding of the increasing numbers of technological, scientific, product, and marketing innovations originating in a Japan that is shedding its reputation of an unimaginative "copy cat."

The outlook is for more, not less, access to the Japanese market. Foreign companies will benefit as deregulation of the business sector slowly but surely continues.

## THE END OF THE JAPANESE
## ECONOMIC MIRACLE IS AT HAND

A combination of faulty economic analysis and wishful thinking by some U.S. analysts has perpetuated an assembly line of erroneous forecasts of an impending demise in Japanese competitiveness. The reasoning, but not the inaccuracy, has changed over the past three decades. The tendency for many Americans to grossly underestimate Japan's underlying competitive strengths and its ability to overcome economic setbacks has been the common thread.

One of the earliest bearish forecasts predicted that rising Japanese wages would undermine an international competitiveness built mainly on cheap labor. On several occasions, beginning in December 1971, yen appreciation against the dollar triggered projections that many Japanese goods soon would be priced out of the U.S. market and U.S. goods would enjoy an upsurge in the Japanese market. In the 1980s, the theory of Japan "hitting the wall" after it caught up with Western technology became popular; it asserted that the lack of Japanese creativity would become a serious problem once that country was forced to stop imitating others and break new ground. Demographics become the next alleged indicator of diminished industrial competitiveness: an aging Japanese population would require more government financial support and the hardworking work force would gradually be replaced by a younger generation, fewer in number and more hedonistic and individualistic because they are unfamiliar with hard times and the need to sacrifice.

In the 1990s, Japanese and U.S. handwringers have predicted that Japan's financial crisis and slower growth would cause a serious cutback in bank loans and an increased emphasis on profits. They believe that the stampede to offshore production by Japan's biggest exporters will hollow out its industrial sector. Even in the post–bubble era, tears should not be shed for a country with a proven ability to work harder and smarter when it is facing tough times and one that has a highly educated work force and a government system that clearly protects and promotes industrial corporations. Japan still exudes a single-minded national compulsion for industrial strength. It continues to allocate relatively large amounts of capital to research and development and to investment in new plants and equipment. These are the kinds of expenditures that support the ability of Japanese industry to move constantly up-market to provide state-of-the-art capital goods that often are unavailable from other sources. As demonstrated by the United States, the ability to develop new products is a far more important determinant of economic succes than the need to shift some old products to offshore production.

## NOTES

1. A pure economic theory variant on the significance of the bilateral trade balance argues that by running consistent deficits, the United States is the clear winner. When the United States is obtaining (on a net basis) real economic resources from Japan in exchange for often-depreciating money that the Japanese must then largely lend back to us, the American people are the net beneficiaries.

2. World Bank, *World Development Report, 1994*; American Express Bank, *Review*, October 1994; International Monetary Fund, *International Financial Statistics*, April 1996.

3.  For additional details, see Robert A. Blecker, *Beyond the Twin Deficits* (Armonk, N.Y.: M. E. Sharpe, Inc., 1992), Chap. 1.

4.  Dick K. Nanto, *Japan's Official Import Barriers*, Congressional Research Service Report, July 11, 1993, p. 15.

5.  Jagdish Bhagwati, "The Fraudulent Case against Japan," *The Wall Street Journal*, January 6, 1992, p. A14.

6.  Masaru Tamamoto, "The Ideology of Nothingness — A Meditation on Japanese National Identity," *World Policy Journal* (Spring 1994), p. 89.

7.  Daikichi Irokawa, *The Culture of the Meiji Period* (Princeton: Princeton University Press, 1985), p. 4.

8.  Fumie Kumagai, *Unmasking Japan Today: The Impact of Values on Modern Japanese Society* (Westport, Conn.: Praeger, 1996), p. 2.

9.  Fumio Matsuo, "Trade with a Moral Compass," *The Wall Street Journal*, December 6, 1994, p. A28.

10.  William K. Tabb, *The Postwar Japanese System — Cultural Economy and Economic Transformation* (New York: Oxford University Press, 1995), pp. 8, 13.

11.  Janet T. Spence, "Achievement American Style — The Rewards and Costs of Individualism," *American Psychologist* (December 1985), p. 1288.

12.  R. Taggart Murphy, *The Weight of the Yen — How Denial Imperils America's Future and Ruins an Alliance* (New York: W. W. Norton, 1996), pp. 263–64.

13.  Eisuke Sakakibara, *Beyond Capitalism — The Japanese Model of Market Economics* (Lanham, MD: University Press of America, 1993), pp. 1, 4, 14, 26.

14.  Quoted in *New York Times*, September 16, 1995, p. 31.

15.  See, for example, "Japanese Tout Their Brand of Capitalism, *Asian Wall Street Journal*, July 20, 1992, p. 22; "The Struggle for Vietnam's Soul," *The Economist*, June 24, 1995, p. 33.

16.  As translated from the Japanese in Kenneth B. Pyle, *The Japanese Question — Power and Purpose in a New Era* (Washington, D.C.: AEI Press, 1992), p. 36.

17.  As quoted in Clyde Prestowitz, Jr., "Beyond Laissez Faire," *Foreign Policy* (Summer 1992), p. 67.

18.  Ichiro Ozawa, *Blueprint for a New Japan — The Rethinking of a Nation* (Tokyo: Kodansha International, 1994), p. 94.

19.  Ichiro Ozawa, "The Third Opening," *The Economist*, March 9, 1996, p. 21.

20.  U.S. Treasury Department, "Statement of Lawrence H. Summers," press release, June 25, 1993, p. 3.

21.  Juha Kahkonen, "Japan's Capital Flows," in Ulrich Baumgartner and Guy Meredith, eds., *Saving Behavior and the Asset Price "Bubble" in Japan*, Occasional Paper Number 124 (Washington, D.C.: International Monetary Fund, 1995), p. 18, Table 3-1.

22.  Interview by telephone with International Monetary Fund official, June 1996.

# II

## WHY IT HAPPENED

# 6

# The Domestic Foundations of
# Japan's Foreign
# Trade Performance

Turning technology into products is where Japan is number one in the
world.

— Akio Morita (1989)

Japan's corporations have, in many cases, sacrificed potential and
legitimate profits in an effort to secure a strong place in the market;
taking razor thin profit margins which no Western company would
be able to tolerate. . . . This surely fails to embrace the *spirit* of competition found in the United States and Europe. . . . Foreign competitors . . . do not have the luxury of a sacrificing labor force and low
dividend outlays.

— Akio Morita (1992)

To understand what has caused Japan's extraordinary foreign trade performance since the late 1960s, one must first look to its source: Japan's
extraordinary domestic economic performance. [For the purposes of this
study, the term "economic performance" is limited to a focus on the cost
structure of the tradeable goods sector and the key domestic variables
influencing it: inflation rates, productivity increases, unit labor costs, cost
of capital, and so forth. International factors affecting the domestic cost
structure, mainly the exchange rate, are implicitly included in the variables.] It achieved extraordinary industrial success by cultivating new talents to complement traditional strengths. This was neither simple good
luck nor master conspiracy. The unequivocal national consensus, beginning in 1945, that short-term sacrifices were needed to assure economic

recovery and to accelerate catching up with the West was the starting point for Japan's economic renaissance. Traditions, intellect, and values then united government, corporations, and labor in an extraordinary cooperative effort to elevate the country from the rubble of war to an industrial superpower. The Japanese government established uniquely favorable conditions for economic expansion. Within this environment emerged a brilliant array of innovative managers and skilled, dedicated workers who spawned world-class corporations in one industry after another. The ability to translate the universal desire for economic growth and industrial competitiveness into reality in less than a generation puts Japan in an ultra-elite category.

Although there is extensive literature seeking to determine what brought about the Japanese economic "miracle," I have yet to find any thesis that exactly matches my assessment of the success dynamic. A unique confluence of internal factors launched Japan's industrial success and indirectly defined its export-generating strength and its low propensity to import manufactured goods. The ascendancy of a great "producer state" resulted from a societal emphasis on group interests and on the preservation of the Japanese character, an acute distrust of the rest of the world, a distinctive corporate structure, important innovations in the manufacturing process, and production-focused official policies. More importantly, these phenomena were mutually reinforcing.

Japan's economic dynamism is an example of synergy, the natural science phenomenon in which a number of substances or organisms combine to achieve greater results than they are capable of achieving individually. If any of the three principal generic ingredients of Japan's industrial strength discussed in this chapter had been absent, its economic recovery would have been radically altered. A holistic approach is the most appropriate methodology for explaining Japan's economic ascendancy — not a single-factor explanation. The Japanese economic process violates a rule of geometry: it is larger than the sum of its parts. Regrettably, no methodology exists for either assigning the various success-inducing factors a precise degree of importance or quantifying the ways each affects the other at any given point in time.

That Japan's economy fully recovered from World War II and kept growing was far from preordained. Indeed, success was improbable. Japan is a small, densely populated island possessing a minimum of natural resources. Among its economic practices that contradict the free market recipe for success are labor immobility and a rigid seniority system, concentrated industries (domination by a relatively few companies), lax antitrust enforcement, and active government involvement in economic planning.

## A THUMBNAIL SKETCH OF JAPAN'S
## ECONOMIC STRUCTURE

The wide spectrum of Japan's economy stretches from the superbly efficient to the dysfunctional. Most foreigners mistakenly assume that the large industrial companies that so successfully have penetrated global markets typify the entire Japanese economy. In fact, they account for very small percentages of total business enterprises and work force. They do contribute disproportionately to increased economic growth rates, living standards, productivity, and industrial sophistication as well as to Japan's visibility in world trade. The often overwhelming export success of these elite corporations conveys a deceptive aura of uniform excellence throughout Japan's economy. Beyond a relatively few — perhaps 100 — industrial companies, Japanese producers set no world standards for efficiency and market domination. The 40 companies with the largest reported export sales in 1994 represented approximately 55 percent of total Japanese exports. The comparable U.S. total was about 28 percent.[1]

Virtually all of the primary sector — agriculture and mining — is relatively inefficient. Services — the tertiary sector — represent neither a paragon of efficiency nor a strong competitor of the United States. The Japanese distribution and retail systems subordinate efficiency to the goals of minimizing unemployment and maximizing producers' control over retailers.[2]

A mixed picture appears even in the industrial sector — the core of Japan's international economic strength. U.S. companies continue to dominate several important information processing sectors, including software, multimedia, and logic chips (microprocessors). Japan's chemical and pharmaceutical industries display only average efficiency compared to U.S. counterparts. A 1993 study found the productivity (output divided by hours worked) in three industries — food processing, soaps and detergents, and beer — to be well below those prevailing in the United States.[3]

A close look behind the relatively few big electronics, automobile, and machinery companies dominating Japan's extraordinarily successful industrial sector reveals their heavy dependence on a network of relatively less-productive primary suppliers and subcontractors. A two-tiered, or dual, economic structure exists. Small and medium-sized enterprises are the norm in Japan's secondary (manufacturing) sector in both quantitative and qualitative terms. Only 0.2 percent of Japanese corporations employ more than 1,000 workers. Almost one-half of the work force, as of the late 1980s, toiled in factories of fewer than 50 workers.[4] Many of the second-tier companies functioning as suppliers and subcontractors of components for large manufacturers are "no more than sweatshops in which husband and wife may work ten or more hours a day."[5]

Competition among small businesses is fierce, bankruptcies are common-place, job security is rare, and workers regularly quit for better positions.

A unique symbiosis exists between Japan's relatively few manufacturing giants and their large network of suppliers. The latter (and their subcontractors) frequently are likened to shock absorbers in that they provide invaluable flexibility to the top-tier industrial companies. Heavy reliance on subcontracting permits the elite Japanese exporters to minimize the number of workers granted lifetime employment, impose price discipline on components, and decentralize the risks of cyclical fluctuations in demand. As part of a vertical *keiretsu*, a primary supplier has relatively little independence. It usually is not allowed to sell to its main customer's competitors. Suppliers and subcontractors are forced to absorb a disproportionate share of the cost-cutting drives that are regularly invoked by large Japanese manufacturers. Unwritten ground rules — based on economic dependence and respect for authority — mandate suppliers to work harder and not complain when their parent firm tells them to reduce prices, accelerate delivery schedules, or improve product quality.

The Japanese belief in reciprocal obligation partially offsets what Westerners perceive as exploitation of the weak by the strong. Primary suppliers can expect a guaranteed market, access to financial and technical assistance, and, in some cases, the large manufacturer may assume part ownership. The ground rules deter a big company from turning to cheaper domestic or foreign suppliers unless the status quo would put it at immediate financial risk. This loyalty creates potential inefficiencies. There are ample data, however, suggesting that market distortions caused by not switching to a lower-cost foreign supplier can be largely recouped through a number of intangibles prevalent in the Japanese economy. Customer-supplier loyalty seems to breed a better record of on-time delivery, quality control, and a more rapid and frictionless two-way communication flow. More importantly, the unique Japanese sense of obligation breeds contractors who possess a stoic willingness to spare no effort to be responsive to constant demands for cheaper goods and better performance — a patience based more on honor than economics.

Reciprocity, long-term commitments, . . . mutual trust, and the sharing of risks, costs, and benefits . . . help to hold together Japan's dual-structure economy; the relationship between large parent companies and their network of subcontractors and subsidiaries would be very different if Japanese buyers and suppliers did not adhere to this set of relational norms. The emphasis on collective goals . . . fits in well . . . with the capacity of government and business to form an identity of interests and reach consensus on a common set of collective goals.[6]

## THE ROLES OF HISTORICAL CIRCUMSTANCE AND CULTURAL FACTORS

The ultimate driving force behind Japanese economic behavior is the country's long-standing, collective dedication to keeping the rest of the world at arm's length. This far from universally accepted interpretation does not imply that the entire country wishes categorically to exclude foreign ideas, influence, and physical presence. Instead, the argument suggests a relatively fervent desire to maximize local control over the terms and extent of their influx. Maximum leverage over the external environment minimizes the ability of foreigners to disrupt Japan's internal affairs. A strong economy based on competitive industry and mastery of all important state-of-the-art technologies is more a means of guaranteeing social autonomy — that is, preserving the essence of their highly cherished Japanese-ness — than a materialist pursuit of higher living standards. If one does accept the control hypothesis, a lot of things fall into place: government policies, corporate strategies, and workers' attitudes in Japan all become elements of a behavior pattern that assists the largest group, the country, in its successful effort to keep outsiders at arm's length by means of industrial power.

The fusion of unique cultural, historical, and social factors was a major reason for Japan's developing a distinctive strain of capitalism as well as a cause of its success. This conclusion emanates from the school of thought that a society's value system provides more direction to its economy than its price mechanism. A sociohistorical approach seems especially relevant to Japan, where technical economic concepts seem singularly inadequate for explaining the speed and extent of the country's industrial successes. In a kind of oversize version of the Hegelian dialectic, modern Japanese history has unfolded as a conflict between a Japanese particularism determined to keep the core tenets of their culture unchanged and concerns about pervasive intrusion by Western values. The synthesis that emerged in the aftermath of both the Meiji Restoration and defeat in World War II was identical: the creation of a strong industrial base to neutralize the overwhelming power of the outside world and to control the inflow of foreign influences. The major difference between these two efforts is that military power was a large part of the equation until 1945.

Japan is the outstanding example of a country where economic modernization has neither diminished the veneration of societal values nor diluted the determination to protect them. The compulsion to preserve those values has led to a system of strong government that is less interested in protecting individual liberty than in assuring order and predictability. The quest for these two social conditions was infinitely complicated by the arrival of Commodore Perry's black ships in the 1850s.

This event formally ended Japan's physical and economic isolation, causing the permanent loss of its ability to control unconditionally the outside
world's access to the home islands and to the Japanese society. Uncontrollable, potentially unfriendly foreign forces have always represented
something between a potential and real threat to the nation's physical
security and value system.[7]

It is hard to exaggerate how much the feelings of insecurity and insularity have influenced modern Japan's thinking and economic behavior.
They are responsible for two dominant themes of the country's nine-
teenth- and twentieth-century history: catch up to and overtake the West
economically and be sufficiently powerful to expel unwanted traces of the
"foreign barbarians." In *The Enigma of Japanese Power*, Karel van Wolferen
wrote: "To a degree virtually inconceivable to Westerners, many Japanese
— with no religion beyond mere socio-political demands — found the
ultimate meaning of life, their existential lodestar, in the survival and welfare of the nation."[8]

Japanese leaders since 1868 have believed that the country's survival
required its becoming a modern Western state in a physical, but not cultural or spiritual, sense. Most Western values were and are demeaned, but
Western science and technology have been deemed vital necessities. A
Japanese-born scholar has written that the phrase *wakon yosai* — Japanese
spirit and Western ability — symbolizes the strong, unceasing Japanese
desire to "retain their culture, their way of life, the specific relationship
between superior and inferior, and their family structure, yet simultaneously to build a modern nation endowed with power that is comparable
to that of Western countries."[9] Japan has long manifested a love-hate attitude toward other countries that incorporates feelings of arrogance and
vulnerability along with attitudes of superiority and inferiority. Again, to
quote van Wolferen, "Men who do not appeal to universal rules in protecting their flanks at home are unlikely to believe that internationally
accepted rules, treaties, agreements, or promises are ultimately reliable.
Japan strives for industrial dominance because power is the only guarantee for safety; and military power is . . . for a long time to come, not feasible. Hence the continued voracity for foreign market shares and foreign
technology."[10]

Japan has twice played the role of an industrial latecomer consumed
with the desire to catch up with the West (after the Meiji Restoration and
after World War II). This goal shaped the country's institutions and the
general policy of government intervention in the economy. "Every country that has caught up with others has had to do so by rigging its rules:
extracting money from its people, steering it into industrialists' hands."[11]
Market forces and the theory of comparative advantage took a back seat
to nationalistic fears that if Japan failed to stay ahead of the West in the
race for economic and technological preeminence, the country would be

forced to the "periphery of economic activity, doomed to subordinate status as an industrial has-been."[12]

Defensive modernization for Japan has been successfully achieved in part because its leaders encouraged the assiduous study of the intellectual fruits of more powerful countries. Japan, for many centuries, has grafted useful foreign knowledge onto the immutable bedrock of traditional Japanese values. Michio Morishima believes that "By adapting . . . imported culture to her own cultural heritage and to local conditions, Japan was able to pursue her own unique development."[13] This statement was written in reference to Japan's absorbtion of portions of Chinese culture in the sixth century, but it describes precisely the results of the comprehensive surveys of Western institutions and scientific and technological advances initiated after the Meiji Restoration and intensified after World War II.

Citing culture as a factor in Japan's domestic economic success is subject to qualification. How to define the term and what elements to include in it are uncertain, as is the exact extent to which culture rather than circumstances prevailing at any given time determines national behavior. Japanese culture has changed over the country's long history, and deviations from behavioral norms are common, for example, militant labor activities during the 1950s. In any event, culture is broadly defined here as "a system of inter-related values, active enough to condition perception, judgment, communication, and behaviour in a given society."[14] On a more specific basis, culture accounts for "that middle ground between universal characteristics of our species and the individual's idiosyncratic characteristics." The term encompasses the traits, behavior, and modes of thinking shared by members of one nation-state that are distinguishable from those of other countries.[15] Under either definition, a number of unchanging values and behavioral patterns have been important components of the synergy creating and shaping the Japanese model of economic development.

Many of the important values and behavioral traits of modern Japan became ingrained during the two and one-half centuries of the Tokugawa period. From 1600 until 1868, the government imposed near-total isolation of Japan from the rest of the world to prevent potential dissidents from acquiring foreign ideas and weapons. The overriding political objective of the ruling shoguns during this period was the preservation of their absolute rule. To this end, the Tokugawa shogunate emphasized regimentation and established a centralized feudal structure controlled by regional lords (daimyo). The social order, stressing the concept of hierarchy, was based on a rigid class system with the samurai at the top. The samurai, or warrior class, epitomized the moral virtues of absolute loyalty to their lord, righteousness, and subjugation of self.

When the samurai were transformed into government and business leaders after the Meiji Restoration, they became proselytizers as well as practitioners of these values. They urged farmers, tradesmen, and artisans to vigorously adhere to the notion of group loyalty and the other Confucian ethics that had guided the samurai tradition. Central to Japanese interpretation of Confucian values is the belief, as described by a nineteenth century Japanese scholar, that "the meaning of social life lay not in seeking salvation in another world . . . but in cultivating relationships among members of society built on trust, a fundamental sense of one's humaneness, and, above all, a commitment to loyal action on behalf of others."[16]

A gradual but inevitable consequence of the continued emphasis on obedience to authority and to ritual was the suppression of individualism. In Tokugawa Japan, individual identity and self-esteem became a function of social class and ability to serve the regional lord. Again quoting Morishima, "Throughout Japanese history up to the present, individualism has never prospered. . . . The Japanese have been required to obey their rulers, to serve their parents . . . and to act in accordance with the majority factions in society," thereby leaving little time for problems of conscience.[17]

The prevailing feudal system emphasized unselfishness and derivation of self-identity by relating oneself to a group or organization. Individual happiness or unhappiness became a secondary consideration to the group, be it family, company, or nation-state. Within Japan's regimented society, no one could be self-made. "Thus the competitive, adventurous Japanese of the sixteenth century became, by the nineteenth century, a docile people depending mainly on their rulers for leadership and following all orders from above with few questions."[18] Collective goals became the norm.

As Edwin Reischauer wrote, "Each person, each thing, fits into an accepted order of prestige and power. Position on this scale must be clear so that one can distinguish the superior from the inferior and know where the authority lies."[19] The gradations of politeness and deference in the Japanese vocabulary reinforce the concept of hierarchy. As they go through life, Japanese people are bombarded with explicit and implicit messages about fitting in with the group and about harmonizing their intellectual and psychological growth with group needs. To sugarcoat the pill, this supposedly collective will is presented by parents and bosses as benevolent, devoid of power, and wholly determined by a unique culture.[20] A U.S. social psychologist concludes that "in dealings with outsiders or alien groups, the Japanese undoubtedly have an equally well-defined boundary between themselves and others. But within the context of groups with which the individual is identified, the Japanese . . . *me* becomes merged with the *we*, and the reactions of others to one's behaviors gain priority over one's own evaluations."[21]

Whining about being deprived of personal rewards or comforts suggests immaturity and selfishness, characteristics inimical to the collective good. At school or on the job, the Japanese people comply stoically with demands that U.S. culture would brand as unjustifiable burdens, exploitation, or unacceptable intrusions into individual prerogatives.

For centuries, social and economic morality in Japan has been grounded on respect, duty, obligations, and responsibility within permanent reference groups.[22] In Japan, values, such as personal sacrifice, perseverance in the face of adversity, patience and endurance, loyalty, and subordination of individual desires to the interests of a larger community, are viewed as virtues to be equated with strength of character and true maturity, not with submissiveness.[23]

A number of specific Japanese values, still revered after hundreds of years, have been integral to economic success. On one level, these values are similar to the Protestant ethic: commitment to hard work, honesty, and frugality. The shape and spirit of Japanese capitalism also have been molded by a second level of values that include emphasis on the group over the individual; stress on social harmony; simultaneous competition and cooperation among different groups; a deep sense of obligation; respect for hierarchy; mutual trust and belief in long-term, binding, and reciprocal obligations; and a desire to share risks and benefits.[24] Although these values do not permeate U.S. culture as a whole, they are not unknown to elite specialized groups built on teamwork. Consider the similarity between Japanese values and a Marine Corps officer's explanation that U.S. Marine Corps spirit is "derived from a core of values: tenacity, resilience, fortitude, integrity, loyalty, honor, courage and commitment."[25]

Commitments to loyalty and reciprocal obligations explain the extraordinary durability of the long-term ties in Japan that bond government and industry, lead banks and corporations, companies within a horizontal *keiretsu*, and parent firms and their suppliers and subcontractors.[26] These commitments can lead to costly rigidities and economic inefficiencies. In many cases, however, the disadvantages of simply not accepting the lowest bid are more than offset by such benefits as mutual involvement of producer and supplier in product development, absolutely dependable quality and just-in-time delivery, and responsiveness by subcontractors to recurring demands by assembly firms for better or cheaper components.

Prominent in the third and most abstract level of cultural values (but now less openly articulated) is the uncommonly strong Japanese belief that they are a vastly different race set far apart and above the others. For many centuries, a fierce aversion to assimilation has sustained a complex set of attitudes toward foreigners and concerns that the outside world poses a danger to the inner workings of Japan's social order. Masao

Miyamoto, a trained psychoanalyst, emphasizes the uniqueness and importance of the twin concepts of inside (*uchi*) and outside (*soto*) that carry over from ancient village life and make modern Japan one of the most exclusionary countries. Unless a Japanese person is fully drawn into and accepted by a specific group, he or she remains on the outside and "can never cross over and come in." Foreigners are always "outside" no matter how deep they understand Japanese culture or how similar their lifestyle is to that of the Japanese around them.[27]

The Japanese value system simply does not embrace the U.S. belief that efficient domestic production and a liberal foreign trade policy should, first and foremost, serve the ends of maximizing consumption, lowering prices, and increasing the variety of goods available to consumers. Increased consumption is not spurned; it simply is not the highest priority. Japan has never conformed to the free-market, consumer-gratification model that most Americans assume prevails in all capitalist countries. In response to a question by the author, a one-time senior Ministry of International Trade and Industry (MITI) official stated that the primary purpose of economic activity is to give meaning to and enhance the value of life — hardly the response of a Western economist. The implication is that hard work is its own reward. This might explain why rigid adherence to the seniority system has done little to stifle economic dynamism in Japan, as it would if applied in the U.S. business sector. James Fallows has argued that the Japanese "believe — like all good Confucianists — that you cannot get a decent, moral society, not even an efficient society, simply out of the mechanisms of the market powered by the motivational fuel of self-interest. . . . The morality has got to come from the hearts, the wills and motives of the individuals in it."[28]

Individuals in every society are subject to peer group pressures. The average person wants to fit in with friends and coworkers and not be branded as deviant. In some societies this means pressing for big wage demands and fighting all changes in work rules. In Japan it means subordinating personal interests to needs of the group (the company), performing after-hours work in quality circles, fearing utilization of all of one's allotted vacation time, and attending company-sponsored social events. This does not equate with contentment. As noted below, many Japanese are bitterly dissatisfied with their work environment and complain in conformity with socially sanctioned protocol.

None of these values require the Japanese people to take vows of poverty and self-denial. They do, however, encourage intense group loyalty and relatively less emphasis on pursuit of such U.S. priorities as maximizing individual income and pursuing instant self-gratification.

## THE ROLES OF BUSINESS STRATEGIES
## AND MANUFACTURING SKILLS

An appealing single-factor explanation for Japan's industrial success is the ability of many of its corporations to produce better products at lower prices than their foreign competition. The combination of brilliant management strategies and overall corporate excellence is probably the single most important contributing factor. Certain corporate strengths — for example, a commitment to constantly improve production techniques and a stronger work ethic than most of their foreign competition — have been essential to the ascent of Japanese companies to world-class status. Nevertheless, corporate behavior and labor-management relations do not develop in a vacuum. Japanese industrialists function in a political and social environment where regulations and institutions are unequivocally producer- and growth-friendly. For all their advanced technologies and production know-how, the big corporations reap important benefits from a compliant labor force and the abovementioned leverage exerted over diligent suppliers and subcontractors. When the yen doubled in value against the U.S. dollar between 1985 and 1987, subcontractors, in effect, were ordered to bear a share of the pain. The latter had to cut their prices and profit margins so that their larger customers could minimize dollar-denominated price increases in their efforts to retain foreign market shares.[29]

### Growth before Profits

Japanese business executives are charged with the universally applicable responsibilities of assuring that their companies remain competitive, financially healthy, and responsive to their customers. Beyond these surface similarities, Japanese executives face different priorities, opportunities, and constraints than do most of their U.S. and European counterparts. Different rewards and disincentives breed different corporate strategies. Japanese managers, and other life-time workers, in a large company realize personal identity largely through their place of employment. Because employees will stay until retirement, the long-term success of their company is inextricably linked with their own. As one Japanese executive reputedly said, U.S. and Japanese management are 95 percent alike but differ in all important respects.[30]

The primary indication of successful corporate performance in postwar Japan has been increased market share, mainly because companies with the larger increases in production of a given product were most likely to become the low-cost producers. An absolute increase in sales in a rapidly expanding market, as was the case in Japan for most of the postwar period, was necessary but not sufficient to assure either long-term corporate competitiveness or profits. In addition to keeping marginal production costs competitive with other companies, maximum increases in sales were needed to offset high fixed costs. The latter were the inevitable by-products of, first, a lifetime employment commitment that kept the labor force of large companies fixed in size, and, second, large interest rate repayments associated with heavy reliance on bank borrowing by Japanese companies through the early 1980s. Profits are important, but they are not ends in themselves.

The growth ethic can encourage a corporate strategy that, in turn, can produce a self-fulfilling prophecy in companies that avoid major mistakes:

Managements with a bias toward growth have distinct mind-sets which include the expectation of continued growth [and] decisions and plans formulated to produce growth. . . . Companies with a bias toward growth add physical and human capacity ahead of demand. Prices are set not at the level that the market will bear, but as low as necessary to expand the market to fit the available capacity. Costs are programmed to come down to support the pricing policies, and investments are made in anticipation of increased demand.[31]

A simple, practical explanation for Japanese corporate freedom to think long-term and discount the need for short-term profits is the relatively limited role of shareholders. Commercial bank borrowing has been a far more important source of investment capital to the typical Japanese company than sale of equity (common stock) has been for U.S. companies. Japanese banks, especially if they are members of the same *keiretsu* as borrowers, have placed primary emphasis on long-term market share growth, not short-term profitability, as the means of gauging creditworthiness. The financial component of industrial policy often nudged interest rates below what they would have been under free-market conditions, further reducing the need by targeted industries to pursue quick returns on investment.[32]

Two other factors contribute to the subordinate role of shareholders. Companies in the same *keiretsu* hold considerable amounts of each others' stock to form what is known as an interlocking directorate. They, too, look upon growth as more important than immediate profits and rising dividends. In addition, most outside shareholders prefer appreciation of share prices to dividends because individuals pay relatively low long-term capital gains taxes on profits from sales of stocks. All these factors contribute to the tendency of Japanese companies — particularly in more competitive foreign markets — to price their goods to sell rather than to generate profits. (Emphasis on market share maintenance partially explains the many accusations of dumping against Japanese exporters, that is, overseas sales at less than fair value.)

The business sector's emphasis on growth materializes in two key corporate spending priorities. The first is capital investment for new plants and updating existing equipment. A critical determinant of a manufacturer's productivity is the extent to which it has upgraded to state-of-the-art production equipment. Relatively high growth rates have brought Japan's capital investment outlays, expressed in dollars, to approximate parity with those of the larger U.S. economy. (Comparisons vary with years and whether a nominal or purchasing power parity exchange rate is used.) While the United States enjoyed an unusually high rate of investment in 1994 (12 percent of GDP and about $2,500 per capita), the recession-mired Japanese economy was investing 18 percent of its GDP, or $5,700 per capita. Despite the common belief that "America is back," the average age in 1994 of plant and capital equipment in Japan was only 5.8 years as compared to 8.7 in the United States.[33] Japan has the world's highest productivity in certain industrial sectors partly because companies are constantly modernizing capital equipment and partly because they excel in designing products and organizing employee tasks that maximize simplicity in the assembly process.[34]

The second critical barometer of future growth and competitiveness is research and development. Japanese industry displays an excellent record in increasing its research and development outlays for commercial manufacturing (as opposed to aerospace and defense) — so much so that it has narrowed the one-time large gap with the larger U.S. industrial sector. By way of crude comparison, the estimated U.S. industrial research and development in 1992 was $119 billion, an inflated figure because of large expenditures by defense contractors. The comparable total for Japan was about $90 billion, also a somewhat inflated figure because it is converted at a nominal exchange rate that ignores relative buying power.[35]

## Manufacturing Genius

By the early 1980s, learning how to make things cheaper, better, and quicker made a number of Japanese companies masters of the manufacturing process. A study of Japanese corporations published in 1985 estimated that Japanese manufacturing innovations were yielding cost advantages "in the range of 30 percent" over their foreign competition.[36] Although they had once been the teachers, U.S. managers found that they were now the students.

Process technology is defined as the total planning and execution of the manufacturing process, from product design through final assembly. Advances in this field over the past 30 years were overwhelmingly the result of Japan's corporate brainpower, ambition, and patient trial and error. Government bureaucrats did not engineer the ongoing revolution on Japan's factory floors. Cultural factors provide only a marginal explanation of the exceptional Japanese track record in mastering process technology. For example, a centuries-old sense of insecurity might explain why their companies are never satisfied with any level of cost cutting and quality control and, therefore, can never feel enough confidence to suspend even briefly ever-present efforts to achieve better results. *Kaizen*, the word used to describe Japan's unquenchable thirst for permanent incremental improvement in production processes, was vividly illustrated on a visit made to a Hitachi plant near Tokyo by a Motorola executive. Asking about the "P200" message emblazoned on a flag flying outside the factory, he learned it stood for the lofty 200 percent productivity improvement the plant hoped to achieve that year; the plant manager expressed disappointment that they had so far reached a productivity increase of "only" 160 percent. The U.S. executive quickly sent a warning back to his corporate headquarters because Motorola at the time considered a 20 percent annual productivity increase for pocket pagers to be pretty impressive and ahead of its competition.[37]

An early postwar stratagem consisted of private sector and government agencies resurrecting the Meiji era initiative to assiduously monitor U.S. and European production techniques, technological breakthroughs, and scientific discoveries — and then to import, adapt, and improve upon them. Imitation eventually was supplanted by original contributions to the economics of manufacturing. One example was the emphasis on large, sustained increases in production runs for such goods as steel and television sets. Maintaining market share in the rapidly growing domestic market and rapid export growth produced sufficient increases in volume to allow large Japanese companies to excel at achieving economies of scale. The constantly expanding production base allowed many Japanese companies to move steadily down the learning curve as problems were overcome and shortcuts mastered in the manufacturing process. Sustained increases in production volume also reduced unit prices by allowing Japanese companies to amortize fixed costs (labor, interest payments, and research and development) over a larger base and by encouraging the purchase of the latest available machinery when they expanded capacity. The slow-down in domestic growth rates and saturated export markets that have prevailed since the early 1990s threaten this formula and raise questions about Japanese companies' ability to retain their edge.

Another important managerial innovation was the breakthrough in enhanced quality control. Many of the Japanese techniques here can be traced to W. Edwards Deming, an American whose ideas on how simultaneously to increase productivity and quality were originally ignored in his own country. As part of their ongoing, comprehensive, global search for good ideas, Japanese industrialists en masse found and embraced Deming's quality assurance principles such as:

refuse to allow commonly accepted periods of delay for mistakes, defective material, and faulty workmanship;

reduce the number of suppliers and buy on statistical evidence of dependability, not price;

search continually for problems in the system and seek ways to improve it;

break down barriers between departments and encourage problem solving through teamwork;

institute modern methods of training, and keep workers abreast of new developments in materials, methods, and technologies; and

use statistical methods for continuous improvement of quality and productivity.[38]

Manufacturing high quality goods that work properly from the start proved to be a classic case of the best of two worlds. First, high grades from consumers for product dependability boosted global sales. Second, production line efforts to prevent defects in the first place and to avoid repairing a finished product after it has been assembled or sold to a customer reduce costs in the long term. In effect, enhancing levels of quality can be cost-less. Quality control in the typical Japanese factory is implemented by well-educated, well-trained, dedicated employees who usually are responsible for setting production standards. The goal of zero defects is pursued by "quality circles" composed of production line workers who identify problems and make suggestions for improving assembly line procedures. Japan's extensive use of robotics on the production line further enhances quality control.

A later series of production line innovations carried Japanese manufacturing efficiency beyond economies of scale. Flexible manufacturing, as it usually is called, facilitates complex production schedules, the assembly of many different models of a product on the same production line, and the introduction of new models and styles in the most rapid and lowest-cost manner possible. Many of these techniques involve nothing more exotic than reconfiguring capital equipment or the position of machines on the assembly line floor so that a single worker can operate more than one machine. Toyota sought to reduce to one minute the changeover of a machine from making one part to making another part.[39]

A simple, but ingenious improvement in the manufacturing process consisted simply of bringing together all phases of the production process to work simultaneously on refinements of existing products and the development of new ones. This strategy cuts costs, improves product quality, and quickens introduction of new products. The effort to produce new or upgraded products is managed by a team of workers from research, engineering, assembly line production, marketing, and major suppliers. By making design and production a unified rather than sequential process, less time and money are spent on assembly line trial and error and on product redesigns to fix unanticipated glitches. Integrated teamwork facilitates an optimal production layout, fewer parts, and speedier transition of new models and new products from drafting board to delivery to market.

Yet another Japanese corporate innovation is just-in-time delivery (kanban). The practice of scheduling deliveries of parts from suppliers to arrive on the day they are to be assembled into the final product seems relatively unimportant, but, in fact, it dramatically increases efficiency and cuts costs in many phases of manufacturing. In addition to eliminating the costs of maintaining inventories, just-in-time deliveries reduce the numbers of factory workers needed, reduce the need for factory floor space, streamline the handling of materials, shorten production schedules, and increase pressure on suppliers to attain zero defects.

Toyota is the very embodiment of the competitive strengths of Japanese process technology innovations. The company is recognized as the pioneer and exemplary practitioner of lean manufacturing. It uses fewer of the resources needed by traditional mass production: "half the human effort in the factory, half the manufacturing space, half the investment in tools, half the engineering hours to develop a new product in half the time," and fewer defects. Rather than the "good enough" quality standards of mass production, lean producers' ultimate goal is perfection: continually declining costs, zero defects, zero inventories, and endless variety.[40] An MIT study team in 1990 concluded that traditional mass production techniques then being used by the U.S. automobile industry were "simply not competitive with a new set of ideas pioneered by Japanese companies" that "provides better products in wider variety at lower cost."[41] It also concluded that an assembly process organized as efficiently as Toyota's can outproduce competitors that enjoy lower cost labor and use more automation.[42]

In 1996, the financial press was still reporting major cost-cutting moves by Toyota, a company that would seem to have no more fat left to trim and no inefficiencies left to correct. Perhaps driven to remain competitive no matter how far the yen appreciated, Toyota reported that it was able to cut total production costs by the equivalent of about $1 billion annually from 1993 through 1995.[43] Toyota's place at the forefront of Japanese efficiency explains its improbable success — alluded to in Chapter 1 — in continuing to export light pickup trucks to the United States despite high tariffs, yen appreciation, and U.S. competitors imitating its production techniques. [To keep things in perspective, I relate some of the problems that developed in a Lexus 300 "luxury car" purchased new by someone known to the author. The automatic transmission gave out after less than 40,000 miles of driving. The power steering had to be replaced two weeks later. Within the next 30 months, the water pump had to be replaced, the air conditioning unit failed, and a serious fluid leak necessitated the installation of a third transmission.]

The automobile industry is one of Japan's best and is, therefore, not the fairest benchmark of its industrial efficiency. All Japanese companies are capable of making major mistakes by producing goods the consumer does not want or has grown tired of. The simpler the manufacturing process, the less likely it is that Japanese industry will be able to exhibit superior international competitiveness through lean production and higher productivity. This is the case in the production of paper and some chemicals, for example. It is usually only when demanding assembly and engineering are required that Japanese companies become international stars.

### Workers: Kings or Pawns?

Japanese industrial corporations would be hard-pressed to design a more desirable work force than the one they have. As a whole, their workers are well-educated; highly skilled; industrious; loyal; eager to improve production techniques; respectful of authority; and relatively unaggressive in demands for increased wages, fringe benefits, and better working conditions. The overriding question is whether workers are patsies manipulated by their bosses, or are masters of their domain — the factory. When Westerners look through the *Rashomon* lens, both of these contradictory visions appear. Japanese management practices "a philosophy of involvement that is either quite clever or devilishly insidious, depending on your point of view."[44]

By U.S. standards, most Japanese workers are exploited through long working hours, mandatory overtime, the need to subordinate family and friends to company needs, low salary increases relative to productivity increases, high-priced consumer goods and services, and a relatively underdeveloped social infrastructure (inadequate housing, parks, roads, and so on). A passionate clinging to company symbols, such as the corporate ideology, the singing of the company song, and group calisthenics, wrote long-time Japan observer Karel van Wolferen, are all "symbolic acts designed to reassure the employee of his membership in the company." To justify the workers' personal sacrifices and to maximize their loyalty, "the company must appear to be something more than an organisation established for the purpose of making a profit."[45]

Workers in the large manufacturing companies also are burdened with an informal mandate to oversee and deliver constant improvements in the production process, which, in effect, puts them midway between the standard blue- and white-collar worker designations. Japanese unions in the private sector are organized by individual company rather than the industry as a whole, and their leaders are approved by management. This status not only limits their leverage in improving benefits and working conditions but also explains organized labor's relative unimportance in the national political arena. Although the average Japanese, today, lives better in material terms (diet, home appliances, clothing, travel, and so forth) than he or she did 20 years ago, most city-dwellers still have lower real spending power and fewer physical comforts than their U.S. and West European counterparts.

Social pressure, not some genetically inspired need for hard work and self-denial, is the cause of Japanese workers' unusually deep subjugation of self to corporate needs. It is in management's interest to perpetuate the credo that employers' interests supersede personal interests for the simple reason that it helps lower production costs and increase output. The apparently frequent use of the workers' prerogative to criticize bosses (to their faces) after hours when under the influence of alcohol, and public opinion surveys that frequently find relatively low job satisfaction suggest something other than selflessness lies behind the facade of the smiling Japanese worker.

The opposite version of labor's status characterizes Japanese employees as sovereign entities in a system sometimes described as a "peoplism" management style. Big companies are said to follow a "stakeholders" strategy because management is more concerned with employee welfare and the health of their suppliers than with maximizing returns to shareholders. In addition to lifetime employment status, many workers at big companies are eligible for subsidized housing and use of company resorts. Relative to most Western workers, they are viewed by management as valuable long-term resources and as important decision makers in assembly line operations.

No matter which side benefits most, Japanese industrial workers' long-term "partnership" with big companies enhances productivity. Unlike most of their Western counterparts, Japanese workers with lifetime employment have no reason to oppose introduction of labor-saving capital equipment. Their permanence encourages companies to invest in continuous training and skills enhancement programs. Lack of worker turnover also enhances the quantity and quality of production line output.[46]

As seen from abroad, an informal social contract exists in Japan. Industrial workers are the guarantors of Japan's economic strength and the earners of vitally needed foreign exchange to pay for imported raw materials. Japanese workers do not mimic their U.S. counterparts' efforts in previous years to grab all the wage and benefits increases that oligopoly (or monopoly) union negotiating practices would allow. Productivity increases in the United States do not necessarily establish a ceiling on wage increases. Conversely, the data suggest that productivity increases in Japan do not establish a minimum level of wage increases. The competitive and financial positions of individual companies and the overall health of the Japanese economy — as judged by management — appear to be the main determinants of annual wage increases.

In Marxian terms, Japanese industries have maximized the surplus value of labor — the difference between what workers produce and what they are paid. When social conscience causes industrial sector workers to accept limited wage increases, Japanese producers derive an important international competitive advantage. Domestically, the failure of these workers to secure wage gains commensurate with productivity gains has amounted to a de facto subsidy to the relatively inefficient but labor-absorbing service sectors, such as distribution and retailing. This self-denial is related to the national consensus that full employment is an important means to the priority goals of a stable social order and group harmony at the national level.[47] Even if they deserved greater salary increases, Japanese industrial workers are not poorly paid, especially when expressed in dollars. Hourly compensation costs for manufacturing in the United States in 1995 were calculated to be $17.20, while the Japanese rate was $23.66.[48]

Japanese manufacturers have been blessed with workers who have the best record for increases in productivity among major industrial countries and with one of the best records for stability of unit labor costs (total wage costs divided by output). As shown in Table 6.1, Japan's increase in manufacturing productivity of 80 percent between 1980 and 1994 was well above the U.S. increase of 48 percent. During the same period, unit labor costs in Japan were virtually unchanged, but they increased by 25 percent in the United States (see Table 6.2). Much of this differential is because of relatively slower wage increases in Japan. Between 1977 and 1994, hourly compensation costs for manufacturing workers (expressed in national currency terms) increased in Japan by an impressive 107 percent, but this still trailed productivity gains in manufacturing of 115 percent. U.S.

**TABLE 6.1**
**Output per Hour (Productivity) in Manufacturing**
**(1982 = 100)**

| Year | Japan | United States | Germany | France | United Kingdom |
|------|-------|---------------|---------|--------|----------------|
| 1960 | 18.5  | NA            | 37.1    | 29.6   | 50.3           |
| 1970 | 50.3  | NA            | 66.4    | 58.6   | 72.1           |
| 1980 | 91.1  | 92.9          | 98.5    | 90.8   | 91.0           |
| 1990 | 149.1 | 122.1         | 125.6   | 127.6  | 140.1          |
| 1994 | 164.2 | 137.4         | 140.0   | 142.4  | 165.7          |

*Source*: U.S. Department of Labor, "International Comparisons of Manufacturing Productivity and Unit Labor Cost Trends, 1994." Press release, September 8, 1995.

**TABLE 6.2**
**Unit Labor Costs in Manufacturing**
            **(in national currencies; 1982 = 100 for all countries)**

| Year | Japan | United States | Germany | France | United Kingdom |
|------|-------|---------------|---------|--------|----------------|
| 1960 | 35.5  | NA            | 36.4    | 25.7   | 14.2           |
| 1970 | 49.7  | NA            | 51.9    | 31.5   | 20.4           |
| 1980 | 97.8  | 89.7          | 90.6    | 80.1   | 86.7           |
| 1990 | 92.7  | 110.4         | 117.8   | 126.4  | 128.9          |
| 1994 | 98.8  | 112.5         | 132.7   | 130.8  | 147.8          |

*Source*: U.S. Department of Labor, "International Comparisons of Manufacturing Productivity and Unit Labor Cost Trends, 1994." Press release, September 8, 1995.

manufacturing productivity increased in the same period by only 40 percent, but hourly labor compensation costs jumped by 125 percent.[49]

In sum, an important determinant of Japanese industrial competitiveness relative to the United States through the 1980s was the discrepancy in the need for (or willingness of) management in the two countries to reward labor for gains in productivity. Dollar depreciation after 1985 partially offset relatively greater Japanese productivity gains and lower wage increases, but the fact remains that labor-management relations are conducted quite differently in the two countries. Investment, the raw material of increased labor productivity, is, in turn, dependent on a country's savings rate: the more savings, the greater the supply of capital and the greater the probability of relatively low borrowing costs (that is, low interest rates). Once again, the Japanese performance has been superb.

Japan and the United States have long had among the highest and lowest savings rates, respectively, of the major industrial countries. Data for the mid-1980s indicate that the Japanese saved at a rate three times as great as Americans did (see the analysis of industrial policy, later in this chapter, for details on Japanese motivations to save). In 1995, for example, Japan's net household saving as a percentage of disposable household income was 13.4 percent, nearly three times the U.S. rate of 4.7 percent. In another measure of saving, Japan's gross national saving as a percentage of nominal GDP, is slightly more than double the U.S. rate.[50]

## THE ROLE OF GOVERNMENT POLICIES

Japan's extraordinary economic success since the late 1950s was not solely the result of free-market forces. Enlightened governmental policies also played varying roles. Japan's bureaucratic mandarins did not design, manufacture, or market the relatively low-cost, high-quality goods avidly bought by companies and consumers around the world. Like civil servants everywhere, they produced paperwork promulgating laws, policies, regulations, and exhortations. Direct cause and effect relationships between these efforts and Japan's industrial maturation cannot be demonstrated scientifically.

After World War II, Japanese civil servants, like U.S. policymakers, believed in the private enterprise system and a strong business sector. Unlike their U.S. counterparts, however, they presided over a war-shattered economy that rekindled Japan's worst fear: being subject to control by stronger foreign forces. Like their predecessors after the Meiji Restoration, contemporary Japanese economic policymakers saw themselves integral to realizing the national priority of catching up with the West. Still not trusting the vagaries of free markets to accomplish this goal, senior civil servants, with the passive acquiescence of elected politicians and voters, again sought a leading role in the economic recovery. Their task was to provide the full support of the state to industrial corporations, the agents assigned front-line duty in the mission to restore Japan's economic strength and global prestige.

## Macroeconomic Policy

There is relatively little disagreement with the premise that Japan's Ministry of Finance deserves effusive praise for administering macroeconomic policies conducive to economic growth during the immediate postwar years. Unqualified pursuit of industrial efficiency and economic growth has been the first order of business in Japanese monetary and fiscal policies far more so than the pursuit of a more equitable society, civil rights, or workers' rights.

The initial objective of postwar Japanese monetary policy was to stimulate a massive supply of saving to provide relatively low interest rates to corporate borrowers. This was done through a variety of means, including lenient tax treatment of interest earned on bank deposits, limited old-age entitlements, and encouragement of large corporations to pay large bonuses once or twice a year in lieu of higher weekly wages. Monetary authorities also sought to induce high prices for durable consumer goods (through protection of small, inefficient retail outlets) and housing (through inefficient metropolitan land policies) so as to force workers to accumulate savings in order to pay for many necessities.[51] (Purchases by credit card and installment plans became popular only in the 1980s.)

Another monetary policy objective was to assure a sufficiently large flow of loan capital to finance fast-growing Japanese industries. Some of this lending came from the government-owned Japan Development Bank and quasi-official long-term credit institutions (for example, the Industrial Bank of Japan). The majority of capital came from a private banking sector operating under clearly demarcated official guidelines. Through its assurances that the credit window at the Bank of Japan would be available in an emergency, the Ministry of Finance (which controlled the central bank) signalled commercial banks that none of them would risk insolvency through too much lending to industries targeted for official nurturing. Virtually assured profits for commercial banks that lent to them meant that targeted high-growth industries had access to ample amounts of capital at relatively low interest rates.

Fiscal policy was biased to encourage capital formation and industrial growth. Generous tax deductions were and are provided for "desirable" business expenses, such as accelerated depreciation of capital equipment (to encourage continuous modernization) and research and development expenditures.[52]

## Industrial Policy

A far more controversial element of Japan's economic miracle is industrial policy, defined here as the use of government authority and resources to try to promote development in specified industrial sectors, technologies, and, occasionally, companies that would not have occurred at the same rate if free-market forces alone had been relied upon. Observers looking through the *Rashomon* lens have assessed the impact of Japanese government intervention on economic growth in two diametrically different ways. Americans who believe in the unassailable power of the marketplace in all capitalist economies brand Japanese industrial policy as irrelevant, at best, and an expensive failure, at worst. They conclude that Japan prospered despite industrial policy rather than because of it. Japanese government officials, having a vested interest in discrediting the notion that their intervention could improve market forces and give manufacturers an edge over foreign competition, heavily discount the power and influence of the economic ministries on corporate decisions and growth.

An opposite assessment concludes that industrial policies, collectively, have been the critical element in Japan's domestic and foreign economic successes. Chalmers Johnson has categorized Japan as a developmental state, in which the government concerns itself with substantive social and economic goals. Conversely, he called the United States a regulatory state, in which the government concerns itself mainly with rules of economic competition, but not with enhancing the structure and global competitiveness of domestic industry.[53] In his much discussed book, *MITI and the Japanese Economic Miracle,* Johnson claims that, although he cannot "prove" that a given Japanese industry would not or could not have thrived without the benefits of industrial policy, it was possible to calculate how "foreign currency quotas and controlled trade suppress potential domestic demand to the level of the supply capacity of an infant industry; how high tariffs suppress the price competitiveness of a foreign industry to the level of a domestic industry; [and] how an industry borrows capital in excess of its borrowing capacity from governmental and government-guaranteed banks in order to expand production and bring down unit costs."[54]

"Whether it is joint planning of expansion in capital-intensive industries to avoid excess capacity and to assure the introduction of plants of sufficient size to capture scale economies, or joint research on generic technologies, or reallocation of domestic market share in the aluminum industry to firms that move production offshore," wrote Laura D'Andrea Tyson and John Zysman, "the evidence is overwhelming that competition is bounded and orchestrated. . . . Market outcomes are certainly different because such mechanisms for collaboration, collusion, and bargains exist."[55]

Contemporary Japanese policymakers have seen their role as catalysts for inducing competitive advantage and have rejected a static theory of comparative advantage that views as immutable a country's endowments of the factors of production. They have seen themselves not as guarantors of free markets but as gatekeepers who temper disruptive forces, notably excessive competition, and rising imports. There has been no need to defend government activism from criticism by elected officials or voters; none existed because it was widely accepted as necessary and very seldom regarded as an undesirable intrusion in the marketplace.

Because the creation of internationally competitive industries is a central rationale for industrial policy, Japan's use of import barriers in support of the infant industry strategy and export promotion programs (see Chapters 4 and 8 for details) was inevitable. Import protection and restrictions on foreign direct investment were retained until the major companies of targeted industries became strong enough to hold up well against intensified foreign competition.

In an unusually candid speech in 1970, Yoshihisa Ojimi, then vice minister of MITI, said that if Japan had obeyed basic market forces in the 1950s, it would have relied on the labor-intensive industries that had "manufactured and exported masses of junk before the war." Continued specialization based on comparative advantage, he argued, would have relegated Japan to stagnation and poverty. The government and the bureaucrats decided it was necessary to alter the "natural" course of Japan's economic history. In Ojimi's words, the following chain of events unfolded:

The Ministry of International Trade and Industry decided to establish in Japan industries which require intensive employment of capital and technology, industries that in consideration of comparative cost of production should be the most inappropriate for Japan, industries such as steel, oil refining, petrochemicals, automobiles, aircraft, all sorts of industrial machinery, and electronics, including electronic computers. From a short-run, static viewpoint, encouragement of such industries would seem to conflict with economic rationalism. But, from a long-range viewpoint, these are precisely the industries of which income elasticity of demand is high, technological progress is rapid, and labor productivity rises fast. . . . Without these industries it would be difficult to employ a population of 100 million and raise their standard of living to that of Europe and America with light industries alone. . . . In judging what makes a growth industry, banks relied on the judgment of the MITI as one of their chief criteria."[56]

Laissez-faire economic principles have never dominated Japanese thinking. Efforts to improve the workings of the market mechanism came naturally to the Japanese government as far back as the Meiji Restoration in the late 1860s. The shogunate was deposed to preserve Japanese social traditions through the rapid development of an economy sufficiently strong and sophisticated to resist excessive intrusion by the Western powers. Day-to-day management and extensive ownership of the economy was in the hands of an elite group of powerful bureaucrats, often former samurai, who ruled in the emperor's name without specific statutory authority.

In the early 1880s, the economic policymakers switched from direct control to indirect protection of industry by virtually giving away what it had developed. An economic oligarchy evolved, consisting of politically privileged financial houses that were beholden to the ruling elite. "The *jinmyaku* networks — built on kinship, marriage, bribes, or friendships dating from school — that played such a striking role in the course of Japan's modern economic development" were functioning by the beginning of the twentieth century.[57] Privatization of direct management did not cause officialdom to relinquish much real power over the economy.

The cumulative impact of official policies has been somewhere between irrelevance and critical importance. Exactly where it lies on the continuum is difficult to say, because generalizations about aggregate costs and benefits are of dubious validity in the presence of both notable successes and failures. Even when performed on a disaggregated basis, determination of the impact of government involvement is hard to calculate. Different means of support were provided by different ministries. Within a single ministry, industrial policies varied by sector and over time. Evaluating Japan's efforts to promote targeted industries is further complicated because, to some extent, effective industrial policy depends on larger forces, namely, monetary and fiscal policies that promote price stability and encourage saving over consumption.

Examples of expensive failure can be cited. Some of the Japanese industries that received substantial government assistance did not remain, or never became, world-class competitors (aircraft, for example).

In other sectors, for example, aluminum, government financial support led to misguided, inefficient allocations of resources. Some very competitive Japanese industries (commercial ceramics, for example) received little or no direct benefits as far as is known.

On the positive side, evidence abounds that government efforts to enhance the invisible hand of the marketplace were at least a moderate success in several key, high-tech sectors. Industrial policy inspired companies in two critical information technology sectors, computers and semiconductors, to reach levels of accomplishment and to progress at speeds that would have been inconceivable in the absence of government efforts to reduce their financial risks.

Industrial policy was a necessary but insufficient factor in assuring the development of an internationally competitive computer industry in Japan.[58] One would be hard-pressed to demonstrate that Japanese companies would have decided to take on IBM in the 1960s without meaningful government encouragement. IBM, at the time, had a dominant, world-wide market share for a product noted for rapid obsolescence, mammoth capital requirements, and a growing list of financially-ailing producers dropping out of the market. MITI's policies attracted corporate interest in building computers by reducing risks and costs, increasing profit expectations, and providing incentives to invest in technology and improve quality. After the official and private sectors agreed that computers should be targeted, several specific policy actions ensued: import quotas were imposed and tariffs were raised; cost-reducing government assistance was provided in the form of research subsidies, low interest loans, tax benefits, and loan guarantees; and cooperative research projects were organized to minimize overlapping corporate efforts. Simultaneously, MITI sought to preserve aggressive market forces by such devices as tying official assistance to sales results: "A firm that was not competitive could expect to be cut off from future subsidized R&D."[59]

The rise of the semiconductor industry in Japan, says Kenneth Flamm, is a "textbook example of how industry and government can cooperate to foster the rapid development of a high-technology industry."[60] Over a period of years, MITI provided the intensely competitive companies in the industry with a full range of support: research and development subsidies, low interest loans from government-controlled development banks for capital investment, special depreciation breaks, restrictions on the operations in Japan of U.S. semiconductor companies, and jawboning Japanese end-users into buying locally produced chips. The ministry also was the major contributor to the Very Large Scale Integration research and development projects (to produce a new generation of semiconductor technology) in which MITI mandated a division of labor by dividing electronics companies into specific, theme-related research consortia.[61]

However, in the final analysis, corporate efforts put them at the forefront of semiconductor manufacturing technology and quality standards.

### Administering Industrial Policy

Japanese industrial policies between the early 1960s and the 1980s arguably set the global standard for constructive government intervention. Conventional techniques were used, but they collectively flourished in a uniquely Japanese environment that has precluded widespread replication of their model. Well-designed, single-minded efforts to promote industrial growth meshed seamlessly with the two other critical components of Japan's domestic success: a brilliant performance by industrial companies and a unified and receptive Japanese social order conditioned to accept the wisdom and benevolence of its government's leadership on economic issues.

Official assistance to the industrial sector was well isolated from politicians and their propensity to dole out money on the basis of constituents' political clout rather than the technical criteria used by career civil servants in MITI and the Ministry of Finance. Japan's indicative planning avoided inventing or thwarting market trends. Instead of supporting a single "national champion" in targeted high-tech industries, industrial policy never eliminated intense market share competition among Japanese companies. Industrial policy was guided by extensive dialogue between industry and bureaucracy rather than government decree. The Industrial Structure Council and other advisory bodies assured private sector influence in shaping both economic priorities and broad policy strategy. Critics mistakenly focus on MITI's relatively few conflicts with corporate Japan instead of concentrating on its more impressive record of fostering industry-government consensus.

MITI was extremely adept at understanding corporate needs and providing targeted industries with a resilient safety net comprised of abundant working capital, restricted foreign competition, and promises of government purchases.[62] When corporate executives voluntarily responded to government efforts to promote new industries, they knew their risks had been minimized, their rewards had been maximized, and that the rules of the game would not be changed in mid-stream by political favoritism or vacillating bureaucrats. Advancing into the technologies of the future was a win-win situation for companies: it enhanced corporate size, strength, and prestige, while contributing to Japan's economic independence. By some Western standards, however, industrial policy also involves a Faustian bargain, since MITI's largesse is not without strings. The quid pro quo for economic benefits is considerable MITI power ranging from formal orders to nonstatutory pressure through what is euphemistically known as administrative guidance. When short-term problems threaten MITI's perception of the collective interest in the industrial sector, it will "advise" corporations to modify their behavior and will occasionally propose mergers. MITI's advice has usually, but not always, been followed by industry.

Rather than trying to pick winners, Japanese industrial policy sought to target a limited number of strategic industries with above-average economic value. They usually were chosen only after a careful review of data showed they met such economic criteria as:

The industry would likely produce increasing "returns to scale," that is, after a large initial investment in plant and equipment, the average cost of production would be significantly lowered as the volume of output increased.

A relatively high income elasticity of demand for the product was probable.

The industry's output could be expected to sell successfully in foreign markets, earning needed foreign exchange while helping domestic production achieve economies of scale.

The industry should promote economic expansion in general and generate positive externalities, that is, contribute to technological progress or cost cutting in related and "downstream" industries incorporating the product.[63]

Designation of strategic industries has passed through three broadly defined stages since the late 1950s. The first stage targeted heavy industries, such as steel, automobiles, shipbuilding, and consumer electronics. The second stage commenced in the 1960s and favored knowledge-intensive, low-polluting industries like semiconductors and computers. Since the 1980s, MITI has focused on advanced high-tech sectors, such as biotechnology, software, and composite materials.

Japan's industrial policy took the form of indicative planning and goal setting, not the force of law dictating corporate output. The periodic publication of MITI visions is the government's effort to publicize consensus goals for the optimal future course of the Japanese economy. These statements grow out of consultations among MITI and the manufacturing sector, the financial community, and the government as well as selected politicians, labor officials, scholars, and members of the business press. MITI's version of indicative planning was far less than an exercise in precision forecasting, but it was often good enough to become a self-fulfilling prophecy because industry agreed with the new directions proposed.

The exact mix of benefits usually reflected individual MITI surveys of the needs of each industry targeted for official nurturing and consultations with these industries. Industrial policy at various times included the following measures: tax breaks and tax incentives for new investment, research and development subsidies and government-sponsored research projects, exemptions from antitrust laws (mainly for collaborative research and limiting competition in market segments), protection from

foreign competition, subsidized sale of government-owned land for factories, promises of government procurement of domestic production, and
assistance to companies negotiating technology licensing agreements
with foreign companies on the best possible terms. One of the more cre-
ative forms of industrial policy was channeling portions of the profits
generated by government-operated betting on bicycle and motorcycle
races to companies producing industrial machinery.

Those who dismiss the beneficial effects of industrial policy usually
forget that some industries, such as automobiles, may not have received
large government subsidies, but they did benefit from protectionist trade
policies; plentiful, low-interest bank capital; and government assistance
to the auto parts industry. Discounting the impact of industrial policy
may be a dubious proposition because of the possibility that the industrial support activities of MITI and other ministries have not yet been fully
revealed.

Industrial policy, in general, and administrative guidance, in particular, are also aimed at "sunset" industries that are no longer competitive
because of high labor costs, their energy-intensive nature, and so forth.
Government help to rationalize the industry has been provided when the
relevant companies agree to shrink their output by progressively shutting
down their least efficient factories and equipment (at rates that may or
may not be equal to what market forces would have induced).

The ongoing commercial, financial, and trade liberalization of Japan's
economy, together with the emergence of large, powerful corporations is
eroding the role of industrial policy, in general, and the importance of
government subsidies for research and development and investment, in
particular. However, the informal power of the civil servants is still solid.
Although few corporate chieftains look favorably upon interference by
the ministry that oversees their industry, even fewer want a Western-
style, no-holds-barred, free-market battleground. The economic ministries retain thousands of levers of power through almost 11,000
administrative regulations. Japan's ministries have a long institutional
memory and are likely to take revenge against a defiant company — perhaps on something as mundane as not promptly issuing a license. The
government retains excellent inside information on corporate activities
through the continuing tradition of placing retiring civil servants in the
industries they formerly regulated. The historical tradition in Japan of
respecting government institutions as protectors of the public interest will
not soon disappear. MITI and the Ministry of Finance still have no trouble attracting the top graduates from the country's most prestigious universities. Official funding for research in advanced technologies is still
large in absolute terms even though it is now dwarfed relative to corporate outlays.

## THE JAPANESE ECONOMY HITS A ROUGH PATCH

In late 1989, the Bank of Japan decided to prick the speculative bubble that had driven prices of stocks and land to levels well beyond economic logic. The higher interest rates that ensued set into motion an economic turbulence that soon debunked the 1980s myths of unstoppable increases in Japan's financial wealth, corporate profits, and global competitiveness. What began as a simple unwinding from speculative excess escalated into a real threat that the Japanese economy would implode amid widespread price deflation. All at once, Japan was sent reeling from a multitrillion-dollar downturn in stock and real estate prices (the Japanese urban land index price in mid-1996 was less than one-third its level of mid-1990), a slow-down in growth,[64] a surge in nonperforming bank loans to the $400 to $800 billion range,[65] and rising unemployment. In the early 1990s, the super-strong yen spurred Japanese manufacturers to invest rapidly overseas, and analysts began speaking of the hollowing out of the industrial sector. With exports stagnant in real terms and domestic demand flat or declining, some Japanese companies so aggressively pressured employees to retire early that thin cracks appeared in the facade of lifetime employment.

International money markets in the mid-1990s became so worried about Japan's financial stability that they increased interest rates on short-term loans to its major banks, that is, they imposed a "Japan premium" lest a full-blown financial crisis impair repayment. "The irony of the situation was almost surreal. Japan, the world's greatest creditor nation, holding in excess of $600 billion in net global assets and possessing the world's deepest pool of savings, was singled out for its poor financial regulatory system. . . . There could be no more damning verdict on the [Finance Ministry's] policies."[66] The once sacrosanct Ministry of Finance was hit with such a torrent of criticism that the government summoned the nerve to propose disbursing portions of its presumably excessive regulatory authority to other agencies. The ministry, however, was left with the responsibility for drafting appropriate statutory language.

Large and widespread losses were incurred from Japanese corporate and real estate acquisitions in the United States. Many of the purchases made during the 1980s — Rockefeller Center, Pebble Beach Golf Club, two Hollywood movie studios, hotels in Hawaii and Los Angeles, and so on — turned sour. The common denominator was timing: Japanese buyers had come in at the top of the market and grossly overpaid.

The economic malaise lingered long enough to suggest that many of the institutions and polices that worked so well for Japan for so long (a strong bureaucracy, stakeholder capitalism, and so on) had passed their peak. To some, the old development-state model was in urgent need of modernization to cope with a new era of slower growth, higher production costs, an accelerating pace of technological change in the all-important information processing sector, and an aging population.[67]

## CONCLUSION

Japan's strong domestic economic base was primarily the outgrowth of a unique meshing of a supportive cultural environment; supportive government economic policies; and, more importantly, aggressive, shrewd business strategies. The absence of any one of these three components would have changed economic history. As was first demonstrated after the Meiji Restoration, Japan's burning ambition for economic strength has benefitted from the government's ability to recognize national economic weaknesses and to calculate the most effective methods of overcoming them. The Japanese worried more about the future than other countries, they worked harder, and they prepared better. The paucity of serious, uncorrectable economic or business mistakes in Japan helped considerably, as did a mostly liberal international trading system and relatively small military expenditures.

Japan's industrial sector has benefitted from a domestic economic order that, for historical, social, and ideological reasons, strongly favors large manufacturing corporations over individuals. The Japanese public accepts government support of corporate interests and tolerance of collusive business behavior to a degree that a majority of Americans surely would denounce as antithetical to an optimal and equitable allocation of economic resources.

The historical, social, corporate, and policy factors explaining Japan's domestic economic resurgence also shaped its contemporary export and import patterns. Contemporary attitudes toward imports were based on internal factors, the most important of which are the historical desire to keep the outside world at arm's length, mainly through maximum industrial self-sufficiency, and an economic catch-up strategy based on infant industry protection. The large trade surpluses that have long rankled Japan's trading partners are natural outgrowths of a society with deep insecurities fueled by a relatively high dependence on imported raw materials and by the belief that increased consumption is not the primary purpose of economic activity.

Japan's bureaucratic planners articulated a strategic vision that played to the country's strengths. More often than not, they knew exactly which buttons to push to overcome competitive jealousies and elicit maximum corporate cooperation in the collective drive to maximize Japan's industrial power. Some Japanese industries would not have prospered in the absence of governmental encouragement, and others would have been less successful. For its part, the business sector was responsible for the physical production of low-cost, high-quality goods and the implementation of successful overseas marketing strategies. A skilled, devoted labor force literally forged the tools of economic strength. Japanese export success mostly — but not entirely — reflected the manufacturing talents and strategies of individual corporations.

Those who isolate cultural factors as the sole source of Japan's postwar resurgence forget that these values are many centuries older than Japan's relatively recent emergence as an international economic superpower. Those who ascribe economic success only to government planning still have not explained why other countries (with the possible exception of South Korea, a Japanese colony for most of the first half of the twentieth century) have not replicated the Japanese economic miracle by simply cloning the directives, incentives, subsidies, and techniques for communicating with the private sector adopted by the Japanese government. If the Japanese economic development model were transferable, it surely would have been transplanted to many less successful countries. Finally, the argument that nothing but management excellence, hard work, and thrift were responsible for economic success is dubious. Japan's industrial managers and engineers are very good, but they received important benefits from factors beyond the assembly line. Government support and a pliant labor force made their jobs easier.

Catching up with the United States was easy compared to determining national goals as an economic superpower and solving the problems of the post–bubble era. Still, forecasts of a "setting sun" have proven incorrect, largely because the most valuable resource of all — a determined, intelligent population with a drive to excel in industry — remains at the base of the synergy that created and sustains Japan's economic strength.

## NOTES

1. Calculated from corporate export data in Asahi Shimbun, *Japan Almanac 1996*, pp. 89–92 (for Japan), and *Fortune*, November 13, 1995, pp. 74–76 (for the United States).

2. A U.S. economist has estimated that Japan's retail sector employs 4 million more people than it would need if the sector were as productive as its U.S. counterpart. (David Hale, as cited in *New York Times*, July 11, 1996, p. D2.)

3. The McKinsey Global Institute, *Manufacturing Productivity*, October 1993.

4. Karel van Wolferen, *The Enigma of Japanese Power* (New York: Alfred A. Knopf, 1989), p. 171.

5. Ibid.

6. Daniel Okimoto, *Between MITI and the Market* (Stanford, Calif.: Stanford University Press, 1989), p. 237.

7. van Wolferen, *Enigma of Japanese Power*, p. 375.

8. Ibid., p. 376.

9. Michio Morishima, *Why Has Japan "Succeeded"?* (Cambridge: Cambridge University Press, 1982), p. 52.

10.   Van Wolferen, *Enigma of Japanese Power*, p. 405.

11.   James Fallows, *Looking at the Sun — The Rise of the New East Asian Economic and Political System* (New York: Vintage Press, 1995), p. 204.

12.   Okimoto, *Between MITI and the Market*, p. 29.

13.   Morishima, *Why Has Japan "Succeeded"?* p. 20.

14.   Ali A. Mazrui, *Cultural Forces in World Politics* (London: James Currey, 1990), p. 30.

15.   William K. Tabb, *The Postwar Japanese System — Cultural Economy and Economic Transformation* (New York: Oxford University Press, 1995), p. 26.

16.   Shigeki Nishimura, quoted in Robert J. Smith, *Japanese Society — Tradition, Self, and the Social Order* (Cambridge: Cambridge University Press, 1983), p. 16.

17.   Morishima, *Why Has Japan "Succeeded"?* p. 8.

18.   Mitsuyuki Masatsugu, *The Modern Samurai Society* (New York: American Management Association, 1982), p. 9.

19.   Edwin O. Reischauer, *The United States and Japan* (Cambridge, Mass.: Harvard University Press, 1965), p. 163.

20.   Van Wolferen, *Enigma of Japanese Power*, p. 3.

21.   Janet T. Spence, "Achievement American Style — The Rewards and Costs of Individualism," *American Psychologist* (December 1985), p. 1288.

22.   Merry White, *The Japanese Educational Challenge* (Tokyo: Kodansha International, 1987), p. 48.

23.   Smith, *Japanese Society*, p. 98.

24.   Okimoto, *Between MITI and the Market*, p. 237.

25.   As quoted in "Corps of Champions," *Washington Post*, February 22, 1997, p. D1.

26.   Daniel I. Okimoto and Thomas P. Rohlen, eds., "Afterword," in *Inside the Japanese System — Readings on Contemporary Society and Political Economy* (Stanford, Calif.: Stanford University Press, 1988), p. 265.

27.   Masao Miyamoto, *Straitjacket Society — An Insider's Irreverent View of Bureaucratic Japan* (Tokyo: Kodansha International, 1994), p. 129. One of the few U.S. examples of this phenomenon is the "Semper Fi" mentality that seems to bind current and former members of the Marine Corps and differentiates them in their own minds from non-Marines, no matter how friendly to the corps' traditions.

28.   James Fallows, "The Japanese Difference," *Washington Post*, February 5, 1989, p. D1.

29.   Van Wolferen, *Enigma of Japanese Power*, p. 171.

30.   Japanese executives place an exceptionally high priority on increasing the prestige and reputation of their company within the home market as well as abroad. Possessed of a very competitive society demanding high-quality goods and meticulous after-sales service, Japan is not a market in which the half-hearted flourish.

31.   James C. Abegglen and George Stalk, Jr., *Kaisha: The Japanese Corporation* (New York: Basic Books, 1985), p. 6.

32.   The crucial role of bank lending to larger companies declined in importance in the 1980s when they enjoyed strong cash flows and found that they could borrow at low cost in the Euro-bond markets.

33.   Kenneth Courtis, "The New Agenda and Its Four Forces," *The National Times* (August–September 1995), p. 24.

34.   McKinsey Global Institute, *Manufacturing Productivity*, pp. 2–3.

35.   National Science Board, *Science & Engineering Indicators 1996* (Washington, D.C.: U.S. Government Printing Office, 1996), p. 6/17.

36.   Abegglen and Stalk, *Kaisha*, p. 273.

37.   Ronald Henkoff, "What Motorola Learns from Japan," *Fortune*, April 24, 1989, p. 168.

38.   House Committee on Science, Space, and Technology, Technology Policy Task Force, *Technology Policy and Its Effect on the National Economy* (December 1988), p. 214.

39.   Abegglen and Stalk, *Kaisha*, p. 96.

40.   James P. Womack, Daniel Jones, and Daniel Roos, *The Machine that Changed the World* (New York: Rawson Associates, 1990), pp. 13–14.

41.   Ibid., pp. 3, 225.

42.   Ibid., pp. 94, 260.

43.   "The Kindergarten that Will Change the World," *The Economist*, March 4, 1995, p. 63; *New York Times*, May 24, 1996, p. D8. No data are available to determine what percentage of this cost cutting came from pain inflicted on Toyota's suppliers as opposed to in-factory improvements.

44.   Tabb, *Postwar Japanese System*, p. 159.

45.   Van Wolferen, *Enigma of Japanese Power*, pp. 167–68.

46.   Employees having lifetime employment status have an additional reason for not changing jobs: very limited lateral movement. Japanese companies are not enthusiastic about hiring what would be viewed as a "disloyal" employee willing to abandon a lifetime job for higher income.

47.   The belief that labor is being exploited and alienated by being denied their "just desserts" would be mainly a Western value judgment.

48.   U.S. Labor Department, "International Comparisons of Hourly Compensation Costs for Production Workers in Manufacturing, 1975–1995," report, June, 1996.

49.   U.S. Labor Department, "International Comparisons of Manufacturing Productivity and Unit Labor Cost Trends, 1994," press release, September 8, 1995.

50.   Organization for Economic Cooperation and Development, *OECD Economic Outlook*, June 1996. Differences in calculating the saving rate explain some, but not all, of this gap.

51.   Much of this large pool of saving was deposited for tax reasons in the government-controlled postal savings system, eventually creating the world's largest savings bank.

52.   Deductions for start-up costs for overseas market development were phased out after emergence of Japan's trade surpluses. A major exception to the pro-business tilt of fiscal policy is the relatively high rates applicable to the corporate income tax.

53.   Chalmers Johnson, *MITI and the Japanese Miracle* (Stanford, Calif.: Stanford University Press, 1982), p. 19.

54.   Ibid., p. 30.

55.   Laura D'Andrea Tyson and John Zysman, "Development Strategy and Innovation in Japan," in Chalmers Johnson, Laura D'Andrea Tyson, and John Zysman, eds., *Politics and Productivity — How Japan's Development Strategy Works* (New York: Ballinger Publishers, 1989), p. 77.

56.   Yoshihisa Ojima, speech delivered to the OECD Industry Committee, June 1970, mimeographed.

57.   Van Wolferen, *Enigma of Japanese Power*, p. 377.

58.   Marie Anchordoguy, "Mastering the Market: Japanese Government Targeting of the Computer Industry," *International Organization* (Summer 1988), p. 513.

59.   Ibid., p. 526.

60.   Kenneth Flamm, "Making New Rules — High-Tech Trade Friction and the Semiconductor Industry," *Brookings Review* (Spring 1991), p. 23.

61.   Ibid., pp. 24–25; also see Kenneth Flamm, *Mismanaged Trade? Strategic Trade Policy and the Semiconductor Industry* (Washington, D.C.: Brookings Institution, 1996), pp. 53–54.

62.   When the Japanese government enticed companies to move into a targeted technology with the promise "if you build it, we will buy it," they employed the same technique used by the U.S. Department of Defense in the 1950s to accelerate the early development of semiconductors (see, for example, Flamm, *Mismanaged Trade?* pp. 27–36).

63.   Hiroya Ueno, "The Conception and Evaluation of Japanese Industrial Policy," in Kazuo Sato, ed., *Industry and Business in Japan* (White Plains, N.Y.: M. E. Sharpe, 1980), pp. 382–83, 396.

64.   The perception that Japan was mired in recession during the early 1990s is grossly exaggerated. In the formal sense of the term, no recession occurred. Real GDP growth of 3.6 percent in 1996 was the highest among the Group of Seven countries.

65.   Dick K. Nanto, "Japan's Banking Crisis: Causes and Probable Effects," Congressional Research Service Report, October 6, 1995, p. 1.

66.   David L. Asher, "What Became of the Japanese 'Miracle,'" *Orbis* (Spring 1996), p. 225.

67.   As if to suggest that the gods were angry at Japan, the post-bubble years also saw the country hit with a major earthquake, poison gas attacks in the Tokyo subway, an epidemic of food poisoning, and two world-class financial scandals involving massive illegal trades in currency and copper. Even the most chauvinistic of Japanese lost some of the sense of economic invulnerability that had swelled in the roaring 1980s.

# 7

# The Domestic Foundations of U.S. Foreign Trade Performance

I've always believed that this blessed land was set apart in a special way — that some divine plan placed this great continent here between the oceans to be found by people from every corner of the earth who had a special love for freedom.

— Ronald Reagan (1982)

New Yorkers can have their pooches transported to groomers, vets or even the airport in Lincoln Town Cars or limousines by Princess Car Service. Pet transport, which costs $30 an hour plus 20% tip, is now 25% of Princess' business.

— *The Wall Street Journal* (1990)

Regulators ordered a bank in Kansas City to install a Braille keypad on a drive-through automatic teller machine.

— Murray Weidenbaum (1995)

To understand the less-than-stellar U.S. foreign trade performance over the past three decades, one should first look to its main source: the United States' very uneven domestic economic performance.[1] The changing internal conditions that characterized three broad stages of the U.S. economy since 1945 heavily influenced trends in U.S. international competitiveness, in general, and bilateral trade relations with Japan, in particular.

The United States emerged from World War II as an economic colossus. Its economic size and strength were so superior to other countries that, in retrospect, one could argue that the ensuing sense of over-confidence meant that the United States was too strong for its own good. It was inevitable that this discrepancy in relative economic power would diminish, especially in labor-intensive, low-tech industries like apparel and footwear, as other countries recovered from the war. The critical questions were how fast and how far would be the relative decline of U.S. industrial might.

The answers began to materialize in the latter part of the 1960s when the U.S. economy began to demonstrate a negative synergy — the exact opposite of the Japanese experience at this time. Macro- and microeconomic policies, corporate strategies and management practices, and cultural norms were usually incompatible and often somewhere between indifferent and outright detrimental to increased U.S. industrial strength. Priorities lay elsewhere: fighting the cold war, increased social justice at home, and maximization of equity stock prices. Most Americans believed these goals to be vastly more important than the trade balance. Inevitably, the unsentimental laws of economics caused U.S. industry to become vulnerable to competition from countries with a more clearly defined priority of maximizing manufacturing success rather than national security and social equality and the knack for doing all the right things to achieve this priority. Japan was far and away at the top of the list of the very few countries meeting these criteria.

## A THUMBNAIL SKETCH OF THE
## U.S. ECONOMIC STRUCTURE

With a GDP approaching $8 trillion, the United States is the world's largest national economy by far. When national economic output is divided by total number of hours worked, the United States is the most productive country on earth (even though increases in productivity have declined relative to previous years and to other industrialized countries).[2]

Among major economies, the United States is unique in terms of the small percentage of GDP represented by merchandise imports (about 10 percent) and exports (about 7.5 percent). Simply stated, the U.S. foreign trade sector is smaller relative to total output (GDP) than elsewhere and, therefore, has relatively less impact.

Just as the contemporary Japanese economy was never strong in every sector, the U.S. economy has not been universally weak and stagnant since the late 1960s. The U.S. economic order has been big and strong enough to compete reasonably well against countries other than Japan, except in periods of significant dollar over-valuation. The majority of the primary sector, most notably agriculture, has long been among the most efficient in the world. The tertiary, or services, sector has been productive, innovative, and rapidly expanding. If services can ever be exported as extensively as goods, the United States eventually might be able to rely on this sector to offset a large structural merchandise trade deficit. Pockets of competitive strength have persisted in the U.S. industrial sector, for example, computers, aerospace, and scientific instruments. None of these localized strengths negate what, overall, was a second-rate manufacturing performance relative to Japan. From the 1960s through the 1980s, one U.S. industry after another came to be at risk from Japan's well-oiled industrial and export-generating machines.

Then, with no advance notice, the much-maligned U.S. economy confounded the gloom-sayers by shaking off its malaise and reinvigorating itself. Manifestations of the third (and current) postwar phase of U.S. domestic economic performance first appeared in the early 1990s, shortly after a significant percentage of the U.S. industrial sector reduced production costs and developed important new technologies. The magnitude and duration of this rebound and its ability to ameliorate U.S.-Japanese trade frictions cannot be predicted. In any event, progress did not come fast enough by the mid-1990s to eradicate either the "triple digit" (in the hundreds of billions of dollars) U.S. multilateral trade deficits or the large bilateral deficits with Japan. Despite the apparent rebound of the U.S. economy, analysts looking through the *Rashomon* lens report seeing two different versions of U.S. economic strength: the United States as the world's most efficient economy and a country unable to pay its way in the global marketplace because of an entrenched competitiveness problem.

## THE ROLES OF HISTORICAL CIRCUMSTANCE AND CULTURAL FACTORS

The United States, like Japan, can be characterized as more than a unique country; it, too, is exceptional. It is one of the very few countries in the world today to have emerged from a genuine revolution in both political and intellectual terms. It was "born modern," having never passed through periods of despotism, monarchy, or feudalism. At its birth, the United States was unique in the conspicuous absence of established institutions, that is, there was no official church, no hereditary aristocracy, no standing army, and so on.[3] Its founding faiths, including political freedom, personal liberty, rule of law, social mobility, and egalitarianism, have been constants throughout its relatively brief history.

The United States is the only country formed by people from every other country in the world. A constant influx of immigrants and the ease of acquiring citizenship are the antithesis of the Japanese tradition. Most Americans do not spend time worrying about their culture being unraveled by foreign ideas and influence. Quite the contrary. They exude a self-confidence bordering on jingoism, assuming that the rest of the world is in a constant state of trying to make their countries more like the United

States and that "anyone in the world in his or her right mind should want to live in America."[4]

The United States' sense of self has more to do with common beliefs about what constitutes a good society than with a common history. In the words of the sociologist Seymour Martin Lipset, being an American is an "ideological commitment" rather than "a matter of birth. Those who reject American values are un-American."[5] The United States was founded and largely populated by people escaping the excesses of government authority in other countries. Maximum political, religious, and economic freedom meant limited government. After the American war of independence, a clear consensus existed for a constitution that constructed a permanent separation of powers to prevent concentration of national political power, lest the British king appear in a different form. Japan's Meiji Restoration, the closest that modern Japan has come to a genuine revolution, was designed to assure a government strong enough to mobilize the country for rapid economic modernization; maximizing civil liberties was not a pressing concern. Conversely, the U.S. revolution produced radically new governing institutions consistent with the guideline that the government that governs least, governs best. Government was supposed to serve the needs of the people as defined by the people and their elected representatives.

The priority attached to assuring personal rights and equality indelibly etched individualism and political pluralism onto the U.S. value system. U.S. ideology holds that everyone merits equality of economic opportunity. Children are reared to think for themselves and to "be their own person." Rugged individualism in a spacious, resource-rich country literally conquering new frontiers gave rise to a romanticized vision of a cowboy-like culture where one's career opportunities are limited only by his or her talents, perseverance, and tolerance of risk. The emotional reverence for the personal freedom and opportunity associated with the cowboy lifestyle was exploited by one of the most successful, most widespread advertising campaigns of all time: the Marlboro man. Pluralism is clearly evident in relatively transparent U.S. decision-making systems for economic and social policy. It is a given that all interested parties have the right to offer their views, defend their interests, and try to influence the policymaking process at national and local levels.

For the first 150 years of its existence, the United States maintained a vigorously isolationist attitude toward the rest of the world, similar to Japan before the black ships' arrival. Americans were not concerned about threats from abroad; they were more interested in building a new nation than getting involved in the affairs of other countries. Ironically, the seismic shift in the ideology of U.S. foreign policy was triggered by the Japanese attack on Pearl Harbor. Although the United States emerged from World War II as a military, political, and economic colossus, the depth and breadth of its unfolding messianic zeal as global superpower was considerably magnified by the subsequent cold war crusade to contain the spread of communism. While the Japanese are said to ignore universal values in favor of situational ethics, the U.S. government now subordinated domestic economic interests to defending its key values — democracy, human rights, and free-market capitalism — on a universal basis. U.S. national interests dictated a reverse catch-up strategy: priority was given to accelerating the economic recoveries of noncommunist countries. A willingness to open U.S. markets on a less-than-reciprocal basis to imports from allies became central to a highly accommodating U.S. trade policy in the immediate post–World War II era.[6]

The economic component of the U.S. belief system is built on capitalism and entrepreneurialism. Despite its European roots, the United States spawned a culture that promoted the amassing of personal wealth by all strata of society. Pursuit of the "American dream" is all about leading the good life, measured largely in terms of materialism. The means to this end was, and is, the free play of calculated self-interest in a free-market environment. Not only is the United States the easiest country in the world in which an entrepreneur can become a millionaire (by legal means), it is relatively tolerant of the retention of wealth. No mainstream politician advocates confiscatory taxes, even for the super-rich making tens of millions of dollars annually. At the other extreme, government handouts are frowned upon. Undaunted by a growing income disparity between the wealthiest and poorest segments of the population and by the shrinking number of jobs for the unskilled, U.S. culture remains unenthusiastic about tax-supported welfare for the jobless, unwed mothers, or companies unable to compete against fair import competition.

U.S. values hold that allocation of economic resources and provision of services are best left to the market mechanism. The United States has the only major economy never to have experienced government ownership of telecommunications facilities, radio and television networks, railroads, airlines, or health care. Decisions affecting the economy are supposed to be mainly the prerogative of corporate officials and entrepreneurs. Building new businesses and developing new technologies are the province of the private sector in a society that teaches its people to think for themselves and that "what is not yet done is only what [mankind] has not yet attempted to do."[7]

Corporations are supposed to live or die by their ability to satisfy customers. Government is not supposed to concern itself with excessive competition or corporate decisions to add or lay off workers. What the U.S. belief structure does assign to the federal government is responsibility for assuring that free markets operate properly. This is done primarily by having the government maintain a low profile in terms of intervention in the economy and vigorously enforce antitrust laws designed to prevent business collusion and excessive market power by individual companies. U.S. industrial corporations and the federal government historically have not experienced a close, harmonious working relationship. One tangible result of their discord is that the U.S. Commerce Department is the weakest commercial ministry, as measured by impact on economic policy, of any major industrialized country. Another result is the skepticism with which most Americans view industrial policy. Government officials are not deemed wise enough to decide which industries to promote; providing government financial assistance to a few select companies is widely viewed as intolerable favoritism.

The adversarial relationship that emerged between big business and the U.S. government in the latter part of the nineteenth century is quite at odds with the more harmonious relationships found in the other major industrialized democracies. Its origins can be traced partly to independent-minded corporate executives but mainly to growing populist suspicions that a widening gap existed between the interests of the U.S. people and emerging big companies and the "robber barons" who ran them. Whereas the relatively small-scale nature of private enterprise during the first 100 years of the republic was equated with individual liberty and the opportunity for upward mobility, the arrival of super corporations came to be equated with the threat of unchecked power.[8]

Only in the United States did the rise of big business precede the rise of big government. Unlike Japan, Germany, Great Britain, and France, the United States lacked established governmental or societal institutions to act as a countervailing force on the impact of big corporations. This historical anomaly is a major reason why the big business revolution proceeded so much more rapidly in the United States and why very large enterprises came so much earlier. It also is a primary reason why, beginning in the 1880s, the United States became the first country to enact regulatory (mainly antitrust) legislation directed specifically against big business.[9] Although Japanese and European businesspersons might envy the ability of their U.S. counterparts to make major investment or work force decisions without first consulting government officials, they are baffled by the mutual hostility between two sets of players whom these foreign executives regard as natural allies.[10]

A general belief in laissez-faire notwithstanding, the U.S. economy in operation is not a pure model of the free market or of business-government antipathy. A slight thaw in the icy relationship between U.S. industry and government began in the early 1980s and continues today. Much of the impulse for this shift reflects the determination by both sides that more effective cooperation and communication are needed to respond to increasingly intense foreign (read: Japanese) competition. When facing serious problems, such as severe import competition, U.S. corporations are not above asking for and expecting government assistance. Another example of cooperation between the public and private sectors involves the relationship of major defense and aerospace contractors with the Department of Defense and the National Aeronautics and Space Administration. These can be so close that it is often difficult to disentangle their interests, although this close relationship might help to explain U.S. successes in weaponry and space exploration.

Although the Japanese belief system glorifies efficiency, U.S. policy since the 1960s has tilted toward equity as part of the government's pursuit of a more just society. This is a noble objective, but it collides with the old economic axiom asserting that, for society as a whole, there is no such thing as a free lunch. Production costs have risen at the margin because companies need to comply with laws and regulations that prevent a growing number of business practices deemed to be socially undesirable. Unlike Japan, the United States is never called a producers' country because of laws and regulations dealing with worker safety; equal opportunity hiring practices that prohibit discrimination based on race, gender, disability, age; enforcement of strict environmental laws, and so on. A "let the seller beware" philosophy has spawned a growing casebook of laws establishing detailed rules for product safety standards and truth in packaging, providing for recalls of potentially dangerous products, and easing the way for open-ended product and personal liability lawsuits against corporations.[11] The business community complains that the U.S. legal system operates in a manner that invites lawsuits for grievances, real and frivolous. The result, said the chairman of the Chrysler Corporation, is a tort system costing the United States between $150 billion and $300 billion a year. "Even if you take the low number, that's 2 1/2 times what we spend on police and fire protection. That is a tort tax of $1,200 per American." That is why the Girl Scouts sell 87,000 boxes of cookies just to pay liability insurance.[12]

## THE ROLES OF BUSINESS STRATEGIES AND MANUFACTURING SKILLS

Basking in the glory of their post–World War II global dominance, U.S. industrial managers, as a whole, did not share their Japanese counterparts' zeal for building for the long-term. They were decades late in responding effectively to the unsustainability of the extraordinary competitive edge enjoyed by the United States into the 1960s. By the next decade, many U.S. companies were burdened with bloated production costs and quality control problems, a consequence of paying too little attention to product innovation and improved process technology. The lack-of-foresight syndrome was summarized by an entrepreneur in Silicon Valley:

They didn't invest in the future. The steel industry, the auto industry, the [core] of American industries, their mentality was not to change. They would define the marketplace. It didn't matter what anybody else thought. . . . They weren't prepared to make the changes. . . . The only thing that stays the same is that things change.

The unions are a problem not because they help the workers but because they make costs higher and they don't get the productivity we need. . . . But [if] there were no unions, we still would have lost to the Japanese because we weren't building the right products.[13]

Many aspects of the modern U.S. corporate culture deflected the priorities of U.S. business executives away from the strategies that proved so successful in Japan. Few senior executives have had hands-on experience with assembly line operations. The fastest route to the multimillion dollar salary packages paid to the chairpersons and presidents of industrial companies has been through the marketing or finance divisions, not through production. The best formula for success, once at the top, is to very quickly generate an ever-rising level of profits. The relative importance to U.S. corporations of equity financing (as opposed to debt financing) to raise capital produces intense pressures to please corporate owners, the stockholders. Because their pay and bonuses usually are linked to current stock prices and corporate earnings, most executives choose to concentrate on immediate results instead of long-term projects to increase sales growth and manufacturing productivity, the uncertain payoffs of which are, at best, many years in the future. The fixation on short-term profit maximization caused many chief executives in the 1970s and 1980s to develop a comparative advantage in the speed with which they dropped product lines, for example, consumer electronics, that became less profitable after import competition intensified.

The behavior of U.S. executives is neither irresponsible nor incompetent. They are responding rationally to the reward system in which they operate, flawed as it may be.

Time horizons in corporate boardrooms were further shortened when "casino capitalism" became the business craze beginning in the late 1970s. The mania for mergers, acquisitions (friendly or unfriendly), and leveraged buy-outs further tilted business strategies toward financial and legal maneuvering and away from such "mundane" things as improved process technology, engineering, applied research, and customer satisfaction.

At a time when the Japanese industrial sector emphasized new products, investment, and exports, many U.S. executives were focused on efforts to encourage or repel corporate raiders or to repurchase company stock bought up by so-called greenmailers. Those U.S. companies wanting to be acquired, as well as acquirers who later assumed large debt burdens, often cut back on longer-term necessities — such as capital investment, market development, employee training, and research and development — to dress up the short-term bottom line. "We can't be competitive on a world class basis unless we invest substantially in new technology, and we can't do that with a balance sheet heavily burdened with debt," argued the vice chairman of the Eaton Corporation.[14] Generalizations about these trends are suspect because every corporation is different. Even with the passage of time, however, there is scant evidence to demonstrate that engaging in wholesale asset-shuffling and balance sheet manipulations, which mainly benefit a relatively few shareholders and middlemen (investment bankers and lawyers), was a net plus for the U.S. economy. No data exist to suggest such activities either enlarged or strengthened the U.S. industrial sector.

The breadth and depth of the production malaise that characterized U.S. industry in the 1970s and 1980s was summarized by Akio Morita, cofounder and chairman of the Sony Corporation: "America is by no means lacking in technology. But it does lack the creativity to apply new technologies commercially. This, I believe, is America's biggest problem. On the other hand, it is Japan's strongest point."[15] A comprehensive scholarly study conducted by the interdisciplinary Commission on Industrial Productivity, convened in 1986 by the Massachusetts Institute of Technology, also reached a damning assessment of the U.S. industrial sector's performance in this period:

The verdict is that American industry indeed shows worrisome signs of weakness. In many important sectors of the economy, U.S. firms are losing ground to their competitors abroad.

Determining the causes of these trends and gauging their significance also calls for human judgment. From our industry studies we have concluded that the setbacks many firms suffered are not merely random events or part of the normal process by which firms constantly come and go; they are symptoms of more systematic and pervasive ills. We believe the situation will not be remedied simply by trying harder to do the same things that have failed to work in the past. . . . The weaknesses we discovered concern the way people cooperate, manage, and organize themselves, as well as the ways they use technology, learn a new job, and interact with government.[16]

Although the commission did assign some blame to government economic and regulatory policies, five of the six broad areas of weakness discussed were internal to U.S. companies:

outdated production strategies, with too much emphasis on mass production and too little on flexible manufacturing;

excessively short time horizons;

technological weaknesses in development and production techniques, including poor coordination between the design and assembly functions, lack of

interest in the manufacturing process per se, and inadequate efforts to
improve either products or production techniques;

neglect of human resources, with inadequate education and training of workers;
and

lack of cooperation within the company, between labor and management,
between firms and suppliers, and between firms and customers.

The commission noted examples of well-designed and effective management strategies that drew on the strengths of the U.S. system, but its
two major conclusions were not kind to U.S. management capabilities and
business strategies:

First, relative to other nations and relative to its own history, America does indeed
have a serious productivity problem. This problem in productive performance, as
we call it, is . . . manifested by sluggish productivity growth and by shortcomings
in the quality and innovativeness of the nation's products.

Second, the causes of this problem go well beyond macroeconomic explanations of high capital costs and inadequate savings to the attitudinal and organizational weaknesses that pervade America's production system. These weaknesses
are deeply rooted. They affect the way people and organizations interact with one
another and with new technology; they affect the way businesses deal with long-
term technological and market risks; and they affect the way business, government, and educational institutions go about the task of developing the nation's
most precious asset, its human resources. They introduce rigidities into the
nation's production system at a time of extraordinarily rapid change in the international economic environment.[17]

The MIT commission's findings are consistent with a large body of literature identifying the failure of U.S. industry to use state-of-the-art manufacturing technology as one of the most important reasons it lost ground
to its Japanese competition. Two senior members of the Berkeley Round-
table on the International Economy argued that U.S. industry's basic
shortcoming was not its technology or workers, but how corporations
organized production, used people in the manufacturing process, and set
strategies and goals for product innovation. U.S. industry, they wrote,
"contributed massively to its own undoing," and it "must assume much
of the responsibility for turning things around."[18]

The level of excellence in process technology reached by many
Japanese companies is less a question of investing large sums in new
equipment and automation than how effectively new equipment is used.
General Motors's (GM) estimated $45 billion outlay (an amount larger
than the GDP of many countries) to retool its factories during the 1980s is
literally the largest example of how mastering the production process is
mostly about the application of knowledge. Despite this massive effort to
boost the productivity of its U.S. assembly plants, GM had the dubious

distinction at the end of the decade of being the highest-cost producer among the "Big Three" U.S. auto producers and the operator of 15 of the 16 least-efficient automobile assembly plants in the United States.[19] Inappropriate application of production and design technology, malfunctioning robots, and an apparent resistance to changing its corporate culture limited GM, in the 1980s, to lower productivity increases than those achieved by its two domestic competitors.

Well into the 1980s, only a handful of U.S. corporations responded to increasingly tough Japanese competition by fundamentally modernizing their approach to manufacturing and pushing greater productivity increases and product innovation. The majority reacted passively or demanded the U.S. government restrict the growth of imports from Japan. Most corporate chieftains still viewed themselves as the teachers. They felt they had little to learn from Japan, even as their companies began to trail noticeably in the ability to develop, make, and market at the right price and quality, products able to compete successfully in the world marketplace.

Not all U.S. companies were slow to grasp the importance of production line engineering and of constant improvements in process technology. Some U.S. high-tech firms never lost their competitiveness or their ability to quickly introduce a stream of new products. However, until the resurgence of U.S. industry in the "digital age," they were the exceptions to the rule of a desultory U.S. industrial performance.

Aggressive unions' adversarial relationship with U.S. industry strained labor-management relations throughout the early post–World War II era. As large, industry-wide unions consolidated oligopolistic power, they became increasingly successful in maximizing benefits for their members. They regularly demanded increases in wage rates and fringe benefits with little or no regard for increased worker productivity, employers' long-term competitive health, or the interests of society as a whole. Reductions in existing labor benefits were nonnegotiable, and efforts by management to lower costs by introducing new machinery, part-time workers, or new work rules reflecting technological advances were adamantly opposed by unions as threats to existing jobs. Well-financed union strike funds, access to welfare benefits by striking workers, and public support made work stoppages a regular — and accepted — part of U.S. economic life. Strikes in the United States over salary increases dropped dramatically subsequent to the dissipation of union power associated with the deep recession of 1980–81 and the perception that foreign competition had reached critical mass. Many U.S. industrial workers subsequently began seeking job security over wage increases and were more responsive to modifications in work rules.

Management was hardly blameless for labor's narrow, self-centered agenda. Senior executives in most companies viewed workers not as valuable long-term assets but as expendable inputs who should simply follow their supervisors' instructions and who could be laid off at will and rehired when necessary. Workers responded with indifference, feeling little loyalty to their companies and showing even less concern for the long-term health of a company that they might not be working for in ten years. Whereas prolonged strikes were commonplace, a few industries were prone to capitulate to union demands, confident that higher costs could simply be passed on to consumers. It was no coincidence that the U.S. steel and automobile sectors were early casualties of rising Japanese competitiveness. At the end of the 1970s, wage rates in these sectors were far above the average for the entire U.S. manufacturing sector.

## THE ROLE OF GOVERNMENT POLICIES

The U.S. government has lacked the authority, desire, public support, and expertise to replicate the hands-on economic policymaking approach of Japan's Ministry of International Trade and Industry (MITI) and Ministry of Finance. Except at the highest level of generalization — promotion of sustainable, noninflationary growth — the economic policy of the U.S. government is not to have a comprehensive, proactive set of economic policies. The market mechanism is the designated vehicle for determining development of new commercial goods and technologies, corporate investment and research and development outlays, industrial structure (mergers, spin-offs, new entrants, and company closings), employment levels, and international competitiveness.

Neither U.S. ideology nor institutions in the United States are conducive to systematic government intervention at the sectoral or company levels. The separation of powers written into the Constitution evolved into an economic policymaking process that is highly fragmented, a situation that has inspired neither organizational efficiency nor popular cries for reform. Other than professional economists, few persons fully appreciate the limited power of the executive branch in administering domestic economic policy. The central bank, the Federal Reserve System, independently formulates and administers monetary policy. Congress retains authority over tax legislation and spending authority for all branches of the federal government. The legislative process has become much more convoluted and time-consuming as a result of the decline in the ability of leaders in both parties to control rank-and-file members, the increased numbers of turf-protecting subcommittees, and the proliferation of politically active special interest groups in the private sector. Given the litigious nature of the United States, the judicial branch — including the Supreme Court — periodically becomes a factor in determining the final content of national and international economic policies.

Different priorities, values, and ideologies caused the substance and tenor of U.S. domestic economic policies in the last half of the twentieth century to be radically different from those of Japan. Government minimalists look favorably upon limited official interference with the market mechanism. However, some of us detect an implicit link between shortcomings in U.S. domestic economic policy substance and shortcomings in the U.S. trade performance — just as an implicit link exists between good Japanese domestic economic policy management and a great trade performance. In contradistinction to the Japanese government's developmental approach, the United States remains an example of what Chalmers Johnson called the regulatory, or market-rational, state. The U.S. government has concerned itself with assuring "proper" behavior by firms, perhaps best illustrated by demanding compliance with what arguably are the world's most vigorous sets of antitrust and antidiscriminatory statutes. Government agencies have not sought to collaborate with the private sector to chart visions of the economy's future, target specific industries and technology for nurturing, or designate sectors for being phased out.

## Macroeconomic Policies

U.S. monetary policy over the past half-century has been legally required to regard price stability as its overriding goal. Making low-cost capital available to fledgling industries and seeking an exchange rate conducive to global competitiveness have been minor concerns at best. Unlike the Japanese experience, periodic spiking of interest rates to constrain inflationary pressures regularly caused the "stop and go" phenomenon in the U.S. business cycle. One of the U.S. monetary policy's great failures to prevent inflation occurred when President Lyndon Johnson tried to defy the economic axiom of "guns or butter" and fight a war on poverty at home and a war in Vietnam without raising taxes to pay for them. The overly accommodating monetary policy that accompanied this expansionary fiscal policy was instrumental in unleashing domestic inflationary pressures sufficiently high to cause a secular deterioration in the U.S. trade position. The dollar subsequently became so overvalued that its misalignment was instrumental in the collapse of the Bretton Woods system of fixed exchange rates.

Through the 1980s, articles in the U.S. economic literature asserted that the relatively high cost of borrowed capital caused by relatively high interest rates was a major cause of U.S. companies being put at a competitive cost disadvantage to their Japanese counterparts. In the words of former U.S. Treasury secretary and Wall Street executive Nicholas Brady, high corporate borrowing costs also affect business strategy by making some long-term investments prohibitively costly. High capital costs, he said, mean projects have to pay off more quickly. "But let me tell you what it doesn't mean. It doesn't mean long-term risk-taking. And it doesn't mean competitive prices."[20]

Unusually restrictive U.S. monetary policy in the early 1980s produced extraordinarily high real (inflation-adjusted) interest rates. This action was originally taken to battle the inflationary effects of the second oil shock. It was retained in response to one of the major turning points in modern U.S. economic history: massive federal budget deficits following full implementation of the large reductions in income tax rates approved by Congress in 1981. A well-documented economic argument emerged that accelerating inflation had created a rate of "bracket-creep" in which higher nominal salaries were being pushed into ever higher tax brackets so rapidly that saving and investment were periodically being discouraged. One way to minimize undesirable distortions would be to reform specific sections of the U.S. tax code. However, U.S. fiscal policy and economic logic parted ways as Washington bought into all the exaggerated premises and promises of Reaganomics. Because believers in supply-side economics viewed all taxes as the cause of U.S. economic ills, their answer was to slash the federal tax base across the board — despite the United States' long having had one of the lowest ratios of tax receipts to GDP among the industrialized countries. Supply-siders wrongly predicted that the stimulative effects on economic activity would generate so much new tax revenue that the budgetary implications would soon be negligible, the largest U.S. peacetime military buildup notwithstanding.

Instead, the federal debt tripled as the United States threw itself a $2 trillion economic party during the 1980s and sent the bill to future generations. In contrast to Japan spending less than it produced, the United States was now spending far more than it produced. Triple-digit budget deficits became a long-term fixture of the U.S. economic landscape and kept growing until they peaked in 1992. Although virtual unanimity existed that the deficits were dangerously large and needed to be reduced, the U.S. government lacked the political will to attack the problem head on for several years.

The resulting domestic fiscal policy malaise was important, but it was not the sole cause of the subsequent deterioration of the U.S. trade balance. A second important cause was the unprecedented appreciation in the dollar's exchange rate that presumably reflected the jump in real U.S. interest rates. This is a classic example of U.S. domestic macroeconomic policies being initiated and maintained with little or no regard for the adverse international economic effects. Many foreign-made goods became significantly cheaper in dollar terms while many relatively high-cost U.S.-produced goods were priced out of foreign markets. The damage macroeconomic policies inflicted on the U.S. external sector during most of the 1980s would have been politically intolerable in Japan and elsewhere.

The combination of large budget deficits and inadequate saving to finance them internally has direct implications for a country's external economic position. Because of statistical definitions, the current account balance (goods and services) in any given year will approximately equal the sum of the country's private saving minus net government expenditures (revenues minus outlays) minus investment (see Table 7.1). Unless governmental deficits and private investment outlays are offset by a high rate of saving as they are in Japan (or by a surge in net export sales), a country by definition finances the shortcoming in internal saving through net capital imports. Balance of payments theory and statistical measures, in turn, dictate that a capital account surplus must be offset, that is, financed, by a current account deficit of comparable magnitude.

The U.S. domestic saving rate, already low relative to other industrialized countries, declined to even lower levels in the 1980s and stayed there. The U.S. gross saving rate of 16.2 percent in 1994, for example, was well below its 21.3 percent level in 1979 and barely half of Japan's 1995 gross saving rate of 31.2 percent.[21] Low saving rates can have negative consequences other than contributing to current account deficits. A correlation seems to exist between levels of national saving, investment, and real growth in GDP. The supply of saving can affect interest rates that, in turn, influence corporate investment decisions. Outlays for new plant and capital equipment are major variables determining annual increases in productivity — the most important indicator of a country's abilities to

**TABLE 7.1**

**The U.S. Saving-Investment Imbalance**
**(in billions of U.S. dollars)**

|  | 1985 | 1990 | 1995 |
| --- | --- | --- | --- |
| Private saving | 731.5 | 861.7 | 1,078.1 |
| Government saving* | 15.2 | 43.0 | 80.0 |
| Investment* | −865.0 | −1,000.0 | −1,285.3 |
| Saving-investment imbalance | −118.3 | −95.3 | −133.5 |
| Current account deficit | −124.2 | −94.7 | −148.2 |

*A considerable amount (upwards of $200 billion annually) of federal spending is counted as "investment," thereby causing an overall federal/state/local governmental budget deficit to statistically move into surplus; hence, the government shows positive saving rather than the usually reported dissaving.

Sources: U.S. Commerce Department data presented in the Annual Report of the Council of Economic Advisers, and the Congressional Joint Economic Committee, Economic Indicators, various issues.

increase its standard of living on a noninflationary basis over the long-term and to improve its competitiveness in the global marketplace. U.S. investment rates do not compare favorably with Japan. The latter's investment in nonresidential buildings and capital equipment between 1972 and 1991 increased almost 3.5 times as fast, in real terms, as that of the United States.[22] Japan, with half the population, recorded investment outlays (expressed in nominal dollars) just slightly less (in absolute terms) than did the United States in 1991.[23] During the 1960–90 period, the average annual increase in U.S. productivity (output per hour) in the manufacturing sector was 2.9 percent, the lowest of any major industrial country and less than one-half of Japan's average annual increases of 6.9 percent.[24]

### Assisting and Regulating Industry

Few of the U.S. government's official actions below the level of macro-economic policies have enhanced U.S. industrial efficiency. Prior to the late 1960s, ineffectual economic policies would not have been an immediate cause for concern: the United States was enjoying an unrivaled standard of living, high productivity growth, steadily rising real wages, and undisputed global leadership in basic manufacturing as well as high value-added goods. By 1970, the margin of error for economic policy had shrunk dramatically.

"Industrial policy," designed to bolster the effects of free markets in desired areas of economic growth, has acquired such a negative connotation in official circles that it is discussed in Washington only in terms of the more limited concept of "science and technology policy." In fact, the "non-planning" process in the United States has spawned a back door policy and an uncoordinated series of fragmented industrial policies. Opposition to the idea of the U.S. government's picking winners and losers has not prevented federal financial support for a number of sectors, including defense, space exploration, agriculture, housing, and automobiles (including construction of the interstate highway system and initiation of voluntary export restraints by Japanese automobile makers). The results of government-business cooperation in these sectors appear to have been cost-effective on balance. However, a curious blind spot in the U.S. psyche sustains widespread opposition to the notion of adding high-tech commercial technology to the list of government beneficiaries. Government funding to develop semiconductors with military applications is perfectly acceptable but not for development of chips having commercial applications.

These beliefs have a curious institutional effect: the equivalent of Japan's MITI in the U.S. government has been the Department of Defense, more particularly its Advanced Research Projects Agency, the Pentagon's outlet for financing new weapons and dual-use technology, such as computers, semiconductors, and flat panel displays.[25] (MITI, in some respects, is Japan's equivalent of the Pentagon. For more than half a century, expanding industrial strength has been judged more important to Japan's long-term national security than countering external military threats.) The U.S. government financed an estimated $61 billion worth of research and development in 1995, the majority of which was allocated to defense and space. It also indirectly supported industrial research and development through several billion dollars in tax credits received by the private sector for incremental research and experimentation expenditures.[26] In contrast, only $221 million was appropriated by Congress for fiscal 1996 to the Commerce Department's Advanced Technology Program, the U.S. government's largest civilian program designed specifically for promoting commercial technological and manufacturing innovations.

Research ideas regularly spill over from the defense to the commercial realm, as happened when technology that was developed for military cargo planes was adapted for commercial jumbo jets. The hit-and-miss nature of such spillovers, however, makes industrial policy "by proxy" a second-best approach. The effects of focused targeting can be seen by contrasting the excellence of U.S. defense-related technology with the excellence of Japan's commercial high-tech industries. An early 1980s critique of the U.S. government's haphazard approach to helping the industrial sector by Robert Reich and Ira Magaziner still rings true:

While U.S. defense procurement and defense-related research and development programs have spawned some highly competitive industries, these programs have been undertaken without regard to their effects on the commercial development of civilian markets. . . . [The United States] has clung tenaciously to the notion that government can and should be "neutral" with regard to market adjustments. The vast array of U.S. tariffs, quotas, "voluntary" export agreements, and bail-outs for declining businesses are viewed as isolated exceptions to the rule of neutrality; its defense-related expenditures, tax breaks, and assorted subsidies for other industries are seen as being somehow unrelated to industrial development or to market dynamics. Consequently, the U.S. has neither neutrality nor rationality. Meanwhile, its trading partners are becoming ever more efficient in designing and administering policies to aid their industries in adapting to market changes.[27]

The argument has been made that unnecessary and poorly administered government regulation has negatively affected U.S. productivity and competitiveness. Few have recommended going as far as to repeal, in their entirety, statutes designed to improve social health and welfare, but many have suggested that there is a need to administer regulatory measures with more emphasis on an economic cost-benefit test, especially in the wake of the major upsurge in new federal regulation during the 1970s.

One estimate of the rising costs to the U.S. economy of federal regulation puts the 1995 total at more than $600 billion (in 1991 dollars), much of which is accounted for by industry's complying with Environmental Protection Agency regulations.[28]

### Education

While primary education is not formally a part of economic policy, it is another area of government responsibility that has been a drag on improvement in U.S. industrial performance. World-class manufacturing corporations need workers who can operate sophisticated machinery with minimal supervision and who comprehend the intricacies of the manufacturing process well enough to take the lead in offering suggestions on how to improve it. The United States has a shortage of workers with these skills. According to IBM's chairman, the U.S. business community may be spending as much as $30 billion annually to upgrade the reading and technical skills of the labor force and losing another $25 to $30 billion in lost production because of inadequate literacy among workers.[29]

U.S. public schools have improved only slightly since 1983, when the National Commission on Excellence in Education concluded that "the educational foundations of our society are presently being eroded by a rising tide of mediocrity that threatens our very future as a Nation." The commission's final report argued that because knowledge, training, and skilled intelligence were the "new raw materials of international commerce," the United States needed to reform its primary educational system "if only to keep and improve on the slim competitive edge we still retain in world markets."[30] That this concern has not yet been translated into improved educational performance is suggested repeatedly by relatively poor showings of U.S. students on standardized international tests. In a 1991 assessment of 13-year-olds' proficiency in mathematics, the average scores of U.S. students ranked dead last in a sample group of 14 industrialized and semi-industrialized countries, and thirteenth out of the same 14 in a science proficiency test.[31] Despite the potential drag of an under-performing educational system on future U.S. economic performance, the U.S. propensity to place equity and nondiscrimination ahead of excellence largely explains why about $11 is spent in the United States on educational programs for handicapped children for every one cent allocated to programs for gifted students.[32]

## THE U.S. ECONOMY REBOUNDS

The U.S. industrial sector experienced a renaissance beginning in the late 1980s and continuing into the late 1990s. This improved performance, in sharp contrast to the series of setbacks suffered by Japan's economy in the post–bubble era, was so pronounced that the U.S. economy was designated as the world's most competitive by the 1994 and 1995 annual surveys jointly conducted by the Swiss-based World Economic Forum and the International Institute for Management and Development. The 1996 survey, published separately by the latter, again ranked the United States as number one. (In the 1996 rankings of the World Economic Forum, Japan had dropped to thirteenth place).[33]

Between spring 1991 (the end of a brief downturn in the business cycle) and year-end 1996, the U.S. economy enjoyed an uninterrupted period of noninflationary growth that added more than $800 billion to total GDP in real terms. The net civilian work force expanded by more than 10 million in the first seven years of the 1990s. If the estimated 20 million-plus losses in existing positions is factored in, at least 30 million new jobs were created in the United States during these years. U.S. macroeconomic policies performed extremely well. The chairman of the Federal Reserve's Board of Governors, Alan Greenspan, won the overwhelming confidence of the financial markets and was roundly praised for steering monetary policy along a near-perfect middle ground between anti-inflation and growth-promotion. On the fiscal policy side, three factors substantially reduced government deficits, President Clinton's politically bold tax increase, which barely squeaked through Congress in 1993, increased tax revenues generated by sustained economic growth, and restrained federal spending on many programs. By 1997 the United States could boast that its budget deficit expressed as a percentage of GDP was the lowest of any major industrial country (well under 1 percent).

Silicon Valley became a metaphor for the U.S. economic resurgence. This term symbolizes the unequalled pace of U.S. innovation in important high-tech sectors like computer hardware and software and multimedia and internet technology. Technological advancements seemed to occur on a weekly basis, giving new meaning to product obsolescence. Pleased with the economy and the outlook for increased corporate profits, the U.S. stock market soared upward. The steady upsurge in stock prices increased the estimated market value of U.S. equities by nearly $4 trillion between 1994 and year-end 1996[34] and provided abundant equity financing for hundreds of new start-up companies. Some 3,000 U.S. companies went public by issuing stock between 1992 and mid-1996, as compared with 150 companies in Europe making initial public offerings of stock between 1990 and mid-1996.[35]

With average annual increases of 3.2 percent between 1990 and 1995, the growth in U.S. manufacturing productivity was both above its earlier levels and higher than the average annual increases during this period for Japan (2.2 percent) and Germany (2.7 percent).[36] The number of labor strikes dropped to a 50-year low during the first half of the 1990s.

Increases in total real compensation to U.S. workers was about equal to increased labor productivity. An important hidden strength of the U.S. economy was uncovered in a study by the McKinsey Global Institute that found the United States utilizes its physical capital (machinery and buildings) far more efficiently than either Japan or Germany. U.S. capital productivity was found to be about one-half higher than in these two countries; in other words, a unit of capital input in Japan or Germany has been producing only about two-thirds the amount produced by a unit of capital in the United States. A more efficient use of capital and higher rates of return on invested capital partially compensate for lower U.S. saving and investment rates, thereby explaining the paradox of how the United States is creating greater financial wealth and out-consuming countries who save and invest relatively more than it does.[37]

One of the most important measures of U.S. industry's rebound was the many hundreds of high-tech and basic manufacturing companies that restructured themselves from top to bottom in a relentless drive to increase efficiency, lower production costs, enhance quality control, and accelerate new product development. The single greatest motivating force for these improvements was crushing foreign competition — usually from Japan. Often faced with clear and present threats of financial ruin, these companies belatedly recognized the necessity of emulating the lean production techniques perfected by the Japanese (sometimes in connection with the ideas of U.S. management consultants). Arguably, every improvement in process technology initiated by U.S. industry after 1980 was inspired by Japanese innovations.

The notoriously inefficient U.S. steel and automobile industries confounded critics and free-trade advocates by gradually transforming themselves into world-class competitors while partially shielded from foreign competition by voluntary export restraints. The steel industry became one of the world's low-cost producers thanks to extensive investment to modernize and streamline production techniques, higher labor productivity, the proliferation of ultra-efficient "mini-mills," and a weakened dollar. Ford and Chrysler were reported to have improved their automobile assembly line productivity by more than 30 percent between the early 1980s and early 1990s, virtually erasing the labor cost advantages enjoyed by Japanese auto producers.[38] Chrysler trimmed its normal new model development time by more than a year for the automobiles it introduced in the 1990s by replicating the Japanese team approach for product innovation. Instead of pitting suppliers against one another in competitive bidding, the company, like Japanese firms, has shifted to long-term contracts with key suppliers and has engaged in close consultation with them about component designs and performance criteria.[39]

The Xerox Corporation, original developer of photocopying machines, saw the need for radical action in the 1980s as its world market share for this product plummeted. Its strongest Japanese competitors were producing copy machines at about one-half of Xerox's production costs and with 10 to 30 times fewer defective parts. Furthermore, new products were being introduced in Japan in one-half the time, with one-half as many people on the development team.[40] Xerox subsequently regained market share after it, again, like Japan, streamlined production techniques, enhanced after-sales service, reduced the layers of middle management, slashed the number of suppliers (by almost 90 percent), and increased quality control. In 1989, the company's Business Products and Systems Division won the U.S. Commerce Department's Malcolm Baldrige National Quality Award in recognition of "preeminent quality leadership" by U.S. corporations.

Motorola's experience suggests a strong link between corporate zeal in manufacturing excellence and success at competing head-to-head with Japanese companies, even in their home market. Motorola's global dominance in such products as pocket pagers and cellular telephones reflects a corporate strategy to "out-Japan" Japan, in which Motorola has unstintingly stressed quality control, product innovation, simplified assembly operations, customer satisfaction, worker training, research and development, and a long-term planning horizon.[41] Motorola also has imposed rigid quality control standards on suppliers, in some cases insisting that the latter be good enough to be seriously considered for the Baldrige award. Its manufacturing excellence notwithstanding, Motorola's record is also notable for frequent appeals to the U.S. government for help in getting discriminatory regulatory barriers reduced in Japan.

Despite the torrent of favorable economic news, many Americans, in the mid-1990s, were deeply pessimistic about the future.[42] Widespread corporate downsizing unleashed a virtual epidemic of job insecurity, mostly among white collar workers who rarely had such worries in the past. The perception that the vast majority of new jobs being created are for minimum wage "hamburger flippers" is so widely believed that it overwhelms empirical data showing that more than two-thirds of the net growth in full-time U.S. employment in the mid-1990s came in job categories paying above-median wages and that one-half of the net growth occurred in job categories paying wages in the top 30 percent (mostly in the services sector).[43]

Paul Krugman has noted that "Virtually every statistical measure of economic well-being — real wages, family income, poverty rates, and so on — shows a rapid improvement from 1945 to the early 1970s, but flattens out or declines thereafter."[44] By most measures, average real earnings for production line and nonsupervisory workers fell moderately but steadily from the late 1970s through the mid-1990s.[45] (When fringe benefits, such as health insurance, are included, total real compensation to workers increased by a moderate amount.) To the extent that the consumer price index has not been exaggerating increases in inflation, median family income appears to have been stagnant over the past two decades despite large income increases among the wealthiest 20 percent of Americans. The bottom line is that there are no incontrovertible answers to the questions of the cause, extent, and permanence of U.S. economic prosperity in the 1990s. There is also no definitive answer to the question of whether the United States has a competitiveness problem when competitiveness is defined as a country's ability to simultaneously increase the real incomes of its people and compete successfully in the global marketplace. Any country can improve its trade balance through reductions in living standards induced by lower real wages and currency depreciation.

## CONCLUSION

The pockets of strengths and weaknesses in the U.S. domestic economy have been critical variables determining foreign trade performance, just as in Japan. The two countries' trade fortunes have been dissimilar primarily because of differences in domestic economic institutions, economic ideology, and national priorities. The United States originally achieved economic success through individual initiative, the perfection of mass production techniques, and abundant natural resources — not self-denial in favor of long-term goals, group effort, a propensity for collusion, and other tendencies associated with Japan. An examination of bilateral trade relations since the 1970s tends to exaggerate weaknesses in a fundamentally strong, resilient U.S. economic system. The industrial sector of no other country so consistently and dramatically outcompeted U.S. industry as did that of Japan.

In retrospect, the U.S. government, business, and labor sectors would have suffered fewer economic setbacks if they had shared Japan's intense commitment to thinking about and preparing for the future. While Japan deferred consumption and gave top priority to expanding its economic base, U.S. consumers lived for the present, and U.S. government strategists plotted containment of the Soviet Union. Americans deserve no praise for waiting until the late 1980s, after many companies and whole industries either disappeared or were threatened with extinction from Japanese competition, to mount a credible economic counterattack.

The U.S. idea of economic efficiency — a collection of individuals adhering to an ethos that only personal limitations should limit success, a government should interfere only minimally in the economy, business managers should operate under the strict discipline of maximizing current shareholder equity and profits — was and is a successful system entirely appropriate to the U.S. historical experience. It was not, however, the same as Japan's synergy in making the transition to master producer of low-cost, high quality products that the world wants to buy. The United States' unabashed pursuit of personal enrichment, adversarial government-business relations, and short-term horizons resulted in a relative lack of focus, harmony, and concern for the costs of declining industrial competitiveness, mainly relative to Japan.

Thus far in the 1990s, the U.S. economy has performed far better than it did in the previous two decades. In most respects, it has out-performed the Japanese economy. The merits of free-wheeling U.S. entrepreneurialism in the fast growing fields of information management, vast improvements in process technology invariably adapted from the Japanese, and better macroeconomic policies have been much in evidence. If the positive results of these recent improvements have not been fully felt then the rise in U.S. industrial dynamism has not yet hit its peak.

The U.S. economic performance is still far from exemplary. The United States is saving too little and consuming too much. The overall rate of productivity increase is too low and needs to be increased through higher rates of investment in both human and physical capital. The lesson of cyclical economic performance suggests the most foolish response to favorable U.S. economic trends would be overconfidence and a sense of permanence.

## NOTES

1. See the first page of Chapter 6 for a definition of how this term is used here.

2. Unpublished data by the U.S. Department of Labor estimate that in 1992, with the United States equal to 100, comparative levels of real GDP per employed person were 76.4 in Japan, 89.1 in Germany, and 85.6 in Canada.

3. Thomas K. McCraw, "Business & Government: The Origins of the Adversary Relationship," *California Management Review* (Winter 1984), p. 39.

4. Sanford J. Ungar, *Fresh Blood — The New American Immigrants* (New York: Simon & Schuster, 1995), pp. 366–67.

5. Seymour Martin Lipset, *American Exceptionalism: A Two-Edged Sword* (New York: W. W. Norton, 1996), p. 31.

6. Examples of U.S. tolerance in the 1950s for discriminatory trade treatment included disproportionately high U.S. tariff cuts made in the early rounds of the General Agreement on Tariffs and Trade trade liberalization negotiations and the discriminatory provisions of the European Payments Union.

7. Alexis de Tocqueville as quoted in *Bartlett's Familiar Quotations* (Boston: Little, Brown, and Company, 1982), p. 506.

8. McCraw, "Business & Government," pp. 42, 46.

9. Ibid., pp. 41–43.

10. Ibid., pp. 45–46.

11. When various "nuisance" lawsuits are included, the U.S. legal system had become so convoluted that a book describing its excesses, *The Death of Common Sense*, became a best seller. Subsequent to the book's publication, a customer

who spilled hot coffee on herself sued the McDonalds corporation and was initially awarded a multimillion-dollar judgment by a jury.

12.    Bob Eaton, "No Joking Matter," *Newsweek*, September 23, 1996, p. 20.

13.    Bert Braddock, as quoted in *Washington Post*, October 24, 1982, p. A10.

14.    Stephen R. Hardis, as quoted in *New York Times*, October 30, 1988, p. III-8.

15.    "A Japanese View: Why America Has Fallen Behind," *Fortune*, September 25, 1989, p. 52.

16.    MIT Commission on Industrial Productivity, *Made in America* (Cambridge, Mass.: MIT Press, 1989), pp. 8, 42.

17.    Ibid., p. 166.

18.    Stephen S. Cohen and John Zysman, "Puncture the Myths that Keep American Managers from Competing," *Harvard Business Review* (November-December 1988), p. 98.

19.    "Stuck in Reverse," *New York Times Book Review*, October 29, 1989, p. 38; "Study Says Ford Leads in Efficiency," *New York Times*, January 3, 1990, p. D5.

20.    U.S. Treasury Department, press release, September 12, 1989, p. 4.

21.    Organization for Economic Cooperation and Development, *OECD Economic Outlook*, June 1996, Annex Table 27.

22.    Daniel F. Burton, Jr., "High-Tech Competitiveness," *Foreign Policy* (Fall 1993), p. 118.

23.    Organization for Economic Cooperation and Development, *National Accounts, 1960–1994*. The yen was converted at 125 to the dollar. Note that 1991 was the peak year, thus far, for Japanese domestic investment.

24.    U.S. Labor Department, "International Comparisons of Manufacturing Productivity and Unit Labor Cost Trends, 1990," press release, August 20, 1991.

25.    This agency was originally called DARPA. To connote its concern with commercial technological innovation, the Clinton administration dropped the word "Defense" from the beginning of the agency's name.

26.    National Science Board, *Science & Engineering Indicators 1996* (Washington, D.C.: U.S. Government Printing Office, 1996), pp. 4-6, 4-7.

27.    Ira C. Magaziner and Robert Reich, *Minding America's Business* (New York: Vintage Books, 1983), p. 200.

28.    Alliance for Reasonable Regulation, "Environmental Regulations: In Too Many Instances, Out of Control," press release, March 22, 1995.

29.    Louis Gerstner, Jr., "Our Schools Are Failing. Do We Care?" *New York Times*, May 27, 1994, p. A27.

30.    The National Commission on Excellence in Education, *A Nation at Risk*, April 1983, p. 7.

31.    National Science Board, *Science & Engineering Indicators 1996*, pp. 1-11–1-12, 1-15. These tests were all administered by the U.S.-based Educational Testing Service.

32.    Philip K. Howard, *The Death of Common Sense — How Law Is Suffocating America* (New York: Random House, 1994), p. 151.

33.    "U.S. Is Ranked Most Competitive in World," *The Wall Street Journal*, September 5, 1995, p. A2; "The C-Word Strikes Back," *The Economist*, June 1, 1996, p. 76.

34. Security Industries Association, *1996 Securities Industry Fact Book* (New York: Security Industries Association, n.d.); data provided to the author by telephone.

35. Peter Lynch, "The Upsizing of America," *The Wall Street Journal*, September 20, 1996, p. A14.

36. U.S. Department of Labor, "International Comparisons of Manufacturing Productivity and Unit Labor Cost Trends, 1995," press release, July, 17, 1996.

37. McKinsey Global Institute, *Capital Productivity*, June 1996, pp. 1–5.

38. Thomas H. Klier, "How Lean Manufacturing Changes the Way We Understand the Manufacturing Sector," *Economic Perspectives* [Federal Reserve Bank of Chicago], May-June 1993, p. 3.

39. Ibid., p. 7.

40. MIT Commission on Industrial Productivity, *Made in America*, pp. 119-23.

41. See, for example, "The Rival Japan Respects," *Business Week*, November 13, 1989, pp. 108–18.

42. According to an NBC/*Wall Street Journal* poll conducted in January 1996, a mere 41 percent of U.S. parents polled believed that their children would enjoy a higher standard of living than they (the parents) achieved. "Americans, Especially Baby Boomers, Voice Pessimism for Their Kids' Economic Future," *The Wall Street Journal*, January 19, 1996, p. A12.

43. President's Council of Economic Advisers, "Job Creation and Employment Opportunities: The United States Labor Market, 1993-1996," report, April 23, 1996, p. 6.

44. Paul Krugman, "It's a Wonderful Life," *Washington Monthly* (January-February 1996), p. 49.

45. Brian Blackstone, "What's Happening to Wages and Incomes?" (Washington, D.C.: Coalition of Service Industries, n.d.), p. 1 (newsletter).

# 8

# Divergent International Economic Policy Strategies

The Japanese don't understand why the U.S. doesn't play by their trade rules; the reason is that the U.S. does not realize that it is in a [competitive] race.

— Senior U.S. Commerce Department official (1982)

Thus far, Japan has viewed its economic, technological, and trade policies, including its negotiations with the United States, as a continuation of competition and predation by other means.

— Charles H. Ferguson (1989)

Determination of a country's international trade performance begins with domestic economic and business conditions and then moves to the external dimension, specifically the interaction of international trade, monetary, and investment policies. The substance of U.S.-Japanese post–World War II international economic policies demonstrates little common ground because they were based on dissimilar belief systems, and they reflected different national goals. Once again, when comparing the two countries' experiences, dissimilarity is a constant. Japanese international economic policies have focused with laser-like precision on maximizing exports relative to imports as a means to enhanced domestic industrial strength. Conversely, U.S. international economic policies have demonstrated ambiguity within an unfocused, scattershot effort that sometimes tries to promote foreign policy goals and sometimes tries to promote a liberal international economic order. This chapter explains how and why these contrasting approaches to international trade, monetary, and investment policies contributed to three decades of trade problems.

## JAPANESE FOREIGN TRADE IDEOLOGY AND PRACTICES

When U.S. and Japanese policymakers looked at the international trading system at the conclusion of World War II, they saw different things. The two countries had little in common when it came to needs, memories, traditions, ambitions, and motivations. Only the general desire to make the process of importing and exporting serve what was deemed to be the national interest was shared.

Throughout the post–World War II era, Japan stubbornly clung to an "export or die" mentality. An expanding export sector was considered to be a prerequisite for economic recovery and growth. Exports were necessary to earn the foreign exchange needed to pay for massive amounts of essential raw materials and energy imports for an expanding, but natural resource–poor economy. In addition, exports were needed to provide the incremental sales base needed for domestic manufacturers to achieve economies of scale. Imports of finished goods were tolerated or disdained. Japan's relatively self-centered, narrowly focused view of the international trading system was and is anything but unique. The commitment to promoting a booming export sector as a means to attaining domestic economic goals is also shared by most countries. Japan has been distinctive only in the magnitude of its twin trade successes: expanding exports through manufacturing and marketing excellence and maintaining a dynamic industrial sector despite discouraging import competition through formal and indirect impediments.

In blunt terms, Japan has been a master practitioner of mercantilism, the centuries-old theory that a country enhances its economic prosperity and international political power by running trade surpluses. Viewing trade as a zero-sum game among nations, mercantilists believe markets are too imperfect to be left unregulated. Imports are seen primarily as a threat to domestic prosperity. Western economists have disparaged this still politically appealing concept since 1776, when Adam Smith's classic study, *The Wealth of Nations* first appeared. Their arguments that trade is a positive-sum game and that a nation increases its wealth by being able to provide consumers with goods produced more efficiently abroad often fall on deaf ears, even in the West. For Japan, importing one's way to prosperity is a wholly alien concept.

The ultimate guiding force behind Japan's approach to foreign trade relations since the Meiji Restoration is the priority of preserving its unique value system amid what it has seen as a hostile, undependable, and unpredictable world. Most Japanese view the development and preservation of globally competitive industries as the essence of their country's national security and the principal determinant of its domestic prosperity. From the time that it literally was forced at gunpoint to become part of the Western-dominated trading system, Japan has struggled to overcome the handicaps associated with being an industrial latecomer and being dependent on foreign sources for a majority of its raw materials. Catching up with the West, as measured by the ability to rely on domestic production for an ever-expanding array of state-of-the-art manufactured goods, has been the informal national past-time in Japan for the past 150 years. Personal sacrifices required to close external competitive gaps seemingly are offset by the psychic income accompanying reduced dependence on, and increased respect from, foreigners.

Japan's contemporary success, as measured in industrial size and strength, has not yet erased the country's long-standing feelings of superiority and vulnerability. As a geographically isolated country subject to natural disasters, lacking raw materials, possessing an extraordinary inner drive to preserve its cherished cultural heritage, having only one close overseas political ally, and not giving priority to the goal of maximizing consumer sovereignty, Japan exhibits feelings of nationalism and realpolitik toward foreign trade to an extent not understood in the United States. In the words of Masataka Kosaka:

Ultranationalism was discredited by the Second World War, but the views and experiences of the 1920s and 1930s have remained in Japanese consciousness: as Japan has no natural resources, its first priority must be their acquisition; extraordinary efforts to increase exports are necessary in order to pay for raw materials. . . . Japan is in a disadvantageous position politically because it is the only non-white industrial country. These feelings make up the underpinnings for Japan's defensive and nationalistic international economic policy.[1]

The theoretical construct underlying Japan's trade policy strategy is difficult, if not impossible, for Americans to comprehend. Modern U.S. import policy ideology is framed as a black and white struggle between selfish, inefficient protectionists and a mutually advantageous, Adam Smith–driven pursuit of a liberal international trading order enhancing the wealth of all nations. It is not that simple. Economic activity need not be about increased incomes and consumption for individuals. Long forgotten is Alexander Hamilton's 1791 *Report on the Subject of Manufactures*, one of the earliest treatises on economic nationalism, in which he advised every country to possess within itself "all the essentials of national supply." Hamilton believed that "Not only the wealth, but the independence and security of a country, appear to be materially connected with the prosperity of manufactures."[2]

Japanese trade ideology clearly parallels the nineteenth-century German Historical School of political economy that dismissed the alleged virtues of free trade. One of the leading members of this school, Friedrich List, felt that the British exemplified the hypocrisy of a country staunchly advocating liberal trade — but only after having achieved economic strength through non–laissez-faire, state-supported promotion of infant industries (and occasionally through military conquest of other countries). In other words, Great Britain allegedly pursued protectionist policies until its industrial sector was strong enough to dominate world trade in manufactured goods. This school of thought holds that advocacy of liberal trade at the end of the twentieth century comes exclusively from the dominant industrial countries. Only after being able to pay for imports of relatively low-cost primary goods through exports of sophisticated manufactured goods do these countries become enamored of promoting an open trading system.

Given the Meiji government's determination to prevent the unique social order from being subjugated by the military might of Western powers, Japan could readily identify with List's argument that the highest priority of a sovereign nation is safeguarding and maintaining its independence. "Its duty is to preserve and to develop its prosperity, culture, nationality, and language, and freedom — in short, its entire social and political position in the world."[3] List inferred that foreign trade was a process of the strong versus the weak, not a matter of right versus wrong or of cheating versus playing fair.

The Japanese government's 150-year tilt toward producers rather than consumers echoes List's core argument that in the long run, a society's well-being and its overall wealth are determined by what it can produce, not what it can buy. In strategic terms, countries became dependent or independent based on their ability to make advanced industrial goods — as demonstrated today by the skewed allocation of production between the relatively powerful economies of the North and the relatively weaker ones in the South. Sounding zenlike, List wrote:

The *causes of wealth* are something totally different from *wealth itself.* A person [who] does not possess the power of producing objects of more value than he consumes . . . will become poorer. . . . *The power of producing wealth* is therefore infinitely more important than *wealth itself.* . . . This is still more the case with nations . . . Germany has been devastated in every century by pestilence, by famine, or by civil or foreign wars; she has, nevertheless, always retained a great portion of her powers of production, and has thus quickly reattained some degree of prosperity.[4]

In sum, List felt that the prosperity of a nation is mainly determined by the extent to which it has developed its "powers of production" in the industrial sector.[5]

Japan shared List's dismissal of the notion that the invisible hand of the marketplace would lead inexorably to national economic prosperity and cultural independence. Hence Japan's consistent emphasis on building a strong, export-oriented industrial sector and, until the 1980s, inhibiting imports of any advanced manufactured good that could be produced reasonably efficiently in Japan. Most Japanese traditionally have viewed the international trading system, first and foremost, as a vehicle for assuring national survival, not as a means of making money or helping other countries to bolster their economies.

Japanese trade policymakers do not believe that comparative advantage is linked immutably to a given relative endowment of land, labor, and capital. They do believe that through an elaborate infant industry strategy, a joint government-business effort could induce global competitiveness in most industries. Government assistance to targeted industries would influence private sector allocations of capital and human resources, and it could produce better results than reliance on pure free-market competition.

Utilization of advanced Western technology and manufacturing techniques has been a constant in Japanese trade strategy. After 1945, Japan became particularly adept at identifying advanced technology abroad and gaining access to it through means other than imports and inward foreign direct investment. As part of the syndrome of maximizing domestic control over influences from the outside world, the Japanese government assisted domestic companies in negotiating highly favorable licensing agreements for those foreign ideas and inventions useful to industrial resurgence. By one estimate, the Japanese paid $9 billion between 1950 and 1978 in licensing fees for technology developed in the United States at a cost that may have been as high as $1 trillion.[6] A second estimate of $17 billion in cumulative royalties paid by Japan between 1951 and 1983 noted that this 33-year total was less than the annual U.S. research and development bill for one year in the early 1960s.[7]

The Japanese do not share the U.S. view that import barriers are unfortunate short-term responses to political necessity. Historically, few Japanese leaders have exhibited a genuine philosophical commitment to the concept of global free trade as a desirable end in itself. What they have been committed to is maximum domestic economic strength. Japanese officials do not believe in free trade if that term means allowing foreign companies with a comparative advantage to gain market share in Japan at the expense of less competitive domestic firms. Free-market, liberal trade policies are considered by most Japanese policymakers to be "at best foolish, and at worst grossly negligent" if they allow foreign-owned companies to dominate major sectors of a country's domestic economy.[8] Consistency between domestic industrial policy objectives and international trade performance was infinitely more important to the Japanese than dismantling barriers to imports. This thinking explains the pervasive application of import barriers to manufactured goods after World War II. In addition to a comprehensive system of quotas, Japan's domestic market was protected by an intricate tariff system, with low duties on primary products and capital goods not produced domestically and high rates on most finished and consumer goods.

In contrast with the postwar U.S. ambitions to reshape the international order in its own market-oriented image and resurrect the economies of noncommunist countries, the Japanese practiced case-by-case liberalization measures implemented almost entirely in response to specific pressures exerted by the United States. Lacking aspirations to global leadership, the Japanese did not adopt activist trade policies comparable to those taken by the hegemonic United States. Like most other countries, Japan's policies were reactive. It virtually never promoted an agenda nor tried to change the distant international economic system that appears to Japan to be controlled by foreigners. As explained by one Japanese observer, "There does not exist in Japan a real feeling that Japan and the Japanese, with their individuality, are related with other nations . . . [or] that the Japanese contribute to the civilization of others, and others to the civilization of Japan. . . . The world has been a 'given' surrounding Japan, which makes a real impact on Japan, but which cannot be modified by the efforts of the Japanese."[9]

The unprecedented speed and magnitude of Japan's post–World War II industrial resurgence behind a solid wall of trade barriers suggests flaws in the blanket assertions by liberal trade advocates that protectionism stifles competition, efficiency, and, therefore, the chances of economic success. The Japanese economic miracle took place without benefit of the discipline of vigorous import competition constantly poised to seize domestic market share from less efficient Japanese manufacturers. Conversely, many overconfident U.S. companies were suffering a collapse in their competitiveness despite the discipline imposed by one of the world's most liberal import policies. The world has seen few, if any, examples outside of Japan in which so many companies that were extended infant industry treatment so quickly became world-class competitors that no longer needed formal protection from imports. The peculiarities of its economic system and cultural values apparently exempted it from the need for a genuine open-door import policy to assure peak operating efficiency for domestic corporations.

Although they view imports of manufactured goods with thinly disguised disgust, Japanese government officials and corporate executives believe that a powerful export sector is crucial to achieving sufficient industrial strength to minimize Japan's dependence on foreigners and to maximize its global prestige. If encouraging imports in order to benefit consumers is unfathomable to Japan's elite, so, too, is the idea of imposing export controls in order to promote foreign policy or humanitarian goals in other countries. Until 1970, Japan's drive to increase exports was based on a nearly universal phenomenon: the need for incremental foreign exchange to pay for a greater volume of imports to support a growing domestic economy. By the late 1970s, the effort to expand exports could no longer be explained by the need to pay for incremental imports. Japan had begun amassing what was growing into the world's largest trade surpluses, and the value of exports was one-half again as large as total imports.

In the early postwar years, the Japanese government did not miss a trick in providing maximum assistance to the export promotion effort. It devised a broad range of export incentives, including export subsidies, some of which allowed companies to sell products abroad below production costs; the establishment of the Japan External Trade Organization to provide overseas commercial information; generous export financing facilities; and encouragement of industry export associations. Tax incentives included special deductions for export income and overseas market development costs and accelerated depreciation for capital equipment used to produce exports. As Japanese export strength became a source of contention in the late 1970s, virtually all special incentives were terminated. However, the phaseout of export support measures did no more to switch off the well-oiled Japanese export machine than the phaseout of formal import barriers did to engineer an overall boom in imports.

Most large Japanese manufacturing companies have coveted exports as much as the bureaucracy has. A virtual army of smart, zealous, and patient Japanese business executives went overseas to master foreign tastes, laws, customs, and languages. For the leading companies in such sectors as automobiles, consumer electronics, steel, and precision machinery, exporting represented an overseas extension of their domestic business strategy of maximizing sales and market share rather than short-term profits. Maximizing exports was also relied on to reduce the unit costs of production by spreading fixed costs over a greater sales volume.

For many years Japanese export drives typically began at the cheaper, less glamorous end of a product line that had high-volume sales potential. Since "down-market" products tend to have low profit margins, they seldom were a focus of intense efforts by U.S. producers to protect or reclaim their market share from import competition. Once a beachhead was secured, Japanese companies sought to increase sales volume by moving "up-market," that is, to the middle and upper segments of the product line, all the while maintaining consumer satisfaction through low prices and high quality. By the 1980s, Japanese innovative skills had progressed to the point where many exports to the United States consisted of state-of-the-art consumer goods, machinery, and components that had little or no competition from U.S. producers.

The aggressive pricing tactics of Japanese companies have long inspired the perception in the United States and elsewhere that Japanese exports often were priced at less than fair value, that is, there were repeated accusations of dumping. Guilty or not, Japan has been, by far, the most frequently named country in petitions filed in U.S. antidumping proceedings. Sometimes the onerous cost of distributing goods within the Japanese market had the effect of making home market prices legitimately higher than export prices. Sometimes Japanese companies engaged in dumping on a calculated basis in order to build a sales base for the future or even to decimate overseas competition. Sometimes dumping was unintentional, occurring because honest mistakes were made as to exactly where U.S. antidumping officials would draw the arbitrary dividing line between a fair and unfair price. In still other cases, U.S. producers were hoping to intimidate Japanese competitors into making quick price increases to avoid the uncertainties and expenses of formal antidumping proceedings.

Japan's general trading companies, or *sogo shosha*, provide an additional strength to the country's export capability. These companies specialize in importing and exporting, thereby freeing Japanese manufacturers to concentrate on developing and making products. The general trading companies have built an unmatched, world-wide, commercial intelligence network and miss few outlets for Japanese exports or sources of cheap raw materials to ship back to Japan. Working on small sales commissions and large volume, the larger trading companies operate in well over 100 countries, individually generating export sales valued at tens of billions of dollars annually. The perfecting of the trading company model illustrates, yet again, the Japanese practice of turning weakness into strength. Two Japanese professors explain:

When Japan was opened to international trade in the mid-19th century, it quickly recognised that its lack of preparation was a source of commercial inequality and therefore set out to foster its own trading companies to replace foreign traders in intermediating Japan's exports and imports. . . . The net result has been the emergence of unique mercantile institutions whose performance and efficiency in both intermediating trade and organising overseas ventures are unrivalled in the world. Japan has thus turned its original disadvantage into one of its trump cards for trade and investment.[10]

## U.S. FOREIGN TRADE IDEOLOGY AND PRACTICES

Compared to Japan, the attention given by the U.S. government to foreign trade has amounted to little more than an afterthought. Most U.S.

policymakers view imports as benefitting the all-important consumer, and they exude a lackadaisical attitude toward the economic importance of maximizing exports. Because industrial policy is untouchable, U.S. policymakers do not view foreign trade as part of a larger plan for achieving domestic economic goals. One observer has suggested that "the lack of a set of U.S. industrial goals means that it is impossible to have any trade goals for U.S. policy, other than to exhort other nations to practice laissez faire in the American image."[11]

The heart of modern U.S. trade ideology is suggested in Adam Smith's eighteenth-century dictum that "Consumption is the sole end and purpose of all production; and the interest of the producer ought to be attended to, only so far as it may be necessary for promoting that of the consumer."[12] This philosophy is sustained by the belief, first, that the principle of comparative advantage emerges immutably from countries' relative endowments of land, labor, and capital and, second, that global economic production will be maximized under an international division of labor based on relative efficiency. Import restrictions are believed to frustrate an optimal allocation of resources and are considered annoying but unavoidable political necessities. If relatively inefficient or declining industries with political clout are given temporary protection from intensifying import competition, the rationale is to minimize the adverse social consequences of factory closures and job losses, not to conform with long-term planning. Virtually all U.S. trade officials for the past half a century have wisely believed that the government should minimize efforts to bail out noncompetitive companies and workers by means of import barriers. Import protection equivalent to that extended in Japan would almost certainly have inspired the U.S. basic manufacturing sector — steel, automobiles, textiles, consumer electronics, footwear, and so on — to be even more indifferent to reducing production costs and increasing quality control than they were in the face of stiff external competition.

The United States' emergence as an international superpower in the late 1940s quickly imbued it with a genuinely global sense of purpose in political, military, and economic terms. Its foreign policy elite perceived a unique opportunity to shape the post–World War II international economic order in accordance with U.S. values. Negotiating reciprocal trade liberalization agreements became a central focus of U.S. trade policy. The advent of the cold war between democratic and communist bloc countries elevated trade liberalization to an even higher priority as foreign policy decision makers equated a relatively open U.S. market with promoting political stability in Western Europe and Japan. Accelerated international economic growth was seen as a catalyst for sustaining democracy and capitalism throughout the world. In what amounted to the antithesis of mercantilism, the United States did not demand full reciprocity from its trading partners in the early rounds of multilateral tariff-cutting negotiations that it promoted under the auspices of the General Agreement on Tariffs and Trade. Washington also willingly accepted discriminatory treatment imposed on its goods by Japan as well as by the European Payments Union (a regional economic organization that operated in the 1950s). A clear consensus existed that the best long-term stimulus to U.S. exports, and assurance of national security, was the rejuvenation of the European and Japanese economies.

Until U.S. hegemony first began to be questioned by the Europeans in the mid-1960s, "good" U.S. international economic policy was deemed the equivalent of "good" national security policy. There had been no serious inconsistencies between the goals of the two policies in the 20-year period after 1945. Import competition was no more a source of concern to U.S. industry than export promotion was of interest to the U.S. government. The United States was so strong in material terms that it literally sought to spread its wealth overseas in pursuit of national security objectives.

U.S. trade policies and foreign aid programs were major factors inducing the boom in international trade and capital flows during the 1950s and 1960s, the so-called golden age of the world economy. In retrospect, U.S. international economic policies may have been too generous. The abilities of the Japanese and West European economies to recover were severely underestimated. A serious flaw in postwar U.S. trade policy was the failure to foresee, recognize, and adjust to the unexpectedly rapid increase in relative Japanese and European industrial strength.

The U.S. military effort in Vietnam fanned domestic fires of disillusionment with the costly burden of global responsibilities, in general, and the U.S. international economic position, in particular. The administration of Lyndon Johnson was unable to correct accelerating inflation and a deteriorating foreign trade balance. In contrast, Western Europe and Japan in the late 1960s and early 1970s were enjoying price stability, full employment, structural balance of payments surpluses, strong foreign trade positions, and comparatively low defense costs. These divergent trends eventually had a critical consequence for the international economy: the exchange rate of the world's key currency became seriously overvalued as U.S. competitiveness steadily declined. The U.S. balance of payments deficit ballooned to the point that it was largely responsible for causing the collapse of the fixed exchange rate system.

A fundamental reorientation in U.S. international economic policy to favor domestic over foreign priorities was introduced in August 1971 by President Nixon's New Economic Policy. Among other things, it imposed a 10 percent import surcharge and terminated the U.S. commitment to convert unwanted dollars held by foreign central banks into gold at a fixed rate. The New Economic Policy led to agreements in late 1971 to implement history's largest exchange rate realignment and to prepare for another round of multilateral trade liberalization negotiations. Despite its continuing to be the guiding force behind multilateral liberalization efforts, U.S. import policy for the next 10 to 15 years was characterized by an increased willingness to respond to growing demands for relief from accelerating import competition. Mostly, these efforts took the form of agreements with Japan and the East Asian newly industrialized countriess to voluntarily restrain shipments to the United States of such goods as steel, color television sets, automobiles, machine tools, and textiles. Apologetic U.S. trade officials usually characterized these actions as second-best exceptions to continued commitment to liberal trade, not to be viewed as part of an embrace of protectionism.

The emergence of the largely macroeconomic policy-induced increases in trade deficits in the 1980s caused several interesting innovations in the philosophy and strategy of U.S. trade policy that continued into the next decade. One innovation has been the staunch rejection by both the public and private sectors of the notion that new import barriers are an appropriate means of reducing these large deficits. Congress passed the 1,000-page Omnibus Trade and Competitiveness Act of 1988 devoid of any unilateral trade restrictions at a time of little optimism that substantial reduction in the triple digit ($100 billion-plus) merchandise trade deficits was in sight.[13]

Within a few years, the U.S. government, with the unqualified support of the vast majority of the business community (especially multinational corporations), had become a driving force to draft timetables for inaugurating regional free trade areas in the Pacific Rim and in the Western Hemisphere. Exploratory talks were begun with the European Union about reducing trans-Atlantic trade barriers. Should all three regional trade blocs materialize in the twenty-first century with the United States as a member, the latter would effectively phase out all import barriers to goods shipped by all of its major trading partners, that is, the United States would adopt a virtual free trade posture.

Another important innovation in contemporary U.S. trade policy was the adoption of an aggressive commitment to correct its trade deficit through export expansion rather than import reduction. Reciprocity became the watchword of the priority effort to convince trading partners, beginning with Japan, that the United States could no longer afford and would no longer tolerate foreign trade barriers impeding its export expansion. The results were seen mainly in a series of demands, backed by unilateral threats of retaliation under the Section 301 and Super 301 provisions (see Chapter 2), that foreign import barriers be eased or eliminated. Although the primary U.S. objective was to free the flow of international trade, the Japanese, Europeans, and others intensely disliked high-profile threats of retaliatory trade barriers if they did not respond in a manner deemed satisfactory by U.S. trade officials.[14]

The concentrated campaign that began in 1985 against major foreign barriers to U.S. goods has been the exception to the long-standing rule that the U.S. government pays only lip service to export expansion. No other government has come close to its degree of indifference to, and outright restrictions on, foreign sales. No other government has displayed comparable alacrity in subordinating commercial interests to concerns about national security and foreign policy (nonproliferation of weapons, human rights, antiterrorism, and so on). No other country in the last half of the twentieth century has been quicker to opt for export sanctions as a middle ground between inaction and military attack to penalize what is deemed repugnant behavior by other countries. At various times, U.S. export controls have been imposed on the Soviet Union, Eastern Europe, China, Cuba, North Korea, Afghanistan, South Africa, Iran, Libya, Iraq, Haiti, and Syria, among others. By one estimate, export controls (including those imposed under multilateral agreements) and inadequate funding for export promotion resulted in lost U.S. exports in the range of $21 to $27 billion annually in the early 1990s and possibly as high as $40 billion.[15]

No other country has been so willing to go it alone on export controls, knowing full well that the practical result of unilateral action is that the targeted country simply shifts its orders from U.S. suppliers to foreign companies. No other country has emulated the quixotic U.S. effort to promote a higher level of morality in the world's marketplaces through the passage of a Foreign Corrupt Practices Act prohibiting all manner of illicit payments by U.S. companies to secure overseas contracts. The Clinton administration has greatly eased export controls on dual-use, high-tech goods like computers. However, the United States remains completely alone in threatening the world's fastest growing market, China, with a wide range of trade sanctions in response to alleged violations of trade rules and human rights violations, shipments of weapons of mass destruction, and so on.

Like all countries, the United States operates official programs to promote exports, the most important of which is subsidized and insured loans to assist foreigners in buying U.S. goods with high price tags. To an extent found in no other country, however, U.S. export promotion programs have been widely attacked at home as "welfare for the rich" and subjected to budget cutbacks. Even before the spending cuts, the United States was last or nearly last among eight major industrialized countries in most measures of export promotion spending, for example, per capita outlays and official assistance for industrial exports as a percentage of total industrial exports.[16] (The latter measure partly reflects a disproportionate amount of U.S. government lending in support of agricultural exports.)

There is no simple way to determine whether the unique U.S. approach to export policy is a case of nobility or foolish naïveté.

## INTERNATIONAL MONETARY POLICY AND EXCHANGE RATES

International monetary factors affect the U.S.-Japanese trade relationship on two levels. The first is the broad impact of the extraordinary international role of the dollar on the total U.S. attitude toward foreign trade. The second, narrower level is the repeated inability of the floating exchange rate system to establish a yen-dollar rate capable of inducing and sustaining equilibrium in the bilateral trade balance. Japan's claim since the 1980s to the world's largest current account surpluses (goods and services) and the dubious U.S. claim to the world's largest current account deficits exemplify the extreme differences in the two countries' international financial positions.

For good reason, the United States is unique in its relative lack of urgency about earning foreign exchange. No other country can use its own currency to pay for 100 percent of its imports of raw materials, manufactured goods, and services. Americans can simply divert from the domestic money supply whatever number of dollars are needed as payment for what they want to import. The dollar's role as the world's primary international reserve and transactions currency has exempted the United States from much of the balance of payments discipline imposed on every other country: keeping the value of imports over time roughly in line with earnings from exports. For the past half-century, the United States has been the only country able to incur a persistently large balance of payments deficit without exhausting its foreign exchange reserves.[17] The United States has financed the largest and longest excess of foreign spending over foreign earnings in modern economic history through the willingness — subject to termination at any time — of foreign central banks, businesses, and individuals to hold onto accumulated dollars and put them in their reserves or working capital.

The extraordinary nature of its balance of payments position has been vividly demonstrated since the mid-1980s by the ability of the United States to finance world-record annual current account deficits with equally record-breaking net capital inflows. Even more remarkable was the nearly unbroken increase in the value of the dollar between 1981 and early 1985 against every major currency in the face of a steady, massive deterioration in the U.S. trade deficit. The main international economic effect of sizable dollar appreciation was widespread damage to the U.S. industrial sector by encouraging imports (especially from Japan) and pricing many U.S.-made goods out of overseas markets.

The response to massive dollar appreciation by senior officials in the Reagan White House and Treasury Department had no precedent in modern international economic policy. They expressed delight that the people best able to gauge "proper" exchange rates — millions of investors in the world's financial markets — were registering a vote of confidence in the relative strength of the U.S. economy. This is the exact opposite of the more typical cries of anguish and warnings of economic suffering emanating from Tokyo after the value of the yen soared in the mid-1980s and again in the early 1990s. Given the economic costs imposed on U.S. business, it is not hyperbole to suggest that no parliamentary government in Western Europe or Japan could survive if it were to exhibit comparable indifference and inaction toward a grossly overvalued (in commercial terms) exchange rate.

The seemingly moderate costs (at least in the short term) of U.S. trade deficits raise the question who is conning whom. On the level of economic theory, the United States is fleecing Japan. A country comes out ahead to the extent that it can exchange paper money for real economic resources, that is, goods and services that enhance the national standard of living. Enormous current account deficits have enabled the United States to spend beyond its ability to produce. A large portion of the dollars generated from Japan's large trade surpluses have been invested in, or lent to, the United States. Instead of using capital to improve their underdeveloped infrastructure — such as housing, roads, and parks — or to expand consumption, the Japanese have indirectly subsidized U.S. living standards. They do this by shipping real economic resources worth much more than their purchases of U.S. goods and then returning a significant amount of their net export earnings to the United States.

The already questionable benefits to Japanese living standards of exchanging real economic resources for cash have been further dissipated by periodic depreciations of the dollar against the yen. When this occurs, the yen-denominated value of dollar assets held by Japanese companies drops immediately by the percentage of currency realignment. The upward movement in the value of the yen from the end of the late 1980s through the mid-1990s produced accounting losses on the balance sheets of Japanese corporations from U.S. assets estimated to be as high as $500 billion.[18] Many of the so-called trophy purchases of U.S. real estate (best exemplified by Rockefeller Center and the Pebble Beach Golf Club) went sour. Several corporate takeovers proved not to be bargains. Sony Corporation, in 1994, had to take a $3.2 billion write-off in connection with losses incurred at its Columbia Pictures acquisition.

The United States is not totally exempt from the laws of economics, however. Large structural current account deficits probably are not indefinitely sustainable at a reasonable cost. Eventually, they are likely to cause one or both of two highly undesirable economic changes in order to encourage reluctant foreign investors to continue providing the large net capital inflows necessary to finance current account deficits: sustained dollar depreciation that would reduce real incomes in the United States and rising interest rates that would retard domestic economic growth.

The second important link between the international monetary system and trade flows has been the failure of exchange rate adjustments, specifically yen appreciation relative to the dollar, to reapportion competitiveness between the two countries by the amount necessary to induce equilibrium in the bilateral trade balance. Other things being equal, a country with a depreciating currency experiences increases in prices of imports while the country's exports become cheaper in terms of other countries' currencies. A floating exchange rate system, in theory, is supposed to generate balance of payments adjustment by assuring small but constant exchange rate changes until reaching an equilibrium rate, that is, one that nudges the value of total exports and imports in the direction of approximate balance. This is the reason that U.S. economic officials since the Nixon administration periodically have gone public with their desire to correct bilateral trade grievances by having additional yen appreciation price Japanese goods out of the U.S. market and reduce yen prices of U.S. exports in Japan.

Contrary to popular expectations, the considerable cumulative depreciation in the value of the dollar relative to the yen since 1971 has yet to suppress U.S. demand for Japanese goods or to stimulate Japanese demand for U.S. goods by amounts sufficient to eliminate the U.S. bilateral trade deficits. At best, occasional yen appreciation has temporarily reversed an upturn in the size of the bilateral U.S. deficits or reined in the size of what Japan's trade surpluses otherwise would have been. Long-term adjustment has been hindered by sporadic yen weakness even as Japan's trade surpluses continued. The minimal-to-nonexistent success of what should be a powerful international economic adjustment measure supports the thesis that a systemic economic problem exists. Dollar depreciation has brought about larger, more permanent corrections in relative U.S. trade flows with other geographical areas. For example, with the appropriate lag time, the U.S. trade deficit with the European Union countries returned to surplus for many years after the dollar began depreciating in early 1985.

The most significant reason for the failure of exchange rate adjustments to terminate the bilateral trade disequilibrium is one of the running themes of this book: the extraordinary resiliency and determination of large Japanese manufacturers to retain competitiveness and foreign market share, even under the most trying conditions. Long-successful practitioners of continuous improvement, the dominant exporting companies repeatedly have turned weakness into strength. By slashing production costs and "pricing to market" (that is, holding price increases to a minimum), they have been able to neutralize much of the effects of yen appreciation. All major Japanese exporters boosted productivity, trimmed profit margins, relocated assembly facilities to low-wage Asian nations, and pressured suppliers to reduce prices. Some companies shifted domestic production to more technologically sophisticated goods that tend to be less price sensitive.

A U.S. business consultant calculated that in the 25-year period beginning in 1971, major Japanese industries have reduced their costs at an average compound rate of 5 percent annually — an amount almost as great as the amount of dollar depreciation against the yen over the same time span.[19] Another study found that while the yen appreciated in value against the dollar by almost 40 percent between 1990 and the first three quarters of 1995, the average dollar price of Japanese exports rose by only 15 percent. Consistent with the thesis of two-tiered pricing in the Japanese industrial sector, the average reduction of 20 percent in the yen prices of exports during this time did not result in similar price cuts for the same goods sold within Japan.[20] Consistent with the thesis that cutting costs commensurate with currency appreciation is a specialty of Japanese exporters, *The Economist* several years ago concluded: "With so many options now available to them, big Japanese companies have become, to all intents and purposes, independent of the value of the yen against the dollar."[21]

A number of other economic factors have diminished the ability of yen-dollar exchange rate changes over the long term to alter relative competitiveness and induce bilateral equilibrium, thereby eliminating U.S.-Japanese trade frictions:

U.S. exporters and Japanese importers frequently opt to widen their profit margins by raising their prices in the wake of dollar depreciation that otherwise would lower yen-denominated prices for U.S.-made goods.

U.S. demand for many Japanese products, especially those perceived to be of high quality, for example, automobiles, is not seriously discouraged by price increases.

Japanese consumers and companies respond in a relatively limited way to price reductions in most imports of manufactured goods, including many U.S.-made products. (This tendency partly reflects the previously discussed Japanese corporate preference for preserving long-standing business relationships at almost any cost.)

Exchange rate changes need to be adjusted for inflation differentials. Japanese inflation rates were consistently lower than those of the United States during the 1969–95 period; hence the real yen appreciation has been much less than the nominal appreciation.

Whenever the yen appreciates against the dollar, the yen costs of imported raw materials (which mostly are dollar-denominated) to Japanese companies decline, thereby reducing production costs; Japan's steel industry has been a major example of reduced production costs thanks to cheaper raw materials.

There are no domestic or meaningful foreign alternatives to a growing proportion of goods imported from Japan, for example, customized semiconductor chips, 35 mm cameras, fax machines, video cameras, and computer components.

In theory there is a point at which yen revaluation would be so great as to decimate U.S. demand for Japanese goods and to make the price differential for U.S.-made components so favorable that Japanese producers would be forced to begin buying these components at the expense of long-time domestic suppliers in order to remain competitive. For several reasons, however, there is little or no chance that we will witness such an exchange rate any time soon. In the first place, exchange rates are influenced heavily by non–trade balance considerations like interest rate differentials and speculators' expectations. Second, recent history supports the argument that it is a near certainty that one or both governments will adopt whatever countermeasures are necessary to prevent massive yen appreciation continuing against the dollar. Senior U.S. economic policy officials sometimes do not welcome the likely costs of an unstable dollar, such as the potentially inflationary impact of rising import prices and the nudging up of domestic interest rates by nervous financial markets.

The Clinton administration in mid-1995 did a turnabout and convinced the international financial community that it was genuinely committed to a strong dollar. Fear of grievous damage to its industrial sector's international competitiveness led the Japanese government to buy dollars aggressively in the foreign exchange markets and to apply administrative guidance to Japanese financial institutions when market sentiment caused prolonged yen appreciation in the 1993–95 period. In sum, a completely clean float producing a dollar-yen exchange rate fully offsetting both the extraordinary competitiveness of Japanese industry and U.S. market access problems in Japan is unlikely. Exchange rate changes will remain a necessary but insufficient condition to cure the systemic trade imbalance.

## FOREIGN DIRECT INVESTMENT
## POLICIES AND ACTIVITIES

International commerce can no longer be defined solely in terms of foreign trade among countries. Increasingly, it includes competition among the far-flung operations of multinational corporations. With a book value estimated at $2.4 trillion, foreign direct investment by nearly 40,000 of the world's largest companies has become a major variable determining international trade flows.[22] Sales by foreign affiliates of multinational corporations were estimated at $5.2 trillion in 1992, a figure exceeding the estimated value of trade in goods and services in that year. Intracorporate trade accounts for a large (an estimated 33 percent) and growing percentage of trade flows among the industrialized economies.[23] Companies with overseas production facilities tend to demonstrate healthy increases in exports to overseas subsidiaries from their home countries. These increases mainly consist of components, replacement parts, and models of goods not being manufactured overseas. Incremental home country exports also consist of capital equipment to be used by subsidiaries to manufacture goods. In some cases, the effects on exports can be negative as the output of overseas subsidiaries displaces what otherwise would have been exports by the parent company.

Since the 1950s, U.S. companies have been avid practitioners of defending and expanding overseas sales through the establishment of production facilities in foreign markets. The estimated book value of U.S. foreign direct investment at year-end 1995 was $712 billion, and annual overseas sales of goods and services by all majority-owned U.S. foreign affiliates is well above $1 trillion annually. U.S. parent companies exported $105 billion to their majority-owned foreign affiliates in 1993, almost one-fourth of total U.S. exports.[24]

Until changes in international economic conditions caused a wholesale shift in their overseas marketing strategies, the Japanese displayed none of the U.S. zeal for this activity. Japanese management chose to produce domestically and serve overseas customers through exporting. This preference was motivated partly by their desire to avoid unpredictable business conditions and relatively less-dedicated workers in foreign lands, and partly by the absence of any need to seek lower production costs abroad. Everything changed in the mid-1980s when the Japanese were confronted simultaneously with increases in foreign hostilities toward their exports, yen appreciation, rising domestic labor costs, and the need to dispose of a massive accumulation of dollars. For the first time, Japan adopted an international economic strategy identical to one practiced by the United States: major exporters rapidly shifted to large-scale overseas production. The explanation for this singular similarity may be that the Japanese and U.S. business sectors act somewhat alike outside of Japan.

Japanese foreign direct investment poured into the United States and Western Europe in the 1980s to protect market shares from exchange rate realignments as well as rising threats of new trade barriers. Japanese capital poured into Southeast Asia to cut costs by producing labor-intensive components exported back to Japan for assembly into finished products. The book value of direct investment there jumped from $21.5 billion in 1987 to $74.7 billion as of March 1995.[25] Japanese companies also invested heavily in relatively low-wage Southeast Asian countries, particularly Malaysia and Thailand, to produce labor-intensive manufactures for export to the United States and other markets. Between 1985 and 1995, Japanese companies increased their offshore production of color television sets from 11.4 to 35.5 million units and video cassette recorders from 2 to 20 million units.[26] A conservative estimate of U.S. imports of goods produced by Japanese-owned companies in Southeast Asia was $10 billion annually in the early 1990s.[27] The steady increase in U.S. imports of Japanese-label goods manufactured in third countries has the effect of reducing the U.S. bilateral deficit with Japan, which is calculated on the basis of geography rather than ownership.

One explanation for the relatively weak U.S. trade performance with Japan is the unusually low amount of U.S. foreign direct investment in that country. This phenomenon is not limited to U.S. investors. Japan accounts for about 18 percent of world GDP, but is host to only 1 or 2 percent of world foreign direct investment. Such inward investment amounts to $80 per capita in Japan as compared to $1,618 in the United States. Sales by foreign firms in Japan account for only 1.2 percent of domestic sales, the lowest level among industrialized countries.[28] At the end of the 1995 fiscal year, the reported value of Japan's foreign direct investment abroad ($515 billion) was almost 14 times greater than foreign direct investment within Japan ($38 billion).[29]

Japan, the second largest U.S. trading partner, accounted for only 5.5 percent of the total book value ($712 billion) of U.S. foreign direct investment at year-end 1995. U.S. direct investment in manufacturing in Japan, valued at $17 billion in that year, was just 13 percent of the U.S. total for the European Union (EU) countries and equated to 40 percent of U.S. direct investment in the much smaller Canadian economy. Japanese direct investment in the United States of $109 billion in 1995 was almost three times as great as the value of the comparable U.S. figure in Japan ($39 billion).[30]

A positive correlation between foreign direct investment and export success is suggested by the large-scale presence of U.S.-controlled companies in Western Europe and the perennial U.S. trade surplus with the EU countries.[31] U.S. Commerce Department data show that exports of manufactured goods (mainly semifinished) by U.S. parent companies to their majority-owned manufacturing subsidiaries in Japan are quite low when compared to figures for Canada and the EU. In 1993, such shipments to Japan were virtually identical to those going to manufacturing subsidiaries in the relatively tiny Dutch economy and just a little more than those going to the city-state of Singapore (see Table 8.1).

A white paper on U.S. foreign direct investment published in 1980 by the American Chamber of Commerce in Japan argued the existence of "a clear connection between the small extent of U.S. manufacturing operations in Japan and the continuing U.S. deficit in trade with Japan."[32] The chamber's 1995 white paper asserted the unequalled ability of direct

**TABLE 8.1**
**U.S. Exports of Manufactured Goods Shipped by U.S. Parent Companies to Majority-Owned Foreign Manufacturing Affiliates, 1993**

| Country | Billions of U.S. Dollars |
| --- | --- |
| Japan | 2.3 |
| Canada | 27.7 |
| European Union | |
| Total | 17.0 |
| U.K. | 4.6 |
| Germany | 4.7 |
| Netherlands | 2.3 |
| Belgium | 1.5 |
| Singapore | 1.9 |

*Note*: The totals above do not include manufactured goods shipped to overseas subsidiaries classified as distribution facilities.

*Source*: U.S. Department of Commerce, *U.S. Direct Investment Abroad . . . Preliminary 1993 Estimates*, June 1995, Table III.H 9.

investment to provide a company with detailed insights into the business atmosphere in foreign markets, concluding that "Nowhere else in the world is direct investment as important as it is in Japan, with its unique culture and business practices."[33] According to Harvard Business School Professor Dennis Encarnation, just as Japan's strategic investment policy has limited majority U.S. ownership in Japan, so too has it limited U.S. exports there. "The lower incidence of majority U.S. subsidiaries has effectively denied to American multinationals the same access for U.S. exports that they have enjoyed in other industrialized countries." Export of manufactured goods to "other industrialized countries heavily depends on majority U.S. subsidiaries to create final markets and distribution channels for shipments from their American parents."[34] The large proportion of U.S. exports to and imports from Japan accounted for by majority-owned Japanese subsidiaries in the United States "guarantees Japanese multinationals uncontested control over bilateral trade," claims Encarnation.[35]

The Japanese strategy of inviting foreign corporate technology rather than foreign corporate ownership was discussed earlier in this chapter. Most U.S. companies, finding themselves shut out of the Japanese market by the combination of import restrictions and foreign direct investment controls on everything but minority participation in joint ventures, contented themselves with licensing their technology and patents. In the short run, this practice was an attractive second best. Fees and royalties received were mostly pure profit. However, persons doubting severe long-term costs to U.S. industry from providing Japanese competitors with their "corporate jewels" should ask the RCA Corporation, for example, whether, if they could do it over again, they would have licensed their color television technology so quickly and cheaply to Japanese manufacturers.

A critical question remains: why the dearth of foreign-owned manufacturing subsidiaries in Japan. The reasons are similar to the explanation for the relative dearth of imported manufactured goods. Prior to the 1980s, the answer was simply the existence of impenetrable official barriers. Since the Meiji Restoration, Japanese governments have been concerned that an influx of foreign-owned manufacturing could lead to dominance by foreigners of major sectors of Japanese industry, hardly a pleasant prospect for a country jealously guarding its unique cultural system. Outsiders could not be expected to understand and comply with the unique informal rules of the often collusive Japanese business system. Foreign companies steeped in Western traditions would be more trouble than they were worth as potential contributors to Japan's top priority of industrial leadership and independence from foreigners.

But why does foreign direct investment today still enter in a slow trickle — long after the removal of almost all formal barriers and the initiation of government programs designed to encourage it? As with the case of limited imports, the answer is the uniquely harsh Japanese business environment. The American Chamber of Commerce in Japan says that U.S. corporations are discouraged from investing there because of the extremely high costs of doing business, described by others as cost protectionism. One source of high costs to U.S. companies is indirect factors, such as yen appreciation, expensive land, and difficulties recruiting experienced personnel in a land of lifetime employment. A second source of high costs is the panoply of nonmarket factors, for example, structural impediments, unnecessary and protective regulations, exclusionary business practices, and *keiretsu*.[36] The unusually long time it takes foreign manufacturing ventures to become nationally competitive and profitable in Japan is an especially sensitive impediment. Foreign companies are effectively denied, by law and custom, the shortcut available for gaining a quick foothold in other industrial countries: mergers with and acquisitions of local companies.

## CONCLUSION

The managerial, policy, and attitudinal mismatch causing the systemic trade problem between the U.S. and Japanese economies is mainly, but not totally, caused by internal factors. To the previously discussed differences in domestic economic performance must be added distinctive attitudes regarding international economic relations. Dissimilar international trade, monetary, and investment policies exacerbated fundamental domestic dissimilarities between the two countries. Beyond the rhetoric and marginal changes in trade policies, Japan and the United States remain on different courses. The former luxuriates in running the world's largest trade surpluses, fears appreciation of the yen against the dollar, and attracts relatively little foreign direct investment. The United States tolerates the world's biggest trade deficits (in absolute terms), thinks kindly of dollar depreciation as a means of reducing those deficits, and attracts a large volume of foreign direct investment. Even if major international economic changes ensue, such as sustained dollar depreciation and an upsurge of U.S. direct investment in Japan, they will produce significant and lasting contributions to improvement in the U.S.-Japanese trade disequilibrium only if accompanied by internal economic changes.

The different mentalities responsible for dissimilar domestic and international economic policies also explain divergent approaches to bilateral negotiations that seek to diminish trade frictions and disequilibria. Why the two countries contribute to and tolerate a negotiating process that has failed to solve these problems is the subject of Chapter 9.

## NOTES

1. Masataka Kosaka, "The International Economic Policy of Japan," in Robert A. Scalapino, ed., *The Foreign Policy of Modern Japan* (Berkeley: University of California Press, 1977), p. 214.

2. As quoted in Robert Gilpin, *The Political Economy of International Relations* (Princeton: Princeton University Press, 1987), p. 180.

3. Friedrich List, *The Natural System of Political Economy*, W. O. Henderson, trans. (London: Frank Cass, 1983), p. 31.

4. Friedrich List, *The National System of Political Economy*, Sampson S. Lloyd, trans. (London: Longmans, Green, 1904), p. 108.

5. Ibid., pp. 37, 118.

6. U.S. Senate Committee on Finance, *United States-Japan Structural Impediments Initiative (SII)*, hearings of November 6 and 7, 1989, p. 35.

7. Mark Z. Taylor, "Dominance through Technology," *Foreign Affairs* (November-December 1995), p. 15.

8. John P. Stern, "Government Relations and the Administrative Process: Engineering the Regulatory Environment," in Gerald P. McAlinn, ed., *The Business Guide to Japan* (Tokyo: Butterworth-Heinemann Asia, 1996), p. 50.

9. Kyogoku Junichi, quoted in Kosaka, "The International Economic Policy of Japan," p. 225.

10. Kiyoshi Kojima and Terutomo Ozawa, *Japan's General Trading Companies* (Paris: Organization for Economic Cooperation and Development, 1984), p. 71.

11. Robert Kuttner, *Managed Trade and Economic Sovereignty* (Washington, D.C.: Economic Policy Institute, 1989), p. 4 (pamphlet).

12. As quoted by Milton Friedman in *Washington Post National Weekly Edition*, August 16–22, 1993, p. 29.

13.    The one exception was the limited sanctions imposed on Toshiba and a Norwegian company for violating export control laws and selling high-tech equipment to the Soviet Union, which it used to make its submarines operate more quietly.

14.    However admirable the quest to reduce foreign trade barriers, such a strategy by itself is insufficient to restore U.S. trade balance equilibrium under conditions prevailing in the mid-1990s. U.S. saving rates are still low. Increases in U.S. incomes still produce greater increases in imports than income increases in other countries produce increases in their demand for U.S. exports. As noted in Chapter 3, the relatively high U.S. income elasticity of demand for imports implies that reducing U.S. trade deficits is difficult, if not impossible, if the U.S. economy is growing relatively quickly and the dollar is not depreciating in value.

15.    J. David Richardson, *Sizing up U.S. Export Disincentives* (Washington, D.C.: Institute for International Economics, 1993), pp. 2–3.

16.    U.S. Congress, House Committee on Small Business, *Federal Export Promotion Programs: An Academic Perspective*, Hearing before the Subcommittee on Procurement, Exports, and Business Opportunities, May 23, 1995, p. 115.

17.    The United States suffered a moderate loss of gold reserves in the mid-1960s; otherwise, it has not used reserves to finance its balance of payments deficits as every other country must do.

18.    As cited in David D. Hale, "Is the Currency Market Experiencing a Yen Crisis or a Dollar Crisis?" July, 1995, p. 3, mimeographed.

19.    W. L. Givens, "Economic Cocaine — America's Exchange Rate Addiction," *Foreign Affairs* (July-August 1995), p. 18.

20.    Thomas Klitgaard, "Coping with the Rising Yen: Japan's Recent Export Experience, " report issued by the Federal Reserve Bank of New York, January 1996, pp. 1–2.

21.    "How Japan's Exporters Cope," *The Economist*, March 4, 1989, p. 66.

22.    United Nations Conference on Trade and Development, Division on Transnational Corporations and Investment, *World Investment Report, 1995*, p. 7. Foreign direct investment is generally defined as a company in one country having 10 percent or more ownership of the voting stock in a company incorporated in another country.

23.    Ibid., pp. 3–4.

24.    U.S. Department of Commerce, *Survey of Current Business*, various issues, 1995–96.

25.    Calculated from Japanese Ministry of Finance data reproduced in Diane Manifold, "Japanese Corporate Activities in Asia: Implications for U.S.-Japanese Relations," Occasional Paper of the Program on U.S.-Japan Relations (Cambridge, Mass.: Harvard University, 1996), p. 49.

26.    Electronics Industries Association of Japan, *Perspectives on the Japanese Electronics Industry*, 1996 edition.

27.    Calculated from data in a report by Japan's Ministry of International Trade and Industry, "Summary of 'The Survey of Trends in Overseas Business Activities of Japanese Companies'," January 1996, p. 31.

28.    John Carroll, "Trade Talkers on the Edge . . . ," *Journal of the American Chamber of Commerce in Japan*, January 1995, p. 10. Also see "Japan, Please Note:

Foreign Investment is Really Good for a Nation's Economy," *The Wall Street Journal*, April 8, 1994, p. A10.

29. Japan Economic Institute, Report 34A, Washington, D.C., September 1996.

30. U.S. Department of Commerce, *Survey of Current Business*, July 1996.

31. The traditional U.S. trade surplus with Western Europe was briefly interrupted in the mid-1980s as the result of the massive overvaluation of the dollar.

32. American Chamber of Commerce in Japan, "U.S. Manufacturing Investment in Japan White Paper, 1980," p. 7.

33. American Chamber of Commerce in Japan, "United States-Japan 1995 Trade White Paper," p. 68.

34. Dennis J. Encarnation, *Rivals Beyond Trade — America versus Japan in Global Competition* (Ithaca, N.Y.: Cornell University Press, 1992), pp. 31, 211.

35. Ibid., p. 20.

36. American Chamber of Commerce in Japan, "United States-Japan 1995 Trade White Paper," p. 69.

# 9

# The Asymmetrical Bilateral Negotiating Process

We can improve the well-being of our people and we can enhance the forces for democracy, freedom, peace, and human fulfillment around the world, if we stand up for principles of trade expansion through freer markets among nations. The United States took the lead after World War II in creating an international trading system . . . that limited government's ability to disrupt trade . . . because history had taught us the freer the flow of trade across borders, the greater the world economic progress and the greater the impetus for world peace.

— Ronald Reagan (1983)

Japanese policy should . . . be that of keeping Americans and Europeans as much as possible at arm's length. . . . The Japanese should take every precaution to give as little foothold as possible to foreigners.

— Herbert Spencer (1892)

A permanent dialogue between Japan and the United States developed in the late 1960s to address a new generation of bilateral trade problems. The original negotiating agenda centered around U.S. allegations of Japanese protectionism and complaints about an overly aggressive Japanese export drive. Three exhausting decades later, the negotiating agenda is exactly the same except for the geometric increase in the size of the bilateral deficit with Japan that infuriates so many Americans. The unresolved issues remain the same; only the numbers change.

In negotiations, process meets substance. If this book's central thesis about the existence of systemic imbalances is correct, we should find fundamental differences in the approach to bilateral bargaining. In fact, for three decades, the intense but inconclusive bilateral dialogue has afforded a picture-perfect illustration of what happens when clear-cut differences in priorities, ideology, and policy strategy exist between two countries. One side has been concerned with free-market dynamics, superpower politics, and at least the illusion of progress in bilateral problems. The other side has been concerned with long-term industrial power, controlling the inflow of foreign influences, and the use of the trading system to enhance national security.

## NEGOTIATING SYMPTOMS, NOT CAUSES

Japan and the United States tend to talk *at* each other more than *to* each other. The divergences in both economic situation and cultural orientation have fostered a stopgap form of economic diplomacy in which the same problems of communication repeatedly resurface. Demands, excuses, arguments, and counterarguments are regularly recycled. The limitations and contradictions of the negotiating process became a part of the substantive problem. The negotiations bought time, but they did not — and could not — remedy the underlying managerial, policy, and attitudinal mismatches. As part of the problem, the negotiating process could not cure the frictions caused by the superior performance of Japan's industrial sector and its government's ability to parry and dilute many U.S. demands for greater market access. Japan had no real demands to make on the United States and no inherent desire to open its markets. It did need to demonstrate some good-faith response to U.S. visions of how trade policy should be conducted.

An evaluation of the bilateral negotiating process needs to distinguish between two levels of accomplishment. On the more narrow level, upward of 100 specific liberalization packages and bilateral agreements have been implemented since the late 1960s. The sheer number and regularity of Japanese concessions prevented a serious rupture in bilateral relations and even larger bilateral trade disequilibria. On the broader level of addressing structural problems, the negotiating process has been a failure. No agreement to date has come close to bridging the two countries' basic differences in values, priorities, and economic structures.

Criticism of the futile effort to contain trade frictions needs to be qualified in two respects. First, the causal factors of trade problems are deeply rooted in large-scale domestic trends so complex that only now, after many years, have they emerged clearly. It would be foolish to argue today that trade negotiators should have possessed sufficient wisdom in the

1970s to have anticipated the oncoming structural changes that induced an international realignment of industrial power.

It is likely that at least some trade negotiators somewhere along the line realized the negotiating process needed to include concepts much larger than trade policy. These officials were probably reluctant to speak up because of the scary notion that virtually the entire Japanese and U.S. economic systems lay at the heart of the problem. The burden of negotiating on such a scale would have been awesome. The U.S. government would have been forced to consider radical internal policy changes and to demand changes within Japan so far-reaching as to be unacceptable unless the Japanese were somehow willing to drastically reorder their value system. Negotiating symptoms was better than nothing. Agreements are more easily achieved when directed at narrow, tangible items, and negotiators are charged with achieving results. The need for quick results is especially relevant for U.S. trade negotiators at the political appointee level because of their relatively short tenure in office. Only the Structural Impediments Initiative of 1989 was designed to deal with fundamental issues in the two economic systems. Unfortunately, the talks were never destined to produce major policy changes inasmuch as they lacked a formal legal basis and a formal deadline for reaching hard decisions.

The second reason for the failure of bilateral negotiations to eliminate trade frictions is found in the irony that both countries believed their national interests were served by dealing with the problem on a piece-meal basis instead of taking on the heavier responsibility of correcting underlying causes of frictions. Reduced to its basics, the world market was viewed by Japan as a vehicle for enhancing economic growth at home and, most importantly, as a means of ensuring economic security for itself. Because competitive imports and foreign direct investments diluted control over industrial policy objectives, they were not welcomed. Genuine import liberalization normally was delayed until after infant industries were powerful enough to flourish without the aid of protection from imports. The Japanese government, therefore, sought to use the bilateral negotiating process to keep the pace of internal change to as slow a timetable as possible and to allow it to pursue an essentially mercantilist, self-centered trade strategy with minimal foreign retaliation. None of Japan's numerous concessions to world public opinion either slowed the relative growth of its industrial strength or significantly altered the overall size and product composition of its imports.

The Japanese position that their market had been opened by the late 1970s led them to adopt a negotiating posture built around the request that the United States give them specific examples of protectionism. With the Americans content to respond on this level, the negotiating process typically was relegated to the product-specific level. Again, this was mutually agreeable. Rather than seek radical structural shifts, U.S. nego-tiators were content to induce enough of a Japanese response to placate the trade complaints of specific industries or companies — inevitably, the source of official demands on Japan. Hence, negotiations through the 1980s dealt with the more tangible second-tier issues such as quotas, dumping, Japanese import inspection standards, and other problems related to a specific product or sector.

Refusing, perhaps correctly, to give top priority to export maximiza-tion, U.S. trade strategy instead emphasized more noble and abstract ideas like an open global trading system based on comparative advan-tage, maximum competition in the marketplace, and consumer sover-eignty. U.S. companies and unions seeking import protection from fair competition usually were viewed by Washington officialdom as losers who were victims of their own inefficiency. Import restrictions were viewed with distaste as politically necessitated deviations from the free market. Implicitly, U.S. trade policymakers from the president down have recognized the importance of foreign competition in imparting discipline to domestic management and labor. They discerned that most retaliatory actions taken to punish the Japanese for alleged lack of reciprocity would hurt the U.S. economy, at least in the short term, as much as it hurt Japan. U.S. policymakers have also displayed a belief that foreign policy consid-erations should take a higher priority than export promotion efforts. The White House in the 1980s and the Republican-controlled Congress in the mid-1990s steadfastly argued that the source of U.S. internal economic shortcomings was excessive government interference in the economy. The U.S. government was said to be the source of the problem, not the solution.

Two important elements have been missing in the U.S. negotiating position. The U.S. government has never developed any comprehensive or long-term vision of exactly what it wants from Japan and how to get it. Trade policymakers in all administrations have demonstrated a disincli-nation to retaliate against inadequate, less than full-faith Japanese responses to U.S. economic demands. The relative lack of continuity and urgency in the U.S. bilateral negotiating position minimized the perceived costs to Japan of just going through the motions of making its markets more accessible to imports. While the Japanese publicly congratulated themselves on dozens of politically painful liberalization measures, in many cases they had defused U.S. anger with a minimum of real disrup-tion to domestic producers.

## NEGOTIATING IN CIRCLES

Many specialized negotiating forums have been created since the 1960s to deal with continuing frictions. In some cases, specialized groups bring together narrowly focused delegations under a limited mandate to arrange a product-specific export restraint agreement (for example, steel, color televisions, and automobiles) or market access agreement (agriculture, supercomputers, construction, and so forth). A second category of negotiating group consists of intergovernmental meetings and consultative bodies that discuss the overall state of bilateral trade relations; they convene for periodic meetings from the junior level through the president and prime minister. The private sectors also actively communicate with one another. The annual convocation of senior corporate executives at the Japan-U.S. Business Conference frequently produces analytical reports and joint statements on what both sides see as the tasks ahead.

All of these forums have shared the unfortunate trait of negotiating in circles. The sense of repetition pervades a synopsis of the results of the bilateral negotiating process:

Innumerable "packages" of import liberalization measures, domestic economic policy shifts, studies of further remedies, and so forth, in retrospect, have functioned more as political crisis management tools to defuse U.S. temper tantrums than as levers of real economic change. Japan's announcements of market-opening packages typically include promises that great changes are in store and the suggestion that "this is the final package that can and will be assembled."

A barrage of Japanese public relations activities and inconsequential trade promotion efforts were epitomized by Boatique America, a Japanese ship converted into a floating market of U.S. consumer goods that visited various Japanese ports in 1979.

Gaps between Japanese promises and implementation partly reflect the cumbersome Japanese decision-making process and partly their expertise in sweet-talking Americans. Japan has often made commitments on trade policy changes that take many years to materialize even partially, as demonstrated in the telecommunications equipment sector.

The quixotic nature of the search for permanent harmony in the bilateral relationship is regrettable but understandable. The limited value added generated by the negotiating process accommodated both countries' needs and objectives. The United States was able to portray itself as a paragon of free-market purity, play the role of friend of consumers in both countries, and soothe the anger of most import-impacted U.S. industrial sectors. Japan was able to portray itself as a devotee of liberal trade, serve the interests of its large corporations, and soothe the anger of its most important trading partner. Neither side suffered what it deemed intolerable financial or ideological costs.

The built-in limitations to achieving meaningful results produced a clearly second-best approach to problem solving that seemed to make no real progress. Most U.S. criticisms of Japanese trade policy made in the early 1970s are still being made a quarter of a century later. President Nixon's March 1971 Foreign Policy Report to Congress said "Japan's position as a major beneficiary of a liberal international economic system is not consistent with her slowness in removing the restrictions which limit the access of others to her own vibrant economy." The then-assistant secretary of state for economic affairs, Philip Trezise, argued in 1970 that "in the eyes of the United States, key Japanese foreign economic policies are out of step with the requirements of the international economic system, incompatible with Japan's economic status, and contrary to the interests of the United States and other of Japan's trading partners."[1]

A personal experience provides another illustration of a negotiating process on a tread mill. In doing the research for this book, I found a long-forgotten memorandum I wrote in my capacity as chief economist for the U.S.-Japan Trade Council. Entitled "Executive Branch Attitudes Toward Trade," it says in part:

There is widespread belief that Japan's trade policies are consistent neither with its current economic strength nor with the ground rules of reciprocity which the U.S. feels its own liberal trade policies warrant. The list of Japan's liberalization measures notwithstanding, there is a common assertion that the cards are stacked against American industrial exporters (administrative guidance is a favorite example) and that Japan's idea of liberal trade is limited to assuring open markets for its exports. Regardless of the merits of this line of thinking, it is very real, widely held, and deeply believed. Generally, all that differs among the U.S. officials is the degree of impatience with Japan. State and [Office of the U.S. Trade Representative] people still emphasize the use of negotiations to correct the current situation. The Commerce Department, in general, has lost faith in further talk and feels that the U.S. must now turn to action to spur . . . Japan to take the measures which have long and unsuccessfully been sought by this country.

Despite the large number of exchanges between Japan and the U.S., a real communications gap still seems to exist. Most government officials to whom I've spoken accept the fact that the Japanese are not deliberately trying to live by a special set of trade rules applicable only to Japan. They do feel that the Japanese government sincerely believes that the current pace of liberalization fully demonstrates its good faith. However, they argue that U.S. grievances against Japan are sufficiently numerous and justifiable (as evidenced by the current U.S.-Japan trade balance) to make it very difficult to forestall indefinitely hard line trade policies.

Word for word, the text of these two paragraphs accurately reflects U.S. government thinking in 1997 — a remarkable feat because this memo was written in spring 1970.

An apparent absence of institutional memory led to repetitiveness in the proposal for a special, discriminatory tariff on Japanese goods. The first public mention of this idea occurred in 1971, when an unnamed U.S. Treasury Department source told a reporter that such a duty might be necessary unless the yen were to be revalued to correct its allegedly extreme (up to 20 percent) undervaluation against the dollar.[2] A variant of this idea was proposed in mid-1978 when several members of the House Ways and Means Subcommittee on Trade urged President Carter to invoke the obscure balance of payments authority of the Trade Act of 1974 to impose temporary import surcharges of up to 15 percent to correct the destabilizing bilateral trade imbalance.[3] Senator Lloyd Bentsen of Texas got into the act in 1979; while he was chairman of the Joint Economic Committee of Congress, he suggested "a surcharge or other barriers" against Japanese imports.[4] In March 1985, Senator John Heinz (R., Pa.) introduced a bill (S. 770) that would have imposed a 20 percent tariff surcharge on all imports from Japan.

Countless tough trade bills have been introduced into Congress — not necessarily with expectations of their being enacted into law. Most, like a 1982 proposal to limit U.S. purchases of Japanese goods to the level of U.S. exports to Japan of manufactured and processed agricultural goods, are intended to send a message to Japan. Congress is not as blatantly protectionist as it is often accused of being. Despite its anti-import, anti-Japan posturing, it did not pass a binding, unilateral import-restricting statute between 1969 and early 1997 affecting access of Japanese goods to the U.S. market.[5] Congress has developed a decipherable set of signals to express its judgment that another country's trade practices have gotten too extreme and are in need of moderation. The implication usually is that voluntary action by the other country is preferable, but changes will be instituted by harsh U.S. legislation if the other side wishes to call Congress's bluff. Japan has become proficient in reading these signals and responding sufficiently at the last minute to assure that no punitive legislation is passed.

The pattern of repetition has been so consistent, and likely to remain so, that it is not much of an exaggeration to suggest the existence of a permanent script dealing with the seemingly endless U.S. efforts to eliminate Japan's apparently inexhaustible supply of impediments to imports. It reads like this:

1.   The U.S. private sector complains bitterly of market access problems and lack of reciprocity in Japan's trade practices.

2.   The U.S. government expresses dismay that the Japanese do not realize it is in their own interests to go further in opening their market, thus reducing prospects for a protectionist backlash by its trading partners.

3.   The Japanese envision the reappearance of black ships in Tokyo Bay, accuse the U.S. government of not understanding the openness of the market, and advise Americans to invest more energy in mastering the Japanese market.

4.   Japanese lobbyists and U.S. intellectuals warn that U.S. bullying tactics waste political capital and eventually will undermine Japan's friendship.

5.  Japanese "internationalists" quietly thank Americans for vivid threats, saying that they are useful levers in internal debates.

6.  The government of Japan announces another package of liberalization measures advertised as a cure for U.S. export problems and a cause of political problems for the Japanese politicians approving it. Implementation bears little resemblance to U.S. expectations, and some U.S. interest groups complain about insufficient increases in their exports to Japan.

7.  After a brief interlude, both sides express dismay at the continued enormity of the bilateral trade surplus. The script then repeats itself.

## BUREAUCRATIC MISMATCH

Because the course of bilateral economic relations is so much more important to Japan than to the United States, the Japanese allocate relatively more time, effort, manpower, planning, public relations, and, last but not least, gritty determination to the negotiating process. The United States lacks a long-term strategy regarding Japan, a permanent power center in charge of dealing with Japan, and supportive public opinion for a consistently aggressive position toward Japan. These shortcomings create a bureaucratic mismatch that has frequently tilted the negotiating table in favor of the Japanese, who were more likely to get more and give less. It is relatively unusual for the U.S. trade bureaucracy to agree easily among themselves on a negotiating strategy toward Japan, to maintain unanimity, and not to backpedal when Japanese and U.S. free traders express outrage. Before and during most bilateral trade negotiations, interagency groups in the U.S. government expend enormous amounts of time and energy settling internal arguments about policy substance and disputes over jurisdictional authority.

Clyde Prestowitz, Jr., argued in his insider's look at the negotiating process that "the United States is outclassed. Its negotiators nearly always face a better-staffed, better-trained, and better-organized opponent. That they will not be successful is almost inevitable."[6] In a memorandum written for the incoming Clinton administration, a former official in the U.S. Trade Representative's (USTR) Japan office, Glen Fukushima, lamented that "Japan's elite technocrats will outmaneuver, outnumber and outlast American negotiators who are usually beaten before they begin."[7] More recently, these mandarins have shown that they also can outflank the U.S. government outside the negotiating room. In the midst of the furor over automobiles and parts in 1995, the Japanese government successfully (and somewhat disingenuously) portrayed the Clinton administration in the court of world public opinion as a devotee of anti-market, results-oriented trade agreements requiring quantitative indicators, even after U.S. negotiators had backed down from this position.

The U.S. executive branch's shallow and piecemeal trade policy toward Japan often results in a government so divided that the pickings can be easy for Japanese policymakers. A 1989 report by the U.S. Advisory Committee for Trade Policy and Negotiations noted that "By pitting one U.S. agency against another, the Japanese are able to delay . . . negotiations and prevent a consensus U.S. position from evolving."[8] U.S. departments and agencies are all too willing to cut separate deals with the Japanese, a trait reflecting the presence in Washington of many individual interests, public and private, sharing no single definition of the national interest. The Japanese are masters of the art of playing friendly U.S. bureaucratic ends against the hostile middle.[9]

A three-way cleavage in the U.S. bureaucracy is the norm. The State Department and the National Security Council view the bilateral relationship as part of a larger political-military alliance that needs to be protected from damage by seemingly less important commercial squabbles. The Defense Department is unlikely to advocate a trade confrontation because of strategically important bases in Japan that are largely funded by payments from the Japanese government and the military's dependence on Japan for a number of key weapons components.[10]

A second group is composed of the neoclassical macroeconomists in the Treasury Department, the President's Council of Economic Advisers, and the Office of Management and Budget who see their mandate as protecting the workings of the free market. The Treasury Department gets queasy at the thought of imposing retaliatory trade actions. It fears higher domestic interest rates and, therefore, higher government borrowing costs that would likely stem from Japanese counter-retaliation in the form of slowing capital inflows into the United States or, worse, massive sales of existing holdings of U.S. government bonds. Japan, in the view of the powerful Treasury Department, is less a miscreant on trade than a critically important offset to shortages in domestic saving and to the federal budget deficit.

The third bureaucratic school of thought represents the hard-line approach. The USTR and the Commerce Department are charged with protecting U.S. trading interests, and many officials in these two agencies have intellectual scars from having hit their heads so often against the hard brick wall of Japanese negotiating tactics. Trade hawks are in the minority and likely will remain so indefinitely — even if the disequilibria in the trade balance and competitiveness persist. The hawks tend to speak loudly, but carry relatively small negotiating sticks. They frequently are dismissed by other government agencies as protectionists and shortsighted, overly aggressive, and chauvinistic Japan-bashers possessed of an unattractive negotiating agenda.

Japan's long traditions of an elite bureaucracy and close attention to detail give its government many advantages in negotiating with the

United States. Three of the most important advantages are having a specific strategy, being at the forefront of a national consensus on trade priorities, and presenting a relatively unified face to other governments. An additional advantage is that there are relatively more Japanese officials involved in bilateral trade matters. They invariably speak and read English fluently and are knowledgeable about the subjects of U.S. trade policy and economic trends. By contrast, recent budget constraints have forced a reduction in the numbers of Japanese trade experts in Washington and U.S. foreign commercial service officers stationed in Japan and elsewhere.

Two other Japanese negotiating advantages are interrelated: continuity and institutional memory among senior trade officials. Japan's parliamentary system relies on long-tenured, career officials through the deputy minister level. Details of Japanese negotiating arguments and objectives are meticulously passed from one generation of senior bureaucrats to the next. Because the U.S. system relies on a deep layer of political appointees at the top, senior U.S. trade negotiators average only two to three years in office. There is little time for them to learn historical detail and nuances or to cultivate close working relationships with senior Japanese (and U.S.) career officials. A retired senior official of the Ministry of International Trade and Industry (MITI) has said that most U.S. negotiators "seem like they came in just yesterday. Because their time is limited, they tend not to look at the real facts."[11] With their return to the private sector always looming, most political appointees have a natural tendency to opt for a quick, splashy agreement in lieu of methodical, technical negotiations seeking a more effective, longer-lived agreement.

The continuity of the Japanese trade negotiating process has facilitated creation of a repertoire of tactics that further add to leverage in dealing with U.S. negotiators. The package includes presenting blank faces and long silences in response to Western logic; stonewalling by asking for more time because there is a new prime minister; claiming that additional imports are inconsistent with a slow-down in domestic economic growth; and "offering half-hearted concessions in the last nano-second before the latest final, final deadline."[12]

Japanese negotiators are sometimes overwhelmed by the sheer quantity and ferocity of U.S. demands. They are less seldom overwhelmed with the quality and resolve of U.S. negotiating tactics. The Japanese side tends to be bemused with the twists and turns of U.S. trade tactics under various administrations. Their negotiators often are able to exploit the rapid turnover of U.S. trade negotiators by selling them "the same horse many times over. They know that if an issue is drawn out long enough the U.S. players will change, allowing the Japanese to offer the old proposals once more."[13] In complex, continuing disputes such as purchases of U.S. telecommunications equipment by Nippon Telegraph and Telephone, the lack of high-level U.S. continuity can preclude a solution satisfactory to U.S. producers. In the opinion of a former State Department official, when negotiators are turning over relatively rapidly, the ability to sustain long-running negotiations "is virtually nil. So the N.T.T. problem, almost by institutional definition, becomes insoluble."[14]

Senior U.S. trade officials rarely have detailed knowledge of the industries being discussed. Sometimes such expertise is totally unavailable. Negotiations dealing with U.S. companies' access to Japanese public works construction had to be suspended in March 1988 because the U.S. government had no qualified senior official available to lead its delegation. All in all, the head of the U.S. delegation changed four times during these negotiations; unlike their Japanese counterparts, none of them had any deep knowledge of the construction industry.[15]

Japanese trade negotiators have become expert at recognizing the dividing point between U.S. posturing and intensifying anger capable of triggering retaliatory action. This expertise has been put to its severest test when threats of congressional action loomed. One of the favorite U.S. tactics, now all but abandoned, was for the U.S. executive branch to play the good cop trying to prevent passage of severely protectionist legislation threatened by the bad cop — the legislative branch. To quote Prestowitz again, whenever U.S. trade negotiators tried to frighten Japan with the vision of a Congress about to go out of control, there was a major downside: "Implicitly we were linking ourselves in common cause with the Japanese and creating a false sense that free-traders on both sides were fighting against the black hats in Congress. The negotiation thus changed direction: originally a matter of U.S. government requests, it became one of mutually calibrating just how much action would be necessary to keep Congress leashed. Instead of a negotiator, the U.S. trade team became an adviser to the government of Japan on how to handle the U.S. Congress."[16] Although the legislative branch consistently advocates a more aggressive approach to protecting U.S. trade interests than does the executive branch, Congress's bark has been far worse than its bite. It almost never passes protectionist legislation.

A final aspect of the bureaucratic mismatch is the ease with which Japanese representatives can exploit the relatively open U.S. policymaking system. They have little problem amassing voluminous information about U.S. government intentions; meeting with federal, state, and local officials; and talking with the media. U.S. representatives in Japan are relatively isolated by local traditions that discourage their involvement in the decision-making process and their efforts to influence public opinion.

## LOBBYING MISMATCH

The Japanese system is too methodical and calculating to be tolerant of external surprises. Japan has long felt itself vulnerable to hostile overseas actions directed against its economic interests. More directly, it thinks its most important economic partner does not understand it and views itself as an innocent victim of U.S. persecution. The possibility of retaliatory U.S. economic actions is unacceptably risky when the United States is a $130 billion a year export market and the location of well in excess of $400 billion in Japanese-owned assets in U.S. government bonds, direct investments, land, stocks, and so on.[17]

To protect their flank, the Japanese spend hundreds of millions of dollars annually to maintain, in the United States, the world's largest, most expensive, and most effective foreign-financed lobbying, commercial intelligence, and public relations operation. These efforts are designed to influence policy development in the U.S. government, to distinguish between U.S. bluster and genuine commitment to unilateral action if not appeased, and to explain Japan's side of the argument and promote a positive public image among U.S. officials and citizens that offsets criticism of Japan's trade practices.

The sprawling Japan lobby triggered the perception held by some that its big money is buying America — corrupting policymaking and tainting the thinking of the media, academia, research institutes, the law, and every other target of Japanese largesse. No evidence of any significant illegality or impropriety by the Japanese lobby has materialized. There is no hard evidence of persons altering their views on Japan because of the lure of cash rewards. Nevertheless, the backlash in U.S. concerns hit its zenith after Washington-based policy analyst Pat Choate published *Agents of Influence* in 1990. The book, which received both brutal damnation for sensationalism and lavish praise for its important message by reviewers looking through the *Rashomon* lens, contained a stern warning:

Japan is running an ongoing political campaign in America as if it were a third major political party. . . . Better financed, more extensive, and more effective than either U.S. political party or any domestic industry, union, or special interest group, Japan's campaign . . . serves one very important purpose: to influence the outcome of political decisions in Washington. . . . The Japanese are able to use their purchased political influence in America as a critical element of their corporate and national strategies.[18]

The book also contained appendixes of what is still the most complete published list of the many former federal officials who became representatives of foreign interests. It is not uncommon for some of these ex-officials to make public statements and write articles about bilateral trade relations without openly revealing this connection.

The Japanese thirst for information can reach absurd excesses, as illustrated by Toyota's 1981 decision to retain at least ten different Washington organizations to monitor the auto import quota issue. Not knowing that they had all been given the same general assignment, the lobbyists descended on Capitol Hill seeking answers to identical questions. Exasperated congressional staff members finally told Toyota they would be happy to pass along information directly but refused to deal further with the company's squadron of lobbyists.[19] Japan's willingness to pay for influence was, perhaps, best exhibited by the now legendary $300,000 fee reportedly paid to a politically well-connected economic consultant. Japanese television manufacturers retained him in 1977 for a mere three months of part-time effort to contain the protectionist campaign of the U.S. television industry. Japanese interests spent a reported $3 million in early 1995 just on advertisements in U.S. media to oppose threatened import sanctions on Japanese luxury automobiles.[20]

The sheer volume of money spent by Japanese lobbying efforts has resulted in a distinct imbalance in the abilities of the two countries to influence official thinking and public opinion in the other. The sums reported annually to the U.S. Justice Department under the Foreign Agents Registration Act grossly underestimate total lobbying outlays because of the proliferation of activities exempted from reporting requirements under the law. It is still informative to note that reported payments of $56 million in 1995 from Japan to U.S. lobbyists was more than the combined payments reported by the second and third largest countries (Great Britain and Canada).[21] *Business Week* in the summer of 1988 estimated that total Japanese spending on image making and influence molding in the United States, exclusive of product advertising, would exceed $300 million in that year.[22] Japan lobby-watcher Pat Choate estimated that the annual outlay in 1992 had risen to $500 million.[23]

During election years, candidates in both U.S. parties now receive large contributions from the political action committees formed by U.S. employees of Japanese corporate subsidiaries and Americans retained as lobbyists. Although corporate charity-giving is not a tradition in their home country, Japanese-owned subsidiaries in the United States have sought to become good corporate citizens by organizing a major philanthropic effort that, broadly defined, reached an estimated $500 million annually in the early 1990s.[24]

The growing numbers of organizations and individuals receiving Japanese funding means more vested interests in not unduly offending or attacking Japan, that is, not biting the hand that feeds. The Japanese government established a $375 million Japan-U.S. Global Partnership Fund in 1991 to support bilateral academic, business, cultural, and civic activities. Much, if not most, of U.S.-based scholarly study of Japanese institutions is directly or indirectly sponsored by the objects of their inquiries (at least in part because of inadequate U.S. corporate support of such research). Japanese businesses gave $150 million in gifts to U.S. universities in 1990 alone, according to an estimate by a newsletter covering philanthropic activities.[25] Japanese-funded chairs in leading U.S. universities have become commonplace.

Until laws were passed to delay the ability of retired government officials to lobby their former colleagues, critics had wondered out loud about the objectivity of senior U.S. trade officials while still in office. Growing numbers of them were using the "revolving door" to multiply their salaries by signing on as attorneys, consultants, or lobbyists for Japanese interests. With only a little hyperbole, one writer worried that the Office of the USTR and the Commerce Department had become "virtual training camps" for the Japanese, "whose roster of lawyers, lobbyists, and consultants reads like an all-star team of former U.S. trade specialists."[26] At least one-third of approximately 60 senior USTR officials leaving government in the 1970s and 1980s moved on to represent foreign clients, most of whom were Japanese.[27]

Uneasiness about the lure of big money in a society that respects wealth far more than public service was fueled by numerous cases in the 1980s demonstrating not even a pretense of separation between government service and efforts to cash in on contacts and experience. One of the more flagrant examples involved the deputy assistant secretary of commerce, Robert Watkins, who was a senior member of the team formulating U.S. trade strategy in automobiles and auto parts. While still in office in 1987, he circulated a letter suggesting that, upon his departure from office, Japanese automobile companies hire him to form a trade association to represent their interests in the United States.[28] While still a commissioner on the U.S. International Trade Commission, Daniel Minchew actively solicited consulting business in Tokyo.[29]

Richard Allen, President Reagan's first assistant for national security affairs, had earlier been forced to resign as a campaign adviser after his extensive business relations with Japanese companies became public. He was forced to resign from the White House staff after admitting he accepted $1,000 for helping a Japanese magazine arrange an interview with Mrs. Reagan. He immediately resumed representing Japanese interests.[30] James Lake retained his lucrative lobbying contracts with the Japanese while serving as a senior adviser to George Bush's 1988 presidential campaign.

Not even presidents are exempt from suspicion by some that the allure of Japanese megabucks after retirement has wafted into the Oval Office. Criticism quickly followed Ronald Reagan's acceptance of a reported $2 million from a Japanese media company for a short speaking tour in 1989. While he was still in office, news reports had suggested appearance of a conflict of interest when President Reagan was defending the Sony

Corporation's purchase of Columbia Pictures at the same time his representatives were discussing a contribution from that company to the Reagan library fund.[31] Former President Carter received major funding for his presidential library and humanitarian activities from the controversial Ryoichi Sasakawa, a convicted Japanese war criminal.[32]

An important shift in Japanese lobbying tactics began in the late 1980s when the bulk of responsibility for urging that the U.S. market be kept open to Japanese goods shifted to U.S.-based companies benefitting from trade with that country. This trend has continued for three reasons. First, Japanese lobbyists needed to take a lower profile after the publication of *Agents of Influence*. The second reason was the demonstrated effectiveness of mobilizing as lobbyists U.S. corporate customers as well as Japanese-controlled corporate subsidiaries in the United States and the more than 700,000 Americans they employed.[33] A third reason for the surge in U.S. corporate import lobbying activity is the growing dependence of the United States on Japanese suppliers as exclusive sources for a number of sophisticated components and capital equipment largely unknown to the public.

The first major grass-roots Japanese lobbying initiative was Toshiba Corporation's efforts in 1987–88 to defeat the comprehensive import ban on its products being considered by Congress. This proposed sanction was in retaliation for one of the company's subsidiaries' illegal export of sensitive technology to the Soviet Union that reduced the noise level of Soviet submarines. The "who's who" list of lobbyists retained by Toshiba, estimated to have been paid somewhere between $10 and $30 million, galvanized hundreds of U.S. companies to bombard Washington with the message that, as users of Toshiba-made components, they and their workers would be hurt if imports of all its products were banned. Several thousand U.S. workers in Toshiba's U.S. subsidiaries were urged to express to their senators and congressmen strong opposition to the proposed trade sanctions on the grounds that their jobs were at stake. Clever lobbying changed the image of Toshiba from an easily dispensable seller of consumer electronics to that of an irreplaceable vendor of inputs to U.S. manufacturers. The resulting congressional retreat from its desire to impose strong sanctions on the company provides a vivid illustration of the declining U.S. ability to retaliate against Japanese imports at an acceptable cost.

The Japanese Auto Parts Industries Association, in 1994, adopted a grass-roots campaign unprecedented in scope to oppose the Clinton administration's demands for increased purchases by Japanese automobile makers from U.S.-owned auto parts makers. In this case, tens of thousands of Americans employed in more than 100 U.S. subsidiaries of Japanese-owned auto parts makers were given form letters and talking points for use in telephone calls. They were provided free phone lines and asked to tell their members of Congress that their jobs could be at risk if Japanese automobile companies had to divert business from them to U.S.-owned competitors. Workers were also given written material for arguing their case in the media.[34]

A disquieting, albeit illuminating asymmetry is the failure of both U.S. government and industry to develop a policy-influencing presence in the less open Japanese society that is at least in the same league as Japan's lobbying efforts in this country. A phalanx of pro-import trade associations, law offices, consumer groups, and public relations firms does not exist in Tokyo (or in most capital cities) in anywhere near the magnitude found in Washington, D.C. Japanese decision makers do not share the legal requirement of their U.S. counterparts to formulate trade policy largely in public view.

No revolving door exists in Japan whereby retiring trade officials take jobs publicly promoting imports from the United States. Under the Japanese system of *amakudari* (literally, descent from heaven), retiring civil servants at all levels of seniority are placed in lucrative positions with Japanese companies, usually one that a bureaucrat had previously regulated. The situation has improved a little since the late 1980s, when a MITI official was quoted as saying that if a foreign company hired a retiring senior MITI official to represent it, his former colleagues would not pay him "the slightest heed. We would treat him courteously, but he would become a social leper."[35] Today, most U.S. subsidiaries in Japan are allowed to retain junior level government retirees as low-profile conduits to relevant ministries. However, it is still inconceivable that a retired official would publicly challenge a Japanese government position on behalf of U.S. interests.

The lack of reciprocity in corporate lobbying is not entirely the fault of the Japanese system. Relatively few U.S. companies are willing to incur the enormous expenses of maintaining a government relations office and public relations activities in Tokyo. Housing, education, cost of living, and home travel allowances run well into six figures for Americans working there. Even if active in Tokyo, U.S. companies are prevented by the U.S. Foreign Corrupt Practices Act from following the local custom of currying favor with politicians through large, usually unpublicized, cash gifts for "campaigning."

Despite these obstacles, an embryonic U.S. lobbying movement has emerged in Japan. Bilingual representatives of U.S. companies and trade associations in Tokyo have never been more numerous. Astute U.S. business lobbyists who know the importance of cultivating personal relationships in Japan are learning how to exploit the small but increasing leverage available to them in government and business circles. U.S. corporate lobbying efforts seem to have very high rates of success when they operate in conjunction with allies among domestic Japanese business interests. (Pro-import consumer groups are not yet a political force.) Prior to opening in Japan, McDonalds maximized its lobbying leverage by working closely with the many local businesses, such as real estate companies and restaurant suppliers, who would profit from its success in Japan.[36] The American Chamber of Commerce in Japan, now representing more than 700 companies, is increasingly active and vocal in publicizing specific barriers to exports and direct investment encountered by its members. It also directly discusses grievances with Japanese politicians and civil servants.

## IS BILATERALISM ON THE WANE?

After more than three decades of dealing with U.S. economic demands almost exclusively on a bilateral basis, the Japanese government gives every evidence of wanting to shift much of the dialogue to the multilateral level. The U.S. government's use of *gaiatsu* (external pressure) may have passed its peak of effectiveness. Japanese attitudes were summed up in a direct, perhaps exaggerated, declaration in a March 1996 speech by MITI Vice Minister Yoshihiro Sakamoto, the ministry's top career official: "The era of 'bilateralism' is over."[37] Japan is not yet ready to close the door entirely on bilateral trade negotiations, but the bureaucracy seems increasingly willing to say "no" to Washington. Part of the explanation is the growing self-confidence of, and declining sense of gratitude felt by, a generation of Japanese decision makers who did not personally experience the generous U.S. efforts to revive the Japanese economy after World War II. Diluting emphasis on bilateral negotiations is also likely to parallel the emerging trend of increased Japanese trade and investment activity in Asia. As their companies become relatively less dependent on exporting to the U.S. market, Japanese trade policymakers can be expected to become less determined to keep the U.S. government happy.

Japan's current bilateral trade strategy appears to be aimed specifically at emasculating the U.S. Section 301 statute used for challenging foreign trade barriers. If successful, this approach would curtail unilateral U.S. demands and threats of retaliation if alleged Japanese market access barriers were not reduced or eliminated. Three factors are encouraging the anti-301 maneuver: a further loss of patience with three decades of nonstop U.S. demands; the relatively recent creation of the World Trade Organization (WTO) and worldwide support for assuring the success of its enhanced dispute settlement mechanism; and, with most of Japan's at-the-border barriers reduced, the United States is now increasingly seeking changes in its internal regulatory and competition policies, as seen in the Kodak complaint of exclusionary distribution practices filed against its main Japanese rival, Fuji film. The WTO's current jurisdiction over purely internal policy matters is murky at best. Japan, therefore, stands a good chance of convincing WTO dispute settlement panels to dismiss U.S. claims of discriminatory trade practices based purely on competition policy and regulatory controls.

To some, the end of bilateral U.S. coercion is long overdue. To others, a Japanese rebuff to bilateralism is adding insult to the injury caused by three decades of market-opening measures that were allegedly too little, too late. No matter how good or bad one considers the bilateral negotiating process, it reflected the mutual belief in a special relationship. Both countries felt more comfortable and confident dealing on a private, one-on-one basis than in the more impersonal, uncontrollable environment of a multilateral forum. The larger meaning of any genuine move away from bilateral negotiations is a political diminution in this "special relationship," something potentially more important than any given commercial dispute.

## CONCLUSION

The United States and Japan have endured three decades of failure to correct problems that both deemed destabilizing to their relationship. Whether based on indifference, infinite patience, or cunning calculation, their willingness to live so long with marginal achievement did not bode well for successfully resolving trade disputes. A feverish pace of activity prevented a trade war but failed to eliminate the perceived basic problems of market access or Japan's mammoth trade surpluses. Uncountable negotiations on many issues by many earnest people could not prevent continual recurrences of new frictions or ill feelings.

Because U.S.-Japanese trade disequilibria were geometrically larger in the mid-1990s than in 1969, the three-decades-old process of negotiating in circles could be faulted for failing to preserve even the status quo. U.S. negotiating strategy might have been better advised to avoid half-way ad hockery and go to one of two extremes: being infinitely more tolerant and accommodating or forcefully and repeatedly convincing Japan that severe penalties would definitely result from its failure to adopt greater, more effective market-opening measures.

The negotiating process was tilted in favor of Japan because that country attached greater priority to it. On a deeper level, the reasons for mutual toleration of an asymmetrical, relatively ineffective negotiating process in which the deaf outwitted the blind are part of the reason why a systemic problem exists.

Having completed its analysis of the nature and causes of bilateral differences, this study next evaluates the relative merits of the two countries' actions and self-justifications.

## NOTES

1. Philip H. Trezise, "The Realities of Japan-U.S. Economic Relations," *Pacific Community* (April 1970), pp. 359–60.

2. Edwin Dale, Jr., "A Special Tariff on Japan Weighed," *New York Times*, May 24, 1971, p. 47.

3. U.S. Congress, *Congressional Record*, July 31, 1978, pp. 23499–500.

4. U.S.-Japan Trade Council, "Foreign Economic Legislation: A Year-End Review," December 14, 1979, Washington, D.C.

5. There is one possible exception: the 1988 trade act imposed import sanctions on the Toshiba Machine Company for its illegal sales of machine tools to the Soviet Union.

6. Clyde Prestowitz, Jr., *Trading Places: How We Allowed Japan to Take the Lead* (New York: Basic Books, 1988), p. 260.

7. As quoted in John Carroll, "Trade Talkers on the Edge," *The Journal of the American Chamber of Commerce in Japan*, January 1995, p. 15.

8. Advisory Committee for Trade Policy and Negotiations, "Analysis of the U.S.-Japan Trade Problem," February 1989, p. 112, mimeographed.

9. To be sure, there are rivalries, turf battles, and policy disagreements among Japanese ministries and between the Japanese government and private sector. The differences are that these squabbles are relatively less public, frequent, and severe and that the U.S. government and private sectors are relative amateurs at exploiting them.

10. Chalmers Johnson and E. B. Keehn have labeled the Pentagon "a virtual pawn of the Japan lobby" ("The Pentagon's Ossified Strategy," *Foreign Affairs* [July-August 1995], p. 114).

11. Carroll, "Trade Talkers," p. 15.

12. Ibid., p. 17.

13. Prestowitz, *Trading Places*, p. 259.

14. David Osborne, "Japan's Secret Agents," *New Republic*, October 1, 1984, p. 22.

15. "Trade Session with Japan Delayed," *Washington Post*, March 22, 1988, p. C3; Clyde Prestowitz, Jr., "Japan Talks Trade While America Sleeps," *New York Times*, April 24, 1988, p. III-3.

16. Prestowitz, *Trading Places*, p. 281.

17. Total Japanese-owned assets in the United States could easily be worth as much as $500 billion in 1997, given the shortcomings of the data and the U.S. financial community's assumption that the Japanese purchase many U.S. Treasury bills anonymously through European banks.

18. Pat Choate, *Agents of Influence* (New York: Alfred A. Knopf, 1990), p. xi.

19. Christopher Madison, "Is Japan Trying To Buy Washington or Just Do Business Capital Style?" *National Journal*, October 9, 1982, p. 1711.

20. "U.S., Japan Usher in a Nastier New Era," *The Wall Street Journal*, June 29, 1995, p. A12. The centerpiece of this advertising blitz was an unsubtle TV commercial comparing the threatened automobile sanctions to the policies that led to the Depression and the trade wars of the 1930s.

21. U.S. Department of Justice, *Report of the Attorney General to the Congress on the Administration of the Foreign Agents Registration Act of 1938, as amended, for the*

*Calendar Year 1995.*

22.   "Japan's Clout in the U.S.," *Business Week,* July 11, 1988, p. 64.

23.   Pat Choate, "To Get Our Nations on an Even Footing, Japan Must Pay for its Defense," *New York Times,* July 26, 1992, p. III-13.

24.   See "Japanese Firms Use Philanthropy To Build Image," *Christian Science Monitor,* July 23, 1992, p. 8; "Japanese Firms Embark on a Program of Lavish Giving to American Charities," *The Wall Street Journal,* May 23, 1991, p. B1. Depending on definitions used, some of Japan's corporate charity-giving is also counted in estimates of total political lobbying.

25.   The estimate was made by the "Corporate Philanthropy Report," as cited by the Gannett News Service, December 9, 1990; available from the Lexis-Nexis data base.

26.   Osborne, "Secret Agents," p. 20.

27.   "In Trade Talks, Japan Knows the U.S. Team — Often Too Well," *The Wall Street Journal,* February 23, 1990, p. A1. The General Accounting Office identified 76 high-level executive and legislative branch officials who left government between 1980 and 1985 to work for foreign interests.

28.   See, for example, House Judiciary Committee, *Restrictions on the Post-Employment Activities of Federal Officers and Employees,* hearing held May 4, 1988, p. 77.

29.   Osborne, "Secret Agents," p. 21.

30.   David Osborne, "Lobbying for Japan Inc.," *New York Times Magazine,* December 4, 1983, p. 132.

31.   "Sony Discussing Contribution to Reagan's Library," *New York Times,* October 29, 1989, p. I-4.

32.   Choate, *Agents of Influence,* pp. 178, 179.

33.   Japan External Trade Organization, "Handy Facts on U.S.-Japan Economic Relations," 1994, p. 20.

34.   "U.S. Workers Asked to Lobby for Japan," *Automotive News,* January 17, 1974, pp. 1, 42.

35.   "Japan's Loud Voice in Washington," *New York Times,* December 10, 1989, p. III-1.

36.   "Winning Friends and Influencing People," *Nihon Keizai Shimbun,* February 9, 1991, p. A1 of special section on the United States; available from Lexis-Nexis data bank.

37.   Ministry of International Trade and Industry, press release of speech delivered March 15, 1996, p. 3.

# III

# CONCLUSIONS

# 10

# Synthesizing the Arguments

A plague on both your houses.
— Mercutio, in Shakespeare's *Romeo and Juliet*

When two men fight, both should be punished.
— Traditional Japanese saying

It is time to move beyond passive accommodation of the conflicting diagnoses of what caused and perpetuated three decades of bilateral frictions and disequilibria. This chapter presents a composite explanation of the problem consisting of what I believe to be the valid parts of the two contradictory images most frequently seen when bilateral trade relations are viewed through the *Rashomon* lens. My synthesis of the seemingly mutually exclusive arguments assumes that neither country monopolizes wisdom and truth when defending its position or providing a definitive explanation of what has happened. The uncompromising, black-and-white interpretations depicted in Chapters 3 and 4 each contain elements of accuracy, fiction, half-truths, and exaggeration. Without modification, pro-U.S. and pro-Japanese versions are equally misleading.

Scientifically demonstrable, irrefutable cause-and-effect relationships seldom can be revealed in issues where, in the final analysis, perceptions define truths. In this emotional clash of value judgments, there is no single version of "reality" (a concept perhaps best defined as a "collective hunch"). Neither country deserves unqualified blame for irresponsibility, and neither warrants unqualified praise for enlightenment. Both sides have long misjudged the systemic nature of the problem. The search for accuracy is best served by carefully prorating blame to both sides, not by deciding which country is guilty of what. This method can enhance mutual understanding, but it is unlikely to halt the tendency for different belief systems to cause people to process and interpret identical information in a different manner.

## DIFFERENT INPUTS, DIFFERENT OUTPUTS

To evaluate who did what to whom and why, let us return to the question originally posed in Chapter 1: what exactly has been the problem between the two countries since 1969. The short answer is that the data clearly indicate the existence of two unresolved, systemic problems — one originating in Japan, the other in the United States. The first is the unusual difficulties encountered by foreign companies seeking access to the Japanese market, even those with an excellent product and a carefully crafted marketing plan. The second is the competitive shortcomings of the U.S. industrial sector as demonstrated in part by Japan's record of successfully exporting to the United States a succession of increasingly sophisticated manufactured goods.

The common denominator between the two problems is a mismatch involving profound differences in corporate production strategies, economic policies, and social priorities in the two countries. A second commonality is that both problems are ostensibly economic in nature but must be assessed in the context of political considerations. Ultimately, international trade is a political process. Purely economic arguments as to what is right and wrong in this case have limited real world applicability. Elected officials may wish to follow good economic principles, but they cannot be indifferent when the people who elected them to represent their interests complain of being hurt by foreign competition.

Japan has been in a league of its own in being able to out-think, out-work, outsmart, outflank, and outrun much of the U.S. industrial sector since the 1960s. With skill, luck, a little guile, and a work force willing to make sacrifices, Japan's industrial sector — itself cushioned for many years from the impact of import competition — expanded exports to the extent that painful dislocations were inflicted on U.S. producers. Japan leveraged its economic and social advantages in a determined, carefully calculated pursuit of security and international respectability. The means to this end was a focused effort to maximize industrial strength and minimize dependence on the rest of the world, for whom Japan felt no sense of obligation.

For all of the U.S. economic order's exploitable weaknesses, it has done well in the services sector and in competing against the capital-intensive goods of other countries by relying on a relatively free market and by emphasizing corporate profits, self-initiative, and consumerism. Only in the case of Japan has U.S. industrial competitiveness sputtered badly. For better or worse, the United States was unwilling or unable to match Japan's singular commitment to industrial growth and export expansion. The U.S. government never felt the need to respond to Japan's growing economic strength by revising its macro- and microeconomic policies to encourage more saving, investment, and commercial technological innovation. Successive administrations (rightly or wrongly) were far more concerned with protecting U.S. consumers, the military alliance with Japan, and the tenets of free markets. Until a resurgent Japan was judged a clear and present competitive threat, U.S. industry exhibited no belief in the need to radically alter the manufacturing techniques and marketing methods that had catapulted it to global dominance earlier in the century.

Japan was insensitive and insular. The United States was inefficient and distracted.

Japan sought to minimize dependence on imports of advanced industrial goods, but it ignored the disadvantages of not maintaining harmony with its trading partners.

The United States sought to stay one step ahead of the Soviets, politically and militarily, but it ignored the costs of falling behind the Japanese in industrial competitiveness.

Japan equates industrial strength and self-sufficiency with national security. The United States equates military strength and strong allies with national security. "It is only a slight exaggeration to say that the Japanese will accept higher factor costs for essentially the same reasons that the United States will overpay for its defense systems. It makes each feel more secure."[1]

Ironically, both countries were successful in achieving their number one international policy priority. The United States was victorious in its political-military struggle against the spread of communism by the Soviet Union. Japan was victorious in its commercial struggle to become an industrial and exporting superpower. The two countries were also successful in achieving dissimilar foreign trade policy objectives. The United States promoted trade liberalization in multilateral negotiations and was relatively accommodating of imports in order to enhance foreign policy objectives and consumer choice. Japan minimized unwanted imports of manufactured goods while maximizing both export volume and overseas market shares of its big industrial companies. These sharply contrasting successes go a long way in explaining why both countries were willing to live with a secondary policy failure: inability to end bilateral frictions and restore trade equilibrium.

Neither Japan nor the United States merits effusive praise for the quality of its efforts to deal with the systemic changes in bilateral trading

relations that became visible in the 1970s. Both countries groped unsuccessfully for a modus vivendi that would accommodate Japanese export
"overachieving" to the inability of the United States to rise adequately to
the commercial challenge. An adequate response was still not forthcoming in the closing years of the twentieth century — not for lack of trying,
but for lack of dealing with a systemic problem. Fundamental changes in
the economic policies, corporate strategy, and trade policy objectives of
both countries were necessary, but they were not implemented.

The Japanese put themselves in a fool's paradise by assuming the rest
of the world would welcome their becoming the fastest growing source of
exported manufactured goods while simultaneously tolerating the insularity that led to discouragement of imports. U.S. trade policy foolishly
assumed the Japanese would feel honor-bound to respond to demands
that their economic practices be changed to conform to the Western version of fair play.

Japan opted for the politics of sincerity and the economics of public
relations gestures. The United States adopted the politics of intimidation
and the economics of complacency. Neither opted to meet the problem
head on. Japan was not concerned about the economic disruptions inflicted on other countries by its trade actions. Americans opted for a false
security by first failing to notice the extraordinary rise of Japan's industrial competitiveness and then simplistically interpreting it as based on
temporary factors or unfair trade practices that could be corrected fairly
easily.

On close examination, both sides' defenses of their responsibility for
causing frictions are flawed. The bottom line is that the United States and
Japan deserved each other's scorn. Bilateral economic relations have been
a kind of morality play between two economies sharing only the most
basic disciplines of the capitalist system. The conflicts fed on themselves
as second-best analyses generated second-best policy responses.

The essence of the problem since the 1970s has been that a large, powerful market-oriented economy can be quite unsuccessful competing
against the industrial sector of a smaller, talented, and driven country
where government and business skillfully cooperate in pursuing a crusade for maximization of industrial strength. The story of economic relations between Japan and the United States has been written in extremes.
Japan anticipated and planned for economic change far better than did
the United States. When it came to assuring reciprocal market access to
foreigners, the Japanese did far less than other countries to welcome and
encourage change. The United States is one of the world's most open
economies and societies, and it deeply believes in the theory of liberal
trade. Conversely, Japan was, until recently, one of the world's most
closed capitalist societies.

U.S. companies usually agreed with their government that they were supposed to sink or swim on the basis of market forces. Japan's inspired infant industry policies smothered foreign competition and was frequently able to induce competitive advantage by "socializing risk" for Japanese companies willing to invest in the development of targeted industries. Japan's economic success turned parts of Western economic theory on their heads when some of the world's most competitive industrial sectors emerged from a most unlikely environment. Foreign competition in key industrial sectors was rigidly controlled, cartels were encouraged, and the landscape of domestic competition was frequently sculpted by Ministry of Internationl Trade and Industry guidelines. If the U.S. government had ignored antitrust enforcement, encouraged cartels, and stifled the discipline of foreign competition, the results undoubtedly would have been devastating to domestic economic performance.

The contemporary cowboy and samurai societies exhibit many important differences that overshadow their similarities. Like people everywhere, Americans and Japanese respond to an established reward system, but their reward systems are dissimilar. The Japanese economy operates mainly for the benefit of producers, while the U.S. economy is geared to benefitting consumers. Japanese workers are supposed to give unstintingly of themselves and to demonstrate unquestioning dedication to their employers. U.S. workers take for granted putting self-interests first and extracting maximum financial rewards from their employers. Japanese companies emphasize making quality goods and achieving the largest possible market share. U.S. companies fixate on short-term profits.

The samurai society saves, it cooperates, and it glorifies exports. The cowboy society consumes, it practices adversarial relations between government and business, and it luxuriates in imported goods. The samurai society defines desirable economic behavior normatively by respect for an intricate web of interpersonal loyalties and obligations that often constrain self-gratification. The cowboy society defines desirable economic behavior quantitatively by low prices and high salaries, and it believes in an ever-expanding frontier of opportunity for individual enrichment.

It is no open-and-shut case as to who is the winner in bilateral trade relations. In conventional political and business terms, Japan comes out ahead. When measured in terms of economic theory, the United States has gained the bulk of the benefits from trade. To a Western economic theorist, the question is who is sillier: Americans who complain about the bilateral trade deficits or the Japanese who work long hours and accept a lower standard of living by exchanging real economic resources for an endless flow of the suspect product of the U.S. government's printing presses. Japan's mercantilist tendencies have created a system in which much of the surplus wealth produced by its superb industrial sector has been frittered away by the financial consequences of a structural current account surplus. Hundreds of billions of dollars have had to be written off. Massive Japanese holdings of dollar-denominated assets, such as bonds and stocks, were worth less in yen terms because of losses incurred from dollar depreciation. In addition, Japanese investors frequently paid excessively high prices for real estate, movie studios, and other direct investments in the United States. It would have made far greater economic sense, by Western standards, for Japan to have invested more resources in its lagging infrastructure, that is, housing, roads, recreation facilities, and so on.

Regrettably, the focal point of three decades of trade frictions has been the bilateral trade imbalance. In economic terms, there is nothing necessarily wrong, damaging, or intolerable about a large, self-perpetuating Japanese bilateral trade surplus. The always questionable significance of bilateral trade balances has been further undermined by the globalization of production. Corporations increasingly sell goods in foreign markets through overseas subsidiaries rather than exporting, and Japanese subsidiaries in Asia increasingly are exporting directly to the U.S. market. Good economic analysis emphasizes only the structural causes of the imbalances, namely, lagging U.S. industrial competitiveness and limited foreign access to the Japanese market.

Bilateral trade balances can and do matter under certain circumstances. They take on political importance when one country believes that the other is gaining advantage by consistently violating accepted norms of the trade game. U.S. dissatisfaction with Japan's excessive export exuberance and import inhospitality inevitably led to perceptions of adversarial and non-market Japanese trade practices. Even if Japan's counterarguments to U.S. complaints had been economically flawless, public opinion in the United States still would have perceived an inequitable relationship in the severe dislocations imposed on U.S. companies and workers. As E. H. Carr noted more than 40 years ago, "Economic forces are in fact political forces. . . . The science of economics . . . cannot be profitably studied in isolation from politics."[2] Whatever the pure economic merits may be, a serious bilateral problem has existed in political terms because important factions in the U.S. political system have perceived an unacceptable economic disequilibrium.

Bilateral trade disequilibria are economically significant when they stubbornly persist in the face of implementation of all the traditional adjustment measures available to eliminate them. Japan's repeated adoption of export restraints, import liberalization, fiscal stimulation, and so on all had in common their failure to permanently shrink the large bilateral trade imbalances. Not even the loss of approximately three-fourths of the dollar's value against the yen between 1971 and 1996 could prevent the imbalance from ballooning. In theory one of the most powerful inducers of balance of payments adjustment, exchange rate realignments, has been limited to periodically reducing Japan's bilateral surpluses and U.S. bilateral deficits. Although an infinite amount of dollar depreciation would end the disequilibrium, yen appreciation has been limited and temporary. For example, after an upward surge against the dollar that peaked in mid-1995, the yen then depreciated 50 percent against the dollar by the end of January 1997. After an appropriate lag time, this weakness should cause a reversal in the declining Japanese trade surpluses registered in the mid-1990s that were mainly the result of yen appreciation a few years earlier. At least as important as the yen-dollar exchange rate at any given time are two relative price inelasticities of demand. For a variety of reasons, not all fully understood, U.S. demand for most Japanese imports is relatively price inelastic, that is, it is not significantly reduced when their prices rise, and Japan's demand increases relatively slightly when prices of U.S.-made goods fall.

Despite the extent and frequency of bilateral consultations on economic matters, the two countries understood each other only slightly better in the late 1990s than they did three decades earlier. A better comprehension of the other country's needs, goals, and motives as well as the legitimacy of the other's complaints would not necessarily have produced a harmonious bilateral economic relationship. Understanding is not the same as acceptance. The Japanese would not have accepted a greater presence of manufactured-goods imports or foreign direct investment, even if they fully understood and respected U.S. economic grievances. Japan would not have delayed achievement of domestic economic goals or changed social mores to accommodate U.S. demands. The Japanese take a go-slow approach to deep-rooted internationalization because it poses a threat to the unique cultural base of their economy. Most Americans would not have accepted the burdens of diminished internal production and lost jobs from increased imports even if they had sympathized with Japanese practices and intentions. Political necessity would have prevented the U.S. government from allowing free-market forces to totally determine its trade flows even if it perceived that Japan's economic strength rested entirely on fair practices that could be emulated by the United States. Mutual lack of understanding and a communications gap born of cultural differences compounded a systemic economic problem.

## THE UNITED STATES' WORST
## ENEMY — THE UNITED STATES

It is a gross oversimplification to brand an economically strong and socially flexible United States as either industrial failure or helpless victim of a Japanese conspiracy. It is fair, however, to criticize the U.S. public and private sectors for their belated and inadequate responses to two important contemporary trends. The first trend was the inexorable encroachment by the global economy on what had been an invulnerable U.S. industrial sector. The second trend was the degree to which innovative Japanese industrial companies were radically revising and improving traditional methods of manufacturing. More than any other country in modern times, Japan introduced an obsolescence into U.S. international economic policies and corporate strategies. It was able to gain a significant head start because too many U.S. executives suffered from a perception of continuing postwar invincibility and a myopia that prevented them from promptly realizing that the once-vanquished Japanese had unleashed a manufacturing revolution. If Japan's industrial and exporting resurgence had been no greater than Germany's, the wake up call to U.S. trade policymakers and corporate chieftains would have been much quieter. Japan has been the equivalent of a giant spotlight illuminating the weaknesses of U.S. business practices and economic policies.

The United States lacked the will, not the capacity, to respond more effectively to the increasingly obvious signs of a sustained Japanese industrial surge. The failure of the United States to deal forcefully with a major new challenge, as it often had done before, is partly because Americans did not perceive the need. At the start of the 1970s, the United States exemplified an affliction of the successful: "difficulty in seeing the onset of a new order, the rise of a revolutionary new way of doing things, the coming of a new game that will shatter the world of the comfortable and the complacent."[3] Even if Americans had been less confident about the staying power of their economic prowess, policymakers would have been hard-pressed to design a quick, effective response. Because the Japanese industrial challenge was unprecedented, there was no instruction manual to which these officials could turn. Distracted by national security concerns and a lack of social consensus that enhanced industrial power was an urgent necessity, U.S. policymakers felt no need to realign U.S. priorities simply because a friendly country was increasing its share of world trade in manufactures.

The relatively poor record of the United States in effectively responding to the Japanese economic challenge was mostly self-inflicted. The absence of a tangible, self-evident crisis fostered a U.S. government willingness to rely more on rhetoric than meaningful action to deal with structural economic problems. This is almost exactly the opposite of the U.S. government's response to the Communist challenge when, with the overwhelming support of public opinion, it mobilized vast resources and decisively and doggedly responded to the widely perceived Soviet military threat and later to the space race. Partly because of an ideological blind spot, U.S. policymakers and public opinion did not foresee any country being able to transcend the Western instinct for pursuing short-term individual interests, and then to brilliantly execute a long-term, collective national effort to enhance the market mechanism, minimize dependence on foreigners, and maximize national prestige. If Americans had correctly anticipated the impact on them of Japan's industrial success, presidents might have elevated trade policy to the point that they would have felt compelled to pronounce clearly delineated limits on injurious, unfair trade practices by Japan and other major trading partners as firmly as they pronounced limits of acceptable Soviet military behavior.

If this scenario had developed, more aggressive U.S. trade policies would have been a necessary, but insufficient, condition to allow the United States to respond in kind to the unfolding "Japanese miracle." The right mix of domestic economic policy reforms is far more effective in eliminating structural trade deficits than the relatively limited potential of trade policy. Japan is not responsible for the United States' being well below average among industrialized countries since the 1960s in terms of saving rates and increased productivity. Japan is responsible for neither the U.S. government's willingness to bear the world's largest defense budget and finance multibillion dollar weapons systems nor its reluctance to underwrite basic research in commercial technology. It is not Japan's fault that the U.S. government failed to raise taxes sufficiently or cut federal spending in the latter part of the 1980s to reduce its large budget deficit. Japan cannot be blamed for the lagging U.S. success in curing the social problems, such as crime, substance abuse, and lagging technical skills, that impose a multibillion dollar annual drain on U.S. economic efficiency. Furthermore, Japan did not cause Americans to become fixated in the 1980s with mergers, acquisitions, and leveraged buy-outs, many of which were financed by a mountain of high-risk, appropriately named junk bonds. All of the above are home-grown foibles. What Japan could claim credit for was providing virtually all of the inspiration for the improvements in U.S. process technology initiated from the 1980s through the mid-1990s.

Corporate America did not outshine the federal government in the quality of its response to the rise of Japanese industrial competitiveness. The private sector at first displayed misplaced overconfidence, then made accusations of unfair competition, and only much later exhibited a begrudging desire to learn from and adapt Japan's innovations in process technology. The Japanese had mastered a new generation of production techniques that streamlined the many facets of complex assembly operations; empowered highly skilled, dedicated assemblyline workers with considerable operational authority; lowered manufacturing costs while improving product reliability; and introduced better organized product innovation procedures. In this new world, fundamental rethinking was needed about how U.S. industry organized itself and made things. Adding robots to the production line was not enough. A number of relationships — management and labor, business and education, government and industry — needed to be brought into harmony in a new environment based on collaboration and trust. This did not happen in the United States until the 1990s. As reported in the MIT Commission report discussed in Chapter 7, the U.S. industrial sector suffered well into the 1980s from obsolete theories of manufacturing and relatively inefficient assembly lines organized along decades-old principles of mass production.

The decline in the competitiveness of some U.S. companies was inevitable, especially those involved in labor-intensive production or in "mature" industries in which technology had become standardized and disseminated on a world-wide basis. Japan became a source of supreme irritation because it constantly seemed to be the leading foreign executioner of increasingly sophisticated U.S. industrial sectors. This syndrome began with textiles; moved to basic manufacturing, including automobiles, steel, and consumer electronics; and most recently progressed to high-tech products like computers and memory chips. The resulting trade frictions would have been more moderate if any or all the following contingencies had materialized:

Japan's resurgence had not been so quick,

the U.S. industrial sector's response had been more dynamic,

legitimate market access problems in Japan had been more effectively dealt with, and

more supportive economic policies had emanated from Washington.[4]

The politicization of bilateral trade grievances with Japan inevitably led to some costly U.S. blunders, even though U.S. pressures were critical in pushing an otherwise recalcitrant Japanese government to adopt more liberal import policies. U.S. trade negotiators often did enhance exports, with their greatest successes coming when they were petitioning on behalf of a globally competitive U.S. industry committed for the long-haul to succeeding in the Japanese market and willing to provide the U.S. government with specific, accurate information on the impediments thwarting their export efforts and when intense U.S. political pressure was augmented by the cultivation of allies among Japanese constituencies who perceived benefits from increased U.S. sales or direct investment.[5]

The United States, as a whole, is still incurring relatively limited costs from its large, structural multilateral and bilateral trade deficits. The absence of crushing economic costs has been an important factor limiting pressures on government officials to escalate efforts to terminate the trade deficits. The biggest losses associated with the bilateral trade disequilibrium probably are symbolic: pride and self-confidence. U.S. trade deficits with Japan represented a minute fraction of total domestic production. Jobs lost from import displacement also were a small fraction of the total U.S. work force. The unique U.S. ability to pay for all its imports through foreigners' willingness to increase their dollar holdings is another factor constraining the negative effects of trade deficits on U.S. living standards and, thereby, tempering governmental determination to end the deficits.

Criticism of the United States can only go so far. Even at their worst, U.S. business and policy inadequacies were not sufficient to explain the full measure of the mismatch in bilateral trade relations. The systemic problem unequivocally had an important second dimension: Japan's insularity manifested in deliberate and indirect impediments discouraging imports of manufactures from the United States and elsewhere. Even if one wishes to dismiss outright both the relevance of bilateral trade balances and the overall export competence of U.S. exporters, an objective evaluation of Japan's import propensities and business practices suggests that, at a minimum, something funny has been going on in that market. It was gross hyperbole when a Japanese professor wrote in 1987 that "the American eagle is wounded both economically and spiritually. . . . Instead of simply registering emotional protests and presenting statistical evidence in its defense, Japan must come up quickly with a concrete plan for aiding the wounded eagle."[6] The eagle did incur a number of wounds, but there is ample evidence that not all of them were self-inflicted. Some came from well-aimed salvos from Japan.

## JAPAN'S WORST ENEMY — JAPAN

It is a gross oversimplification to brand a hard-working, insular Japan simply as conspirator seeking to amass industrial power or as blameless target of jealous foreign underachievers. The truth rests predominantly in a multilayered middle ground composed of different shades of gray borrowed from the two extreme views of Japan's economic behavior. Almost every one of its positive economic traits can be at least partially tarnished by citing a negative characteristic. "No other great country," wrote *The Economist*, "open to free inspection, produces such a clash of reactions from those who go to inspect it."[7] It is very easy to come up with half-right assessments of the country. No matter how attractive its products were, Japan deprived itself of the ability to cultivate a favorable external image by lugubriously pursuing an economic mission inspired by intense discomfort with the outside world. Long-held Japanese values inspired a humorless zealousness and compassionless efficiency in a systematic quest for strength through industrial power.

Having abandoned the option of using military force for maximizing economic self-sufficiency and international prominence, the Japanese fortuitously shifted to the industrial-technological path in 1945. The timing could not have been better for such a strategy. It coincided with the revolutionary change in the world order through which economic, not military, strength increasingly came to determine national power and prestige. The entire nation willingly mobilized to achieve economic rebirth. Although not a society of ascetics, the Japanese have not yet felt their industrial renaissance to be so firmly entrenched that they can ease up and more fully enjoy their newly found affluence.

The inward-looking pattern of Japanese thought has exacerbated the difficult task of integrating this unique economy into the international system. The Japanese have only begun to fathom a cardinal political rule of international trade relations: trade is a two-way street. Countries eventually get uncomfortable importing from a country that does not want to import their goods. Japan never accepted the fact that its largely one-way trade success was (to paraphrase an old Japanese saying) a nail sticking up so far that, inevitably, it would be hammered down by aggrieved deficit countries. The extremes between its export and import patterns left Japan with minimal reserves of goodwill with which to defend itself against justified and unjustified foreign complaints.

There is nothing inherently wrong with an affluent country possessed of a high saving rate financing a chronic current account surplus with net capital outflows to low-saving countries. This is exactly what the United States did in the 1950s and 1960s and should be doing now. The problem with Japan is that it gives the impression of being far less interested than the United States in nurturing the export earnings of other countries. It clearly has been unwilling to let the yen become a major international currency. This would mean allowing foreigners to accumulate large yen balances outside of Japan where Japanese monetary authorities cannot control their movement.

Maximum economic strength was essential to Japan's centuries-old compulsion to keep the outside world at bay. Intrusions of foreign ideas, influence, technology, and people are inevitable, but the Japanese have wanted to control their importation as much as possible on their own terms. In pursuing this goal, the postwar elites wanted to make the country internationally competitive in every important sector of advanced commercial technology. There may not be anything unique in this ambition, but Japan *is* unique in the degree to which it succeeded, even as it limited competition through barriers imposed on imported manufactured goods. Like many countries, it has looked favorably upon industrial policy and export maximization. Like very few countries, it has produced excellent results on both counts.

The Japanese have no master plan for global economic domination sitting in file cabinets in Tokyo. The conspiracy dubbed "Japan Incorporated" is an exaggeration of an unusually intense, widespread sense of collective purpose and the desire for cultural self-preservation and national prestige through industrial power. If the Japanese economic system was a thoroughly rigged conspiracy between government and corporate chieftains, formal import barriers would never have been necessary. Should a master plan exist in the minds of government and corporate mandarins who want to dominate the world economy for xeno-phobic reasons, it is very unlikely that it will be realized if it does not also directly serve the economic interests of other countries. The rest of the world could and should accept enlightened Japanese economic leader-ship if operated on a positive-sum basis, but it is unlikely to sit idly by and accept prolonged exploitation from a one-sided Japanese power trip. This argument is mostly academic; ambitions of global economic dominance seem well beyond its economic potential.

The unexpected swiftness and magnitude of Japan's successful drive to industrial superpower status was not the result of any single factor. It was based on a unique application of synergy. The first indispensable driving force of economic achievement was cultural values shaped by historical circumstance. Industrial success came quickly to the Japanese, in part because their traditional values revere the work ethic and indirectly encourage positive work habits like emphasis on teamwork and collective responsibility over personal aggrandizement, meticulous attention to detail, and fierce determination to overcome adversity. Kenneth Pyle observed that a different set of traditional values invited economic strains with the United States and other trading partners: "The Japanese are instinctively more comfortable with collectivist than individualist values, with respect for hierarchy than equality, with productivist than con-sumerist values, with nationalist sentiment than universalist principles. While these preferences are at once a source of strength in their social cohesion and economic pursuits, they often block smooth relations with other peoples."[8]

The social psychology inspiring and perpetuating willingness to make sacrifices for a long-term commitment to economic progress is nurtured by the "strong belief that if you just have the right attitude, you can bear up under any adversity." Japanese people are, therefore, trained from an early age to see how well they can withstand adversity.[9] Any government in North America or Western Europe exhorting its citizens to make the extended sacrifices pressed on the Japanese people would not have sur-vived for long. Consensus on the urgency of economic recovery came rel-atively easily to a racially homogeneous country where a high school educator can tell his students that the purpose of education "isn't to develop your personalities. The purpose is to enable you to conform to society."[10]

Japan's macroeconomic and industrial policies — the second critical element of synergy — successfully encouraged and supported Japanese industrial companies' efforts to break new ground. The elite bureaucratic corps that staffed Japan's postwar economic ministries after World War II developed a vision of where Japan should be heading and then helped get it there by exploiting the population's respect for authority, hierarchy, and status. The Japanese system is an excellent example of how state power is capable of constraining individual choice and shifting economic incentives to industrial corporations as compared with U.S. constraints favoring maximum competition and short-term profit maximization.[11]

After determining that comparative advantage was not absolutely predetermined and fixed, the Japanese government set the standard of excellence for programs successfully coaxing private industry into production decisions not preordained by pure market considerations. What civil servants and politicians absolutely could not do, however, is teach the private sector how to successfully develop, manufacture, and market goods domestically and abroad. Skills associated with unprecedented triumphs in the international marketplace were qualities Japanese executives and workers mastered by themselves. Import barriers may have allowed some Japanese companies to use fat domestic profit margins to lower export prices, but this advantage would have been marginalized in the absence of cost-competitive, high-quality goods.

The third and arguably most important element of the synergistic explanation of Japan's economic success is the private sector, namely brilliant innovations in process technology combined with excellent long-range planning by management. Most of the Japanese industrial sector's superb performance reflects pure intelligence having little or nothing to do with either governmental subsidies or cultural phenomena. I once considered the methods of a Washington friend who, for three decades, has maintained the success of the government policy analysis company he heads: tolerate nothing less than the highest quality service; anticipate and address clients' evolving needs; goad staff to improve the product no matter how well the firm is doing; view competing firms with a visceral fear that they are out to take away everything that you personally hold dear; and instill long-term loyalty in employees by convincing them that they will profit as the firm does. Not by coincidence, all of these methods are identical with much-admired standards of Japanese management. Good management is good management — anywhere.

The positive view of Japan's business acumen goes beyond superb management and production techniques to include the idealized notion of corporations being operated primarily for the benefit of the workers (stakeholders) rather than the shareholders. On the one hand, workers are empowered with the primary responsibility to continuously improve the production process, and in large companies they receive lifetime employment. On the other hand, the extraordinary pressures and long hours imposed on most employees as well as their lack of influence in setting salaries and work rules suggest the absence of anything resembling the Western view of a workers' paradise. Anyone doubting the harsh realities faced by many Japanese workers should read, among other things, a poem written by a victim of *karoshi*, the Japanese term for death by overwork. Its theme is that the contemporary company man in Japan shares all of the dehumanizing experiences faced by slaves of yesteryear. Worse yet, Japan's contemporary "corporate slaves" are denied even "the simplest pleasures that forced-laborers of ages past enjoyed; the right to sit down at the dinner table with their families."[12]

If Japanese companies are not operated for the direct benefit of either their workers or their owners, we are left with the perplexing question of just what is the primary raison d'être of large Japanese corporations. The answer appears to be found in the cultural dimension of synergy. Japanese firms operate differently from U.S. companies because they are motivated by different forces. R. Taggart Murphy has made the insightful observation that "Japanese companies are best seen as alliances for mutual protection in a world where nothing is certain. The usual criteria of profitability provide no meaningful yardstick." To fulfill their promises of security to their loyal work force, large companies are forever trying to increase their status and clout and to bind other institutions to them. The resultant need for market share "is the essence of the Japanese company."[13]

Japanese companies also respond to officially sanctioned economic standards and stimuli not found in the U.S. economy. Perhaps the most important of these unshared characteristics is acceptance of what most Americans would call controlled competition or even a rigged market. The credibility of the argument that the Japanese economy is subject to exactly the same basic market disciplines and, therefore, operates identically to any capitalist country has been undermined by statements to the contrary by knowledgeable Japanese analysts (see Chapters 4 and 5). The vision of Japan as just another market economy also has been dimmed by recurring government interventions in the stock market to support falling share prices.[14]

The post-bubble trauma was made especially severe by the costs of the government's long-time assumption of many responsibilities normally left to market forces. Greater reliance on free-market phenomena to influence business decisions and to penalize companies for mistakes likely would have prevented the speculative bubble from growing as big as it did and would have reduced the severity of its contraction. The Japanese economy's nonmarket bias and the tilt favoring exports over imports are caustically described by R. Taggart Murphy, an American with extensive business experience there:

Large companies are supposed to invest and export not on the basis of their assessments of where money is to be made but as part of their particular roles in the grand push to ensure that Japan need not depend on foreigners, so it is not their responsibility when the cash flow to cover their investments is insufficient or

they find they are suddenly expected to pay back the financing for these investments that they had been told was free.

Japan's administrators could not . . . say to the outside world . . . "We don't
want foreign brokers in Japan because our market is rigged, and they might not
understand that, and we're not sure we can control them," so foreign brokers
were let in and given something to do in the hopes that it would be a minor
sideshow. . . . [Furthermore,] Japanese spokesmen could not . . . say, "We have no
intention of ever allowing any important technology now under Japanese control
to go back under the control of foreigners. And we intend systematically to gain
control of all remaining technologies not now under Japanese management. Thus
no foreign company will ever take over an important Japanese company."[15]

U.S. companies were up against more than just very competent business competitors. Japan's embrace of an industrial manifest destiny led to
a formidable array of official import barriers on manufactured goods that
were servants of industrial policy. Barriers also were imposed as part of a
de facto social contract by which the long-entrenched Liberal Democratic
Party compensated relatively inefficient sectors for not being able to benefit from the massive channeling of the country's resources into rebuild-
ing its industrial sector and growing it into world dominance. The
principal manifestations of this compensation were rigid import barriers
on agricultural products and regulations protecting small retailers. To
minimize social disruptions from rapid industrialization, the Japanese
government willingly sacrificed some economic efficiency and foreign
goodwill for domestic consensus and greater income equality.

The gradual dismantling of formal trade barriers was not sufficient to
grant full reciprocal market access to foreign producers because of an
implicit antimarket bias within the Japanese economy. Japan may be the
only country about which it can be said that the result of removing all
overt trade barriers would be only a relatively modest increase in U.S.
imports and a small reduction in the bilateral trade imbalance. A study by
the American Chamber of Commerce in Japan concluded that only 13 of
the 45 bilateral trade agreements signed since 1980 were successful in significantly increasing sales of U.S. goods in Japan (18 others were deemed
marginally successful and 10 were called failures).[16] To this day, there
may be several major import-discriminatory practices in place that have
never been revealed, the encyclopedia-like compendium of barriers compiled by foreign governments and businesses notwithstanding.

The restrictive business practices condoned by the government have
produced market distortions tantamount to informal discrimination
against foreign-made goods. The inherent corporate preference to deal
with associated firms in one's vertical, horizontal, or distribution *keiretsu*
operates to the detriment of all business newcomers, foreign and domestic. Japanese firms are very comfortable with long-term relationships in
which a tight web of trust and mutual obligation is accepted by both

parties. Hence, most businessmen are at least as interested in protecting relationships with domestic suppliers as they are in passing along cost savings to customers.[17]

Foreign-owned firms have an unusually limited ability to compete purely on the basis of price in Japan. The evidence supporting this thesis begins with the economically inconsistent combination of relatively high prices there and the relative absence of new competitors offering lower-priced goods. Furthermore, a relatively large percentage of U.S. exports to Japan is shipped and distributed by Japanese companies who have a high propensity to impose high price mark-ups. Additional evidence of the anti-price phenomenon is the apparent Japanese ability to discourage foreign suppliers from collectively exceeding 10 to 20 percent market share for a given product. An executive of a U.S. fiber optics company is hardly alone when he complains that even when it manages to gain 5 percent of a customer's business through superior quality and price, his company must "fight like hell" for more; Japanese customers typically "think we should have only so much" in order to be "fair" to local suppliers who have loyally served them for years.[18]

Empirical data do, in fact, show a correlation between low import penetration in Japan and products that have high distribution margins or are procured by local businesses and government agencies rather than individual consumers.[19] Another unofficial impediment, albeit one that has declined in importance since the 1980s, is the belief shared by many companies and all government agencies that importing high-tech goods in a targeted industry instead of buying domestic output is an act of disloyalty that would be harmful to the long-term health of the Japanese economy.[20]

The conclusion is that Japan's implicit trade barriers and domestic market distortions operate like tariffs. They keep prices of many imported goods expensive and discourage market share increases by most imports. However, they are not absolute barriers, and they are not capable of preventing at least some changes in demand in response to significant price reductions or domestic cost pressures.[21] Given enough of a price and performance edge, foreign companies can succeed as well in this market as any other. Even in Japan, the survival of the company comes first. If sticking to domestic sources absolutely threatens to price it out of the market or saddle its products with obsolete technical performance, the typical Japanese company will override the tradition of preserving personal relationships and buy imports.

To quote Paul Krugman's introduction to a National Bureau of Economic Research study, "Japan *is* different." The perception that it imports "less than one might have expected wins on points."[22] The situation is changing for the better. Japan is still different, but the de facto tariff protection of inside-the-border barriers has declined enough in aggregate terms that there is no clear justification for the United States to apply markedly different treatment, that is, managed trade, on an across-the-board basis. Differences have been narrowed to the point that the combination of yen appreciation, trade liberalization, and increased commitment by foreign exporters can frequently stimulate Japanese imports in a "normal" manner. Optimism about improved market access must be tempered by the absence of guarantees of continued import liberalization. Placating the United States is a policy that, for many years, will remain subordinated to the primary goal of preserving the Japanese power structure.

Aside from U.S. government pressures for additional economic reforms, major catalysts for continued positive change include the constant array of economic and technological innovations sweeping the world economy that are beyond the ability of the Japanese government to control. Prime Minister Ryutaro Hashimoto's call in late 1996 for major financial deregulation, for example, was not inspired by his cabinet's sudden conversion to Adam Smith–style free markets. The proposal, the exact fate of which is uncertain, stemmed from mounting worries that Tokyo's financial center was sinking to backwater status because investors and corporate borrowers were increasingly using the more deregulated capital markets in Hong Kong and Singapore.[23] In an example of actual change, the recent boom in sales by U.S. catalogue retailers was made possible by the Japanese lifestyle shift that added credit cards to cash as a socially acceptable means of paying for consumer goods.

Deregulation of the Japanese economy is hardly complete. The remaining differences caused by business collusion and market imperfections are narrowing at a sluggish pace. The insecurity that inspires the Japanese to excel in all important industrial technologies and encourages close-knit business alliances is not about to disappear. Despite the coming of age of a generation who knows nothing but relative affluence, the Japanese are likely to continue to pursue their transcendent goal of controlling their destiny through industrial superiority. The Japanese elite will continue to be uneasy with the prospect of being second best in any critical commercial technology, and they will not encourage adoption of mass relaxation.

Japan's slow pace of change is also a reflection of the absences of a viable opposition political party and a westernized sense of individualism. Japan's producer orientation will not be overthrown by a consumer revolution. Although social criticism is becoming more common, even this biting observation from a best-selling Japanese book is unlikely to have a big impact:

What is the point in manufacturing quality, state-of-the-art products if no one has a comfortable, relaxed enough life to enjoy them? Japanese living conditions resemble nothing so much as a warehouse piled high with world-class products, where people smugly pat themselves on the back and brag of their fancied superiority. It ought to be the goal [of] every society on earth for citizens to enjoy leisure time . . . and pursue their personal goals.

The life philosophy that sees work as a tool for the enrichment of personal life seems to me to be far more humane than a policy of urging people to sacrifice their personal lives for the good of the organization.[24]

The entity most capable of fomenting genuine economic change is still the most resistant to it. The Japanese bureaucracy is not likely to engage in the revolutionary act of voluntarily relinquishing to market forces the broad authority over economic activity that makes the senior civil service a powerful and prestigious career as well as a stepping stone to a well-paying private-sector job in retirement.

An apt metaphor for the problematic pace of the Japanese economy's opening to the outside world is the "two steps ahead, one step backward" syndrome illustrated by the Mitsubishi Corporation's response to an objection voiced by one of its member companies. Asahi Glass was angered and embarrassed, in 1994, by an event that, a few years earlier, would have been unthinkable: it lost a bid to provide window glass for a new Mitsubishi office tower in downtown Tokyo to the ultimate outsider, a U.S. glass company. To soothe the outrage of its *keiretsu* partner, Mitsubishi's management decided on a compromise: Asahi would supply glass for the windows on the front side of the building while the U.S. company's contract was revised to provide glass for the windows in the back.[25]

Asserting that Japanese market access has shifted from nearly impossible to selectively restrictive is not the same thing as saying that Japanese trade surpluses are likely to become a thing of the past (not that this is an important objective). Despite changing economic conditions, their export sector should stay very strong. Whenever yen appreciation threatens their overseas market share, Japan's premier exporters repeatedly have demonstrated the ability to cut production costs, including more offshore procurement of labor-intensive components.

An important, yet usually ignored, contributing factor to the relatively price-inelastic foreign demand for Japanese goods is the increasing propensity for Japanese companies to be monopoly suppliers of high-tech goods and sophisticated components. By one estimate, as much as one-third of Japanese exports to the United States is largely immune to cost increases because alternative suppliers do not yet exist and potential competitors do not have the engineering skills to displace the Japanese anytime soon. Many of the United States' most advanced manufacturing companies are mostly or totally dependent on Japanese suppliers — at any price — for flat panel displays, customized machine tools, robots, laser diodes, molds and dies, camera lenses, carbon fiber, and other commodities that have never been mass-produced outside Japan.[26]

Japan's domination of these and other key technologies is not recognized because they are highly specialized and, therefore, unknown to all but a limited number of producers. Almost no one had heard of a substance called epoxy cresol novolac resin until a 1993 explosion disabled a factory in a remote Japanese town. U.S. electronics industry executives and government officials were horrified to learn that this one plant accounted for nearly 65 percent of the world's supply of a vital ingredient for most kinds of semiconductors.[27] A more expensive alternative technology exists, but it, too, is a virtual Japanese monopoly. In view of all the above, many Japanese exports are largely or totally insulated from any foreseeable amount of yen appreciation. If U.S. production is nonexistent or inadequate to meet demand, Japanese exporters will encounter no entrenched protectionist lobbies. Imports cannot injure domestic production that does not exist or companies afraid to take on entrenched Japanese competition.

In sum, ample evidence exists to suggest that only the willfully blind can deny that a distinct form of Japanese capitalism exists, one that seldom has been either import- or foreign direct investment–friendly. Until Japan's trading partners are convinced it has thoroughly deregulated and genuinely internationalized its economy, they will continue to measure the openness of that market by their frustrations, not by Japanese reassurances. Germany, the other major country with a chronic trade surplus, is not subject to constant external criticism because it is perceived to be pursuing common objectives and seeking economic integration with its major trading partners. Until Japan earns such a reputation, the world will view it suspiciously as a self-centered outsider.

## CONCLUSION

In answering the question of why bilateral trade frictions have continued unabated for three decades, criticism should be amply apportioned to both sides. There is plenty to go around. The actions of both countries are responsible for failing to remedy the systemic problem. It is certainly possible to downplay the danger of these frictions, thanks to what can be described as an institutionalized exercise in damage control. Mutual animosities aside, neither country has suffered grievous economic injury, and no trade war has yet erupted between the two countries. Nevertheless, there is no room for complacency about the future. The continued existence in both countries of the forces responsible for generating the fundamental mismatch raises disquieting prospects about new tensions of unknown severity and consequence. The Japanese system has changed a lot over the past three decades and will likely continue to do so. What really matters, though, is whether it will change fast enough to placate its trading partners.

## NOTES

1. Richard J. Samuels, "Consuming for Production: Japanese National Security, Nuclear Fuel Procurement, and the National Economy," *International Organization* (Autumn 1989), p. 628.

2. Edward H. Carr, *The Twenty Years Crisis, 1919–1939* (New York: Harper & Row, 1964), pp. 116–17.

3. Hedrick Smith, *Rethinking America* (New York: Random House, 1995), p. 5.

4. To this day, only limited credence is given by most U.S. decision makers and economists to the notion that the University of Tokyo school of thought that extols certain forms of industrial policy as well as pragmatic trade policy can run roughshod over the University of Chicago school of thought that extols markets free of government involvement.

5. Merit E. Janow, "U.S.-Japan Trade Relations," in Gerald Curtis, ed., *The United States, Japan, and Asia* (New York: W. W. Norton, 1994), p. 90.

6. Hideo Sato, "Aiding the Wounded Eagle," *Japan Echo* (Autumn 1987), p. 30.

7. "The Road Turns, at Last," *The Economist*, July 13, 1996, p. 3 of special section on Japan.

8. Kenneth B. Pyle, *The Japanese Question: Power and Purpose in a New Era* (Washington, D.C.: AEI Press, 1992), p. 120.

9. Masao Miyamoto, *The Straitjacket Society* (Tokyo: Kodansha International, 1994), p. 166.

10. As quoted in *The Wall Street Journal*, January 9, 1990, p. A10.

11. William K. Tabb, *The Postwar Japanese System — Cultural Economy and Economic Transformation* (New York: Oxford University Press, 1995), pp. 290–91.

12. The poem is reproduced in its entirety in ibid, p. 140.

13. R. Taggart Murphy, *The Weight of the Yen* (New York: W. W. Norton, 1996), p. 60.

14. See, for example, "Deregulation Moves Hit Japanese Stocks," *The Wall Street Journal*, January 10, 1997, p. A5.

15. Murphy, *Weight of the Yen*, pp. 264–65.

16. American Chamber of Commerce in Japan, "16 Years of US-Japan Trade Agreements; What's the Score?" press release, January 1997.

17. Michael Gerlach, "*Keiretsu* Organization in the Japanese Economy — Analysis and Trade Implications," in Chalmers Johnson, Laura D. Tyson, and John Zysman, eds. *Politics and Productivity — How Japan's Development Strategy Works* (New York: Ballinger Publishing Company, 1989), p. 169.

18. David D. Baskerville, of Siecor International Corporation, as quoted in *Washington Post*, January 4, 1992, p. B6. He went on to note that, in the United States, his company can and does lose contracts if its price is only half a percent above a competitor.

19.   Peter A. Petri, "Market Structure, Comparative Advantage, and Japanese Trade under the Strong Yen," in Paul Krugman, ed., *Trade with Japan — Has the Door Opened Wider?* (Chicago: University of Chicago Press, 1991), p. 77.

20.   A third market imperfection has all but disappeared — Japanese consumers believing that foreign-made goods could not possibly have the quality, design, or prestige to meet their demanding tastes. On average, astute foreign producers of consumer goods who set up their own distribution system no longer appear to encounter extraordinary levels of difficulty exporting to Japan compared to other markets.

21.   Robert Z. Lawrence, now at Harvard University, was the first to develop this thesis.

22.   Paul Krugman, ed., *Trade with Japan — Has the Door Opened Wider?* (Chicago: University of Chicago Press, 1991), pp. 4, 8.

23.   A real test of whether the Japanese system is changing is to determine how many of the requested reforms will be enacted if the Ministry of Finance develops serious doubts about the wisdom of their implementation.

24.   Miyamoto, *Straitjacket Society*, p. 114.

25.   Not for attribution interview with U.S. Commerce Department official, November 1996. A similar indicator of a mixed message about the pace of change in Japan is the fact that in 1995, foreigners bought (on a friendly take-over basis) a record number of mostly small Japanese companies; the total of 52 purchases, however, is minuscule by U.S. standards. "How Intuit Navigated Takeover-Wary Japan To Buy Software Firm," *The Wall Street Journal*, December 27, 1996, p. A1.

26.   Eamonn Fingleton, *Blindside — Why Japan Is Still on Track to Overtake the U.S. by the Year 2000* (Boston: Houghton Mifflin, 1995), pp. 67–75.

27.   Ibid., p. 66.

# 11

# Minimizing U.S.-Japanese Trade Frictions in the Future

Those who cannot learn from the past are condemned to repeat it.
— attributed to George Santayana

One step ahead is darkness.
— Traditional Japanese saying

The United States and Japan need to implement more effective policies to reduce their trade balance and competitiveness disequilibria. Suggestions that time will heal bilateral frictions are based more on hope than on sound economic analysis. If two key integrating theses of this book—the existence of systemic bilateral trade problems and the limited relevance of any single explanation for why they occurred—are correct, contemporary bilateral economic frictions are still far from over. The changes necessary to correct lagging U.S. competitiveness and inadequate Japanese market access problems are still not in place.

After a brief forecast of impending changes in the dynamics of the bilateral conflict resolution process, this concluding chapter offers a brief set of proposals for promoting both increased harmony between the two countries and improved real living standards in both. All the recommendations that follow are offered on the assumption that they are economically credible and desirable. They would be inherently desirable even if neither country was under pressure from the other to alter the status quo. All recommendations have been deemed compatible with both economic efficiency and the more important multilateral context in which

U.S.-Japanese trade relations function. Given this book's scholarly standards, immediate political feasibility was not an absolute criterion for
inclusion of a recommendation.

The recommendations that follow implicitly assume that the United
States has an obligation to the world as well as to itself to maintain a
vibrant economy. It has done an excellent overall job in the role of international economic near-hegemon through its willingness to play the roles
of global lender of last resort, import market of last resort, and open global capital market providing vast amounts of dollar balances for use as an
international reserves and transactions currency. The recommendations
also implicitly assume inadequate Japanese adherence to universalist
beliefs and inadequate willingness to make sacrifices for the rest of the
world to the extent necessary for it to adequately replace the United States
as global economic leader.

## THE OUTLOOK: CHANGES AMID
## CONTINUING FRICTIONS

A look into the near future generates scant optimism for the withering
away of U.S.-Japan trade frictions. What is foreseeable is change in the
rules of engagement. Cooperative dialogue will be indispensable because
these rules are likely to change so fast that one cannot assume the
inevitability of the two countries operating within traditional guidelines.
On one hand, the two economies will remain so heavily interdependent
that mutual damage is the alternative to accommodation and constructive
action. On the other hand, the prospect of mutual damage is no longer
sufficient to dismiss the possibility that the United States and Japan could
gradually drift apart. "When the players start making it up as they go
along, the drama could turn quite ugly quite quickly" over relatively
small matters.[1] Although chances of an outright rupture of the bilateral
friendship and alliance are negligible, there well could be a diminution of
the mutual benefits derived from extensive economic and political cooperation between two strong countries with much to offer each other.

U.S.-Japanese trade relations entered a new phase in the mid-1990s. A
clearly visible turning point occurred when the Japanese dug in their
heels and refused, on principle, to respond to what they considered to be
intolerable implications of results-oriented trade agreements pressed by
the Clinton administration. In what may have marked a last hurrah for
U.S. "aggressive unilateralism" using Section 301–backed demands to
open further the Japanese market, the government of Japan gave every
indication of willingness to be hit with severe U.S. sanctions against
exports of luxury automobiles rather than to concede fully to U.S.
demands. Rejected out-of-hand was acceptance of any form of quantitative indicators to gauge market-opening efforts in the automobile and

auto parts sectors. The Japanese also gave every indication that they would follow through on their promise to respond to unilateral sanctions by filing a complaint against the United States in the World Trade Organization (WTO) for illegally abrogating a prior tariff reduction. Shortly thereafter, Japan refused to agree to anything more than a titular extension of the semiconductor agreement and then flatly rejected even the initiation of bilateral discussions on U.S. allegations of collusion in the distribution of photographic film. The Japanese government declared the multilateral WTO dispute settlement process to be the appropriate venue for that dispute.[2]

Cracks in the traditional bilateral mechanism for damage control are taking place in a changing global context. The end of the cold war altered the equation of alliance politics in general and the strategic significance of the U.S.-Japan security treaty in particular. This scenario suggests to some Americans an opportunity for an escalation of more hard-line, uncompromising U.S. trade demands. It is just as likely, however, that the negotiating process could move in the opposite direction if both countries relegate bilateral trade relations to a lower order of importance — the possible result of their being crowded out by new considerations. Japanese industry is giving a high priority to reducing its heavy dependence on the U.S. market (and vulnerability to U.S. retaliatory action) through an increase in trade with, and investment in, other countries. Nowhere is this clearer than in Asia, where a yen bloc and a regional confrontation between U.S. and Japanese business interests might be in the offing. For their part, by the mid-1990s, U.S. government officials and business executives seemed to be exhibiting early signs of "Japan fatigue." This "why bother?" attitude is encouraged by booming business prospects in supposedly more open markets in Asia, especially China; the confidence inspired by a resurgent U.S. industrial sector (probably temporary); and the diminution of Japan's trade surplus (temporary).

A reconfiguration of bilateral trade issues could follow the planned phase-out of formal trade barriers, early in the next century, under the Asia-Pacific Economic Cooperation agreement.[3] However, real changes in U.S.-Japan trade flows under such a regime are more likely to be limited. A regional free trade bloc will guarantee neither an end to informal, indirect Japanese market barriers nor an increase in U.S. corporate export excellence.

Many other imponderables remain. The critical importance currently attached to the information technology sector may or may not be permanent, and the same can be said about current U.S. leadership in it. In an effort to restore Japan's semiconductor industry to world preeminence, the largest government-industry research and development effort since the 1970s has been initiated to develop new technologies in this critical sector. The well-funded Semiconductor Industry Research Institute of

Japan may reinvigorate Japan's information technology industry, or it might come up dry.

The willingness to sacrifice for the group, high saving rates, and manufacturing prowess that allowed a war-torn Japan to rapidly catch up to the West after 1945 may or may not be critical attributes in an age in which increasingly rapid product obsolescence seems to have pushed the importance of creativity, entrepreneurship, risk-taking, and corporate maneuverability ahead of good process technology. Japan may need to develop new talents, or it may get by with merely polishing old ones.

Steven Schlossstein thinks Japan has become a "paper dragon" after being rendered "irrelevant" by the digital revolution.[4] Conversely, R. Taggart Murphy has cautioned against underestimating a country that in the twentieth century has "ended Western colonialism in Asia, risen phoenixlike from the ashes of the Second World War, come storming out of the OPEC-induced . . . recession, financed the Reagan Revolution, and created, with the bubble economy, the greatest wave of peacetime plant and equipment investment ever seen."[5]

The recommendations that follow are based on the author's assumption that the post-bubble trauma is more likely than not to be followed by a healthy Japanese domestic economic metamorphosis induced by corporate cost-cutting strategies, accelerated product innovation, and supportive governmental policies. Because it has long confounded pessimists by being able to change when necessary to correct internal weaknesses, Japan almost certainly will remain the United States' number one overseas competitor through the early decades of the twenty-first century.

There is no permanent finish line in the competitive race between the two strongest, most dynamic, and technologically advanced national economies. With change as a constant, the U.S.-Japanese trade relationship moves in cycles. Neither country stays ahead permanently because there is no final plateau. Successful corporate strategies can be quickly undermined by unforeseen changes in technology and consumer tastes. Predictions in the 1990s that Japan's industrial-technological challenge has permanently peaked will likely be no more accurate than widespread forecasts in the late 1980s that the United States inexorably was heading to permanent industrial decline.

## TASKS FOR BOTH COUNTRIES

If U.S.-Japanese trade frictions and disequilibria are to be permanently diminished, the first task for both countries is to reach a better understanding of causality. As previously discussed, the problem consists of two distinct, albeit related, phenomena. The first phenomenon consists of the production and marketing shortcomings that, heretofore, have limited successful head-to-head competition by many U.S. corporations vis-à-vis their Japanese counterparts. The second phenomenon is Japan's continuing import-unfriendly practices: government controls and discriminatory procurement procedures, collusive business practices, and so on.

Systemic problems, by definition, are removed only by altering fundamental economic policies and business practices. Past assessments that the problem would resolve itself — by such marginalia as the supposed convergence of the two economic systems, the hedonism of the next generation of Japanese workers, the implementation of one more Japanese liberalization package, the further appreciation of the yen, and a reduction in the U.S. federal budget deficit — have continually been wrong. Both sides should admit the inadequacies of wishful thinking and of treating symptoms rather than causes — their unsuccessful approaches of choice for the past three decades. Both need to be more willing to make internal changes in the pursuit of international equilibrium and harmony.

Determination of the day-to-day yen-dollar exchange rate should be left mainly to supply and demand in the foreign exchange market. No one really knows what the right rate is at any given time. Neither U.S. government efforts to talk down the dollar nor Japanese government efforts to artificially prop it up in order to minimize yen appreciation has produced positive long-term economic results. Dollar depreciation is strictly a second-best alternative to complete liberalization of the Japanese market and a quantum leap in the ability of the U.S. industrial sector to produce innovative, high-quality goods at relatively low cost. Without these economically optimal solutions, gradual but persistent yen appreciation would be nothing more than a band-aid to boost Japanese imports and moderate import-induced injury to U.S. industry. Sporadic yen appreciation will not, by itself, induce equilibrium in bilateral trade.

Japan and the United States should agree on what kinds of economic issues will remain within the formal bilateral negotiating process. If one or both countries opt to phase out bilateralism in favor of increased use of the WTO's dispute settlement mechanism, the two governments should agree on the need to expand the authority of that institution. Specifically, the United States and Japan should take the lead in convincing fellow members to amend the WTO's charter to bestow clear jurisdiction over domestic competition policy as it affects imports. Article XXIII of the General Agreement on Tariffs and Trade, dealing with allegations of nullification and impairment of past trade concessions, would be a logical place for this amendment. Japan presumably is serious about wanting to stop further unilateral U.S. threats of retaliation under the Section 301 statute. If it is equally serious about denials of collusive business practices impeding imports, it should have no problem agreeing to strengthen the multilateral dispute settlement process to cover ostensibly domestic issues.

Competition policy is the area in which many, if not most, future U.S. trade complaints against Japan will occur.

As part of a mutual effort to close the persistent communications gap, both countries should jettison the still widely circulating, much-distorted efforts at self-vindication based on false stereotype portrayals of the other. Invective about a Japanese master conspiracy closing in on global economic domination or about a disgruntled former superpower unable to address its deteriorating social and economic order is of little use in resolving bilateral trade frictions. To improve the accuracy of mutual perceptions, the two governments should increase their support — on a completely hands-off, no-strings-attached basis — of independent research by business groups, think tanks, and universities on the full range of bilateral economic and business relations.

Both countries would be well-advised to implement the many excellent, but mostly sidestepped, suggestions for reform offered to each other in the Structural Impediments Initiative talks of the early 1990s.

In many cases, the U.S. government has had a legitimate reason for requesting follow-up consultations on the results of a market-opening agreement. Therefore, ground rules should be established on the criteria — short of specific quantitative indicators — for reaching joint agreement on the success of future Japanese liberalization actions.

## TASKS FOR JAPAN

With one exception, Japan does not need my advice on how to improve its ability to export. It would be well-advised to further strengthen what has been the weak link in its economy for decades: a relatively low propensity to import manufactured goods. Two interesting changes would follow Japan's completion of the process of removing formal trade barriers and implementing extensive deregulation of administrative controls. First, these actions would make Japan's overall industrial sector more efficient. Second, economic theory tells us that import barriers act like a tax on exports. Other things kept constant, more Japanese imports would stimulate Japanese exports because of reduced yen appreciation, less foreign hostility toward Japanese goods, and so on. Increased Japanese imports and exports would be a positive-sum game for international economic efficiency. Other countries would generate more jobs and foreign exchange by increasing sales to Japan of goods that it is relatively inefficient in producing, and then using some of these incremental foreign exchange earnings to buy more of Japan's sophisticated manufactured goods than they can currently afford. By correcting the major flaw — an inhospitable atmosphere for imports of capital-intensive goods — in what has otherwise been an awesome export machine, Japan would promote a more efficient allocation of global resources.

Japan would do well to rethink its preference to endure the financial costs of long-term yen appreciation, most of which springs from structural current account surpluses. The rising yen priced an increasing volume of Japanese exports out of world markets, largely because Japanese policymakers preferred this discomfort to the political pain of altering policies in order to attract significantly more imports. Western economic theory debunks the merits of exchanging vast amounts of real economic resources for paper money. The wisdom of this theory is empirically demonstrated when the currency being accumulated is U.S. dollars; dollar depreciation after 1985 inflicted the yen equivalent of hundreds of billions of dollars in balance sheet losses on Japanese investors and companies. Japan's intense mercantilistic export drive has demonstrated dubious economic judgment in continually subordinating its citizens' living standards to the goal of making companies become ever bigger and more powerful.

To adjust for changing circumstances, Japan should change at the margin its definition of optimal domestic economic and foreign trade formulas. The country has caught up with the West technologically and has become an economic superpower. The time is overdue for Japan to exert greater leadership in the liberalization of the trading system. The time is also overdue for the Japanese people to demand, and the government to aggressively promote, a less regimented, more comfortable lifestyle. It does not need to replicate Western-style greed and self-absorption to accommodate U.S. economic demands. It would suffice for Japan to initiate just a slight reordering of priorities away from what has been the near-equivalent of administering economic policy on the basis of a permanent state of emergency. Japan does not need to become an unabashed acolyte of the invisible hand of the marketplace, nor does it need to totally renounce the theories that have long dominated Japanese trade strategies.

Japan's bureaucracy and business leaders need to reach a genuine consensus (one based on *honne* [reality] not *tatemae* [polite formality or pretense]) that the country's long-term welfare and national security depend more on friendship and compatibility with its major trading partners than on the size of its trade surplus or the extent to which it is self-sufficient in advanced technologies. The Ministry of International Trade and Industry needs to do a better job of sensitizing Japan's horizontal, vertical, and distribution *keiretsu* to the potential costs of mounting foreign anger and further yen appreciation if they do not exert greater efforts to buy foreign-made goods.

A consensus should be reached that it would be in the country's self-interest to accelerate administrative decontrol of the economy and to delegate greater authority to the Japan Fair Trade Commission to ferret out and severely punish the more extreme forms of business collusion, especially those that discriminate against foreign goods. Japan's government, business community, and media should be more forthright in admitting that foreigners occasionally have valid complaints about the difficulty of doing business there. In addition, I would humbly urge Japan's elite to read carefully the passages in this book describing the nature and implications of U.S. overconfidence about its economic prowess in the immediate postwar period. Japanese overconfidence, which continues despite the end of the bubble years, is reminiscent of the earlier U.S. experience. Arguably, the two countries swapped roles of tortoise and hare (see page 1) in the mid-1990s. If the Japanese system languishes in the doldrums and delays reforms until the costs of being outperformed by its main foreign economic competitor become unbearably painful, the parallel with the earlier decline of the U.S. industrial sector will be complete.

There is an entirely different policy option open to Japan. Future leaders may believe that it is inappropriate to compromise further national values, independence, and industrial strength in order to appease a possibly insatiable, unrealistic U.S. vision of a liberal international trade order. Japan should make no more concessions if it believes that further foreign intrusions into its domestic economy are not in its long-run national interests. It may prefer to slow down further economic liberalization on grounds that its mammoth trade surpluses in manufactured goods are fully justified and explainable by macroeconomic forces, second-rate overseas competition, and its own better production methods. Foreign retaliation by trading partners might never materialize as a prohibitively expensive effect of protecting import-sensitive sectors. If this is the prevailing consensus, Japan should avoid hypocrisy, announce its feelings in unambiguous terms, and await responses from overseas — if any.

## TASKS FOR THE UNITED STATES

The burden of effort to reduce the bilateral disequilibrium rests with the United States. It is the country most unhappy with the status quo. It is the world's biggest debtor country. Its rates of saving and productivity increases have trailed those of Japan, and they need to be increased. The United States is the one that has been unable to eliminate triple digit trade deficits despite dollar depreciation, extensive corporate cost-cutting, stagnant real wages among production workers, a resurgent high-tech sector, and a sharp decline in the federal budget deficit. A final reason for placing the burden of action on the United States is the absence of strong indigenous forces in Japan to promote economic reform. Steady U.S. as well as European and Asian pressures for further liberalization and deregulation are essential. The U.S. government's ongoing agenda of demands for economic liberalization in Japan is likely to retain its de facto status as the major opposition party in that country.

Ideology and "isms" have been largely shoved aside by a universal race for economic prosperity in which trade, capital, technology, and business skills have more influence among mainstream states than sizes of national armed forces and weapons stockpiles. The United States ought to embrace more deeply the concept that the definition of "national security" needs to be broad enough to include a strong, growing economy. This should be done without exaggerating the importance of national competitiveness and exports as vehicles for increasing a country's growth rates and living standards; capital investment and productivity growth are far more important determinants. Despite Paul Krugman's warning that competitiveness among countries is a "meaningless" word that has become an "obsession,"[6] increased exports of high-tech goods to Japan, and elsewhere, is an ideal means for the United States to encourage increasing returns to scale in capital-intensive industries, to expedite adjustment in its current account deficit, to create jobs with above average pay scales, to generate additional tax revenue to reduce the saving-investment imbalance, and to improve its terms of trade (the overall ratio of export prices to import prices). High-tech companies generate disproportionate amounts of innovation, research and development, and high-paying jobs. The U.S. government, therefore, should take its export sector very seriously.

On a global basis, the U.S. government should formally accord trade relations equal status with domestic economic and foreign policy priorities in the decision-making process. U.S. embassy staffing should be reordered to increase the size of economic and commercial staffs relative to the now excessively large political-military contingent originally assembled in the cold war era. Requests and demands should be made by U.S. trade negotiators in bilateral, regional, and multilateral forums, as appropriate, to advance the existing strategy that the U.S. trade deficit should be eliminated by export increases, not by import decreases. Official export financing facilities should be adequate to match, approximately, the support provided by other governments.

Americans should retire the red herring argument that the ultimate test of a "level playing field" is an end (or almost an end) to Japan's long-standing bilateral trade surplus. Reducing major market-distorting import barriers overseas should be a central concern of U.S. trade policy; a quixotic effort to correct all large bilateral deficits should not be. Impediments blocking access by U.S. exporters to the Japanese market are partially to blame for the bilateral disequilibrium and are, therefore, a legitimate concern to the U.S. government. Because these impediments distort economic efficiency and political fairness, they should continue to be attacked even if the United States develops a bilateral trade surplus with Japan. Conversely, if and when a U.S. consensus develops in which ease of market access in Japan for foreign-made manufactured goods has achieved true parity with North America and Western Europe, the U.S. government and business community should publicly declare that the primary responsibility for reducing any remaining bilateral trade imbalance has shifted to the U.S. private and public sectors.

In the meantime, the U.S. government and business community need to maintain up-to-the-minute knowledge of improved market access conditions in Japan while being resolute in demanding an end to remaining official regulations and business practices deemed harmful to U.S. commercial interests. U.S. officials from the president down should never lose sight of the dangers of allowing Japanese companies either to function in a large, protected home market (see Chapter 5) or to adopt less than fair value export prices in the attempt to maximize foreign market share. Japanese economic practices are no longer so different, even if successful penetration of this market still requires arduous efforts by exporters, that nontraditional results-oriented trade agreements are required on an everyday basis.

It is not illogical to assume that, in the future, special circumstances will justify the U.S. government's being fully prepared to bypass the WTO and use retaliatory authority[7] to convince an otherwise reluctant Japanese government to adopt "voluntary import expansion" measures. The U.S. government needs to develop clear criteria to determine when it must take an occasional uncompromising stand — perhaps because of clear discrimination against an internationally successful U.S. product. The U.S. government also needs to articulate in a more logical, forceful manner what additional market opening measures it absolutely must have from Japan. The potential for collusive business practices in Japan is still sufficiently strong that U.S. trade officials should monitor results of all major Japanese market-opening agreements without necessarily demanding specific statistical targets as proof of compliance.

U.S. policymakers should correct a weakness in negotiating style by adjusting its Japan policy for a similar idiosyncrasy in U.S. policy toward China identified by Lucian Pye. In his opinion, China's officials have cleverly secured significant advantages by exploiting the United States' "guilt culture" through loud warnings that the bilateral relationship is in trouble. The U.S. mentality has often responded to criticism from China and Japan, among others, "by first checking for one's own possible failings" and then producing domestic voices expressing self-criticism that is sometimes more sophisticated than the original foreign complaints.[8]

Several initiatives are needed to close serious U.S. knowledge gaps. In an effort to increase the effectiveness of monitoring Japanese compliance with their market-opening commitments, the Office of the U.S. Trade Representative should — for the first time — compile in one volume the full texts of all bilateral commercial agreements still in force and make it available to all interested government agencies and to the public. To further improve bilateral negotiating skills, U.S. government agencies should put greater stress on recruiting Japanese-speaking trade negotiators and policy analysts. Additionally, to increase overall knowledge of Japan, more Americans should actively be encouraged to attend universities, to do graduate research, or to work temporarily in that country.

For a stronger U.S. business performance overseas, it is imperative that U.S. companies improve their efficiency and increase their manufacturing and distribution presence in Japan. A genuinely accessible Japanese market would not guarantee additional sales there by U.S. companies if they are not aggressive and able to compete with third country exporters. Joint ventures and reliance on Japanese distributors remain a much less fruitful strategy than owning and operating a subsidiary in Japan. Foreign direct investment provides the generic benefits of increased understanding of, and a faster response to, changing tastes in overseas markets. Manufacturing within Japan also inspires greater local confidence in quality control and meeting just-in-time delivery schedules. The growing importance of intracorporate trade suggests that expansion of U.S.-owned subsidiaries in Japan would stimulate U.S. exports there at least as much as the post-1950s proliferation of U.S. foreign direct investment spurred exports to Western Europe.

To buttress their efforts to reduce trade barriers in Japan, U.S. companies should look more aggressively for allies in the Japanese official and private sectors, then encourage them to participate in a joint effort to change the regulatory status quo in a manner that would be mutually beneficial.

In the final analysis, traditional trade policy is seriously constrained in the extent to which it can permanently reduce or eliminate multilateral trade deficits in general or the U.S. bilateral imbalance with Japan in particular. This assertion in no way suggests U.S. trade policy should turn a blind eye to foreign trade barriers and unfair export practices. None of these practices can be left uncontested for political reasons. A liberal trade regime requires public perception of fairness so that legislators are better able to resist constituent pressures to restrict imports. More specifically, maintenance of a strong liberal trade lobby in the United States is dependent on the business community's belief that they can get a full, fair, and fast hearing in Washington when requesting redress of what they consider to be legitimate trade grievances.

The bulk of the response to its mismatches with Japan must come in the form of changes within the U.S. public and private sectors. Despite the above-average performance of the U.S. economy in the mid-1990s, many problems need to be corrected, even if Japan were to disappear tomorrow as a major competitor. U.S. fiscal policy should further reduce (but not necessarily eliminate by any fixed date) the budget deficit and constrain its growth when the long period of economic growth inevitably turns into recession. The urgent need for a higher rate of saving in the United States points to a need to change the tax code to penalize consumption. To the extent that increased saving can be encouraged through reduced taxes on earned interest and dividends, interest rates should decline and capital investment should increase. The latter is the critical means to what should be another policy priority: increasing by at least a full percentage point the anemic rate of increased U.S. productivity. (Between 1960 and 1973, the average annual increase in productivity in the U.S. nonfarm business sector was 3 percent; the comparable figure for the period between 1973 and 1995 dropped to a mere 1 percent.)[9]

U.S. science and technology policy — a euphemism for industrial policy — must operate in that narrow middle ground between excessive confidence that the market mechanism is perfect and excessive pessimism that the United States cannot remain internationally competitive without massive governmental funding of a Ministry of International Trade and Industry–style industrial policy apparatus. Justification for a relatively small-scale, carefully designed science and technology policy rests on the widely accepted scholarly argument that, because companies will realize only a portion of the total returns on their investments in research and development (the remainder trickles to other companies), they will not invest enough to serve the interests of society as a whole. Innovations from successful research and development efforts serve a nation's economy as major stimulants to increased productivity and as a source of positive spillovers to industries in other sectors, for example, laser technology. Government loans and grants supporting basic research, as opposed to product development, can encourage additional efforts that could compensate for the tendency for social returns from research and development spending to exceed private returns.[10]

It is illogical to assume that scientists and engineers operating outside the political process cannot, with a reasonable rate of success, identify potentially promising new technologies. It is equally illogical to assume that government support of high-risk, basic research in advanced technologies that probably will not lead to quick commercialization inevitably leads to a massive waste of the taxpayers' money. The U.S. government's financial support helped produce impressive results in aerospace, medicine, transportation, agriculture, and military hardware. The relatively small spending increments needed in current federal programs[11] that fund private sector high-tech and process technology research could be paid for, many times over, by modest reductions in price subsidies paid to farmers.

To enhance human capital, major changes need to be made in the U.S. public education system. While American children continue to underperform in international tests, especially math and science, the data increasingly suggest that remedies do not lie only in spending more money, prolonging the school year, or increasing homework. Instead, teaching curricula and techniques need to be brought in line with the emphasis, found in countries scoring high on these tests, on having students master underlying concepts instead of problem solving techniques and formulas. Vocational training programs offered in high schools and community colleges need to be upgraded in recognition of the need for a literate, well-trained, blue-collar work force required to operate the increasingly sophisticated machinery used in everything from basic manufacturing (for example, steel) to state-of-the-art, high-tech goods.

The chronic inability of the U.S. industrial, agricultural, and services sectors to export in sufficient quantities to pay for the country's purchases of imports is a problem that mainly should be corrected by the private sector. U.S. competitive shortcomings cannot be cured solely by government policies or by constant depreciation in the value of the dollar. To persuade more foreigners and Americans to purchase U.S.-made goods while increasing U.S. living standards, U.S.-based companies will need to make continuous progress in such key areas as product innovation, manufacturing techniques (process technology), enhanced quality control, labor skills and motivation, and after-sales service. Because Japanese companies are never satisfied with any given level of achievement, U.S. competitors can never rest on their laurels in any of these areas. The best way for the U.S. government to encourage such positive behavior is to continue exposing domestic companies to maximum import competition and avoiding protectionism.

## CONCLUSION

Japan's stunning industrial renaissance and the image of an inept response by the United States have permeated popular culture. Typical was the disparaging remark — which undoubtedly struck a responsive chord with many people on both sides of the Pacific — delivered by a Japanese detective in a Hollywood movie called *Black Rain*: "Music and movies are all America is good for. . . . We won the peace."[12] The current U.S. economic revival needs to progress long and far enough to discredit such cynicism. In 1857, the first U.S. consul to Japan, Townsend Harris, wrote in his journal that he doubted "the opening of Japan to foreign influences [would] promote the general happiness of the people." The Japanese need to modify their attitudes and disprove this heretofore accurate prediction. For almost 20 years, I have been accurately discounting the chances for sustained bilateral trade equilibrium and harmony because inadequate progress has been made in improving the lagging competitiveness of U.S. industry and in reducing the unique market access problems in Japan faced by foreign producers. Actions by both countries to prove my pessimism wrong are long overdue.

## NOTES

1.   Bruce Stokes, "Divergent Paths: U.S.-Japan Relations toward the Twenty-first Century," *International Affairs* (April 1995), p. 291.

2.   The preference for taking bilateral disputes to the World Trade Organization presumably reflects Japan's calculation that an impartial, multilateral panel would be more sympathetic to its position than U.S. officials.

3.   Although the Asia-Pacific Economic Cooperation forum is a purely informal grouping of Asian and Pacific Rim countries, the heads of government of its 18 member countries have agreed to phase out regional trade barriers and create a regional free trade and investment area no later than the year 2010 among developed country members and 2020 among developing country members.

4.   Steven Schlossstein, "Does the Empire Have No Clothes?" *The International Economy* (July-August 1994), p. 50.

5.   R. Taggart Murphy, *The Weight of the Yen — How Denial Imperils America's Future and Ruins an Alliance* (New York: W. W. Norton, 1996), p. 262.

6.   Paul Krugman, "Competitiveness: A Dangerous Obsession," *Foreign Affairs* (March-April 1994), pp. 28–44.

7.   The legal authority could extend beyond the Section 301 provision and include such other measures as the application of U.S. antitrust law if Japanese business collusion is harming U.S. companies.

8.   Lucian W. Pye, "What China Wants," *New York Times*, November 26, 1996, p. A26.

9.   Unpublished U.S. Labor Department data faxed to the author. The difficulty in measuring increased hourly output in the increasingly important services sector has convinced some economists that statistics are systematically underestimating the rate of U.S. productivity growth.

10.   Council of Economic Advisers, "Supporting Research and Development To Promote Economic Growth: The Federal Government's Role," report, October 1995, pp. 5–7, photocopy.

11.   The principal funding programs are the Advanced Research Projects Agency in the Defense Department and the Advanced Technology Program in the Commerce Department.

12.   As quoted in *New York Times*, November 19, 1989, p. II-17.

# Selected Bibliography

Abegglen, James C., and George Stalk, Jr. *Kaisha: The Japanese Corporation*. New York: Basic Books, 1985.

Advisory Committee for Trade Policy and Negotiations. "Analysis of the US-Japan Trade Problem." Washington, D.C.: Office of the U.S. Trade Representative, 1989.

____. "Major Findings and Policy Recommendations on U.S.-Japan Trade Policy." Washington, D.C.: Office of the U.S. Trade Representative, 1993.

Ahearn, Raymond. *Japan: Prospects for Greater Market Openness*. Washington, D.C.: Congressional Research Service, 1989.

American Chamber of Commerce in Japan. *United States-Japan Trade White Paper*, 1993 and 1995 editions.

Asher, David. "What Became of the Japanese 'Miracle.'" *Orbis*, Spring 1996.

Balassa, Bela, and Marcus Noland. *Japan in the World Economy*. Washington, D.C.: Institute for International Economics, 1988.

Beecher, Henry Ward, quoted in Peter Laurence. *Peter's Quotations — Ideas for Our Time*. New York: William Morrow, 1977.

Benedict, Ruth. *The Chrysanthemum and the Sword*. New York: Meridian Books, 1972.

Bergsten, C. Fred, and William Cline. *The United States-Japan Economic Problem*. Washington, D.C.: Institute for International Economics, 1985.

Bergsten, C. Fred, and Marcus Noland. *Reconcilable Differences? United States-Japan Economic Conflict*. Washington, D.C.: Institute for International Economics, 1993.

Choate, Pat, *Agents of Influence*. New York: Alfred A. Knopf, 1990.

Christopher, Robert C. *The Japanese Mind: The Goliath Explained*. New York: Linden Press, 1983.

Cohen, Stephen S., and John Zysman. *Manufacturing Matters*. New York: Basic Books, 1987.

Destler, I. M., Haruhiro Fukui, and Hideo Sato. *The Textile Wrangle*. Ithaca, N.Y.: Cornell University Press, 1979.

Destler, I. M., and Hideo Sato, eds. *Coping with U.S.-Japanese Economic Conflicts*. Lexington, Mass.: Lexington Books, 1982.

Dietrich, William S. *In the Shadow of the Rising Sun: The Political Roots of American Economic Decline*. University Park, Pa.: Pennsylvania State University Press, 1993.

Dillon, Kenneth J. *Worlds in Collusion: Tthe U.S. and Japan Beyond the Year 2000*. Paper No. 2, April 1989. Washington, D.C.: U.S. State Department Foreign Service Institute, Center for the Study of Foreign Affairs.

Dore, Ronald. *Flexible Rigidities*. London: The Athlone Press, 1986.

____. *Taking Japan Seriously*. London: The Athlone Press, 1987.

Encarnation, Dennis J. *Rivals beyond Trade — America versus Japan in Global Competition*. Ithaca, N.Y.: Cornell University Press, 1992.

Fallows, James. *Looking at the Sun: The Rise of the New East Asian Economic and Political System*. New York: Vintage Press, 1995.

____. "Containing Japan." *Atlantic*, May 1989.

____. "The Hard Life." *Atlantic*, March 1987.

____. "Playing by Different Rules." *Atlantic*, September 1987.

Fingleton, Eamonn. *Blindside — Why Japan Is Still on Track to Overtake the U.S. by the Year 2000*. Boston: Houghton Mifflin, 1995.

Gibney, Frank. *Japan, The Fragile Super Power*. New York: Meridian Books, 1979.

____. *Miracle by Design: The Real Reasons Behind Japan's Economic Success*. New York: Times Books, 1982.

Haitani, Kanji. *The Japanese Economic System*. Lexington, Mass.: Lexington Books, 1976.

Hall, Ivan P. "Samurai Legacies, American Illusions." *The National Interest*, Summer 1992.

Hollerman, Leon. "The Headquarters Nation." *The National Interest*, Fall 1991.

Holstein, William J. *The Japanese Power Game*. New York: Plume Books, 1991.

Howe, Christopher. *The Origins of Japanese Trade Supremacy*. Chicago: University of Chicago Press, 1996.

Hunsberger, Warren S. *Japan and the United States in World Trade*. New York: Harper & Row, 1964.

Ishihara, Shintaro. *The Japan That Can Say No*. New York: Simon & Schuster, 1991.

Johnson, Chalmers. *MITI and the Japanese Miracle*. Stanford, Calif.: Stanford University Press, 1982.

____. *Japan: Who Governs? The Rise of the Development State*. New York: W. W. Norton, 1995.

Johnson, Chalmers, Laura D'Andrea Tyson, and John Zysman, eds. *Politics and Productivity: How Japan's Development Strategy Works*. New York: Ballinger Publishers, 1989.

Kaplan, Eugene J. *Japan: The Government-Business Relationship*. Washington, D.C.: U.S. Department of Commerce, 1972.

Krugman, Paul, ed. *Trade with Japan — Has the Door Opened Wider?* Chicago: University of Chicago Press, 1991.

Kumagai, Fumie. *Unmasking Japan Today: The Impact of Values of Modern Japanese Society*. Westport, Conn.: Praeger, 1996.

Lawrence, Robert Z. "Imports in Japan: Closed Markets or Minds?" *Brookings Papers on Economic Activity*, 2:1987.

Lincoln, Edward J. *Japan's Unequal Trade*. Washington, D.C.: Brookings Institution, 1990.

____. *Japan's New Global Role*. Washington, D.C.: Brookings Institution, 1993.

Lockwood, William W. *The Economic Development of Japan*. Princeton, N.J.: Princeton University Press, 1968.

Masatsugu, Mitsuyuki. *The Modern Samurai Society*. New York: American Management Association, 1982.

MIT Commission on Industrial Productivity. *Made in America — Regaining the Productive Edge*. Cambridge, Mass.: MIT Press, 1989.

Morishima, Michio. *Why Has Japan "Succeeded"?* Cambridge, Mass.: Cambridge University Press, 1982.

Murphy, R. Taggart. "Power without Purpose: The Crisis of Japan's Global Financial Dominance." *Harvard Business Review*, March-April 1989.

____. *The Weight of the Yen — How Denial Imperils America's Future and Ruins an Alliance*. New York: W. W. Norton, 1996.

Nanto, Dick. *Japan's Official Import Barriers*. Washington, D.C.: Congressional Research Service, 1993.

Okimoto, Daniel. *Between MITI and the Market*. Stanford, Calif.: Stanford University Press, 1989.

Okimoto, Daniel, and Thomas P. Rolen, eds. *Inside the Japanese System: Readings on Contemporary Society and Political Economy*. Stanford, Calif.: Stanford University Press, 1988.

Ozaki, Robert. *The Japanese: A Cultural Portrait*. Rutland, Vt.: Charles E. Tuttle, 1978.

Prestowitz, Clyde, Jr. *Trading Places: How We Allowed Japan to Take the Lead*. New York: Basic Books, 1988.

Pyle, Kenneth B. *The Japanese Question: Power and Purpose in a New Era*. Washington, D.C.: AEI Press, 1992.

Reischauer, Edwin O. *The Japanese Today: Change and Continuity*. Cambridge, Mass.: Belknap Press, 1987.

____. *Japan: The Story of a Nation*. New York: Alfred A. Knopf, 1976.

____. *The United States and Japan*. Cambridge, Mass.: Harvard University Press, 1965.

Sakakibara, Eisuke. *Beyond Capitalism: The Japanese Model of Market Economics*. Lanham, Md.: University Press of America, 1993.

Sakimoto, Masao. *Straitjacket Society — An Insider's Irreverent View of Bureaucratic Japan*. Tokyo: Kodansha International, 1994.

Schlossstein, Stephen. *Trade War*. New York: Congdon and Weed, 1984.

Smith, Hedrick. *Rethinking America*. New York: Random House, 1995.

Tabb, William K. *The Postwar Japanese System — Cultural Economy and Economic Transformation*. New York: Oxford University, 1995.

Tasca, Diane, ed. *US-Japanese Economic Relations: Cooperation, Competition, and Confrontation*. New York: Pergamon Press, 1980.

Taylor, Jared. *Shadows of the Rising Sun*. New York: William Morrow, 1983.

U.S. Congress, Joint Economic Committee. *Japan's Economy and Trade with the United States*. December 1985.

_____. *U.S.-Japan Interdependencies*. December 1991.

U.S. Congress, Office of Technology Assessment. *Making Things Better: Competing in Manufacturing*. Washington, D.C.: U.S. Government Printing Office, 1990.

_____. *Paying the Bill: Manufacturing and America's Trade Deficit*. Washington, D.C.: U.S. Government Printing Office, 1988.

van Wolferen, Karel. *The Enigma of Japanese Power*. New York: Alfred A. Knopf, 1989.

Wilkinson, Endymion. *Misunderstanding: Europe versus Japan*. Tokyo: Chuo-koron-sha, 1979.

Womack, James P., Daniel Jones, and Daniel Roos. *The Machine that Changed the World*. New York: Rawson Associates, 1990.

Wood, Christopher. *The End of Japan, Inc.* New York: Simon & Schuster, 1994.

Yamamura, Kozo, ed. *Japan's Economic Structure: Should It Change?* Seattle, Wash.: Society for Japanese Studies, 1990.

# Index

## ABOUT THE AUTHOR

STEPHEN D. COHEN is Professor of International Relations at the American University's School of International Service in Washington, D.C. His earlier books include *The Making of U.S. International Economic Policy: Principles, Problems, and Proposals for Reform* (4th ed., Praeger, 1994) and *Fundamentals of U.S. Foreign Trade Policy: Economics, Politics, Laws, and Issues* (1996).

ISBN 0-275-95686-5

90000>

EAN

9 780275 956868

HARDCOVER BAR CODE